Kiddie Meal Collectibles

Robert J. Sodaro with Alex G. Malloy

Published by

700 East State St., Iola, WI 54990-0001
715-445-2214
www.krause.com

Please, call or write us for our free catalog of antiques and collectibles publications.
To place an order or receive our free catalog, call 800-258-0929. For editorial comment and further information,
use our regular business telephone at (715) 445-2214.

Library of Congress Catalog Number: 00-104624
ISBN: 0-930625-16-1

Printed in the United States of America

A portion of the authors' proceeds from the sale of this book are being donated to the **Comic Book Legal Defense Fund (CBLDF)**.
The **CBLDF** is a non-profit organization dedicated to protecting the First Amendment rights of comic book retailers and professionals.

Parties interested in learning more about the **CBLDF**, or in making their own contributions to the fund, are urged to contact the
CBLDF at:

Comic Book Legal Defense Fund
P.O. Box 693
North Hampton, MA 01061

or visit the **CBLDF** Web site www.cbldf.org, send e-mail to cbldf@compuserve.com or
phone (voice) 1-800-99-CBLDF, (fax) (413) 582-9046

Contents

APPETIZERS

ENTRÉES

DESSERTS

More than a Meal

When going out to grab a bite, do you choose an eatery based upon the type of giveaway you'll receive with your meal purchase? If so, then this book is for you. Long before my kids were old enough to eat solid food I was a big fan of the "Happy Meal" style meal. In fact, I consider a "kid meal with collectible toy" one of the primary food groups long ignored by the FDA. That is to say, there were times when I would buy the kid meal just to get the toy. Now that my kids are old enough to understand that "eating out" means that a toy is quite possibly in the offing, they have begun to pay serious attention to which toy is currently available at which fast-food franchise, and make their food choices accordingly. When she was 4-1/2, my daughter went to a local franchise for lunch with my wife and, upon receiving her toy, inquired if this was the beginning or the end of the promotion, and could they please go back next week to get the next toy.

While I'm totally entertained by this behavior pattern, it drives my wife right around the twist — mostly because my son will inevitably want the toy at one place, while my daughter will want the toy someplace else. Lucky for me, we live just a few short minutes from several chains, so "toy surfing" isn't a real problem. Further, that my kids pay attention to which toy is where helps me in that I now rely on them for informing me when various promotions start.

Over the years the Happy Meal, and its string of imitators, has gone from occasional promotional runs at the various franchises to an everyday event. This has given rise to a rapidly expanding market of secondary buyers and sellers of fast-food toys. Prior to the advent of the Internet, collectors like myself

A&W baby glass mug, with continental USA map around logo, used in 1972-75.

had to rely on specialty shops, toy conventions, yard sales, and the like to locate missing toys for our collections. These days all one has to do is log onto the Net, type in "fast-food toys" and stand back as the information piles up.

The aim of this guide was to assemble a comprehensive listing of the toys issued by fast-food chains. Hopefully, we have achieved this goal — a tough job considering how many franchises issue toys and how so few of them maintain even the simplest of historical records of what they've done in this area. Still, given all the twists and turns this project has taken, I am pleased with how it has turned out.

While my children have come to expect a toy at virtually every meal, my wife and I have begun to relish the concept of enjoying a meal at restaurants that don't include a toy with your entree. Still, so long as the chains issue toys, you'll find me queuing up to score the really cool ones.

— Robert J. Sodaro

Acknowledgments & Credits

As with any undertaking of this magnitude, there were many people who contributed in whole or part to the publication of this tome. Some were involved in the day-to-day research and development, some provided invaluable material — including photos, background and promotional materials, and the like — and still others provided contributions of an inspirational nature. To all of these individuals and companies, I would like to express my heartfelt thanks, for without them this book would not have been possible.

Among those I'd like to thank are, in no particular order: Alex Malloy, who not only helped kickstart this project, but who put up with me (as I did with him), as I struggled to keep it going; Stuart Wells (even though he's a lawyer), for his sage advice, extensive production help, and kindly ear; Allan W. Miller, my editor at Antique Trader Books, (my original publisher) for his patience; and Brian Earnest (my editor at Krause) for his enthusiasm; Floyd Scholz, owner of the McDonald's franchise in Thornwood, NY, for his time, insight, and of course, lunch; Nicla, who graciously allowed me to steal time from other projects to actually assemble the book; John A. Wilcox, for not only his unique mastery over gravity, but because he is, after all, a babe magnet; Mike Raub, owner of Flamingo Books (Norwalk, CT), the coolest place on the planet to buy comics, cards, and toys; and Kevin Cleary and Marc Patton because they each have access to such a vast array of toys. I'd also like to thank the numerous people at the various franchise headquarters and local franchises for providing me with photos, background and promotional material, photography, toys, and other assorted items and information.

Thanks also to Ken Polsson, who stepped in at the last minute and provided us with a bunch of A&W images — visit his Web site listed at the end of the book to see more images; and to Paul Browning, who did the same with Burger Chef info. His site is also listed in the back. Most of all, I'd like to thank Jeff Rovin, who not only set me on this career course, but has at various times during served as boss, mentor, and friend.

On a personal note, I'd like to thank my kids — Dylan James and Kayla Rose. For it is because of them that I now get to go into fast-food places, order kid meals and not get funny looks. Lastly, I'd like to thank my wife, Shelly, for putting up with me, having and raising my children, as well as gently and not-so gently haranguing me to get this book done.

Writer/Editor:	Robert J. Sodaro
Toy Listings & Prices:	Alex G. Malloy
Additional Listings & Prices:	Stuart W. Wells, III
	Ken Clee
	Marcy Rickart
	Robert J. Sodaro
Principle Photography:	Alex G. Malloy
Additional Photography:	Stuart W. Wells, III
	Robert J. Sodaro
Photographer's Lighting Assistant:	Dylan J. Sodaro
Additional Help:	Kayla Rose Sodaro
Copy Editing:	Rochelle L. Welfeld-Sodaro
Toy Consultants:	Dylan J. Sodaro
	Kayla Rose Sodaro

How to Collect Fast-Food Toys & Premiums

To be perfectly honest, I never really understood the point behind "how to collect" articles. You collect stuff by going out and acquiring it, then storing or displaying it somewhere in your place of residence. Simple enough? Probably, but that is only just the start of the collection process. The deeper I got into this book, the more I realized there was to collecting than I had originally thought — and I've been a collector for more years than I can remember.

Collecting is really more than just acquiring stuff. You have to not only have an understanding and love of the stuff you are collecting, but you have to know where to find it, how much it is worth — both to you, the person from whom you are buying it, and, ultimately, the person to whom you eventually sell it. You could probably get away with knowing precious little about stuff you buy and sell, but true collectors will sniff you out and probably patronize someone else. Knowing only superficial information about an item and attempting to pass yourself off as a knowledgeable source can only come back to haunt you.

Collecting is an art. You need to be part detective, part bloodhound, and part packrat to amount to anything as a collector. There are folks who collect stuff simply hoping that the junk they collect will become valuable and they'll be able to retire on the eventual sale of the item(s). Well, if there was any sure-fire way to pre-determine what will eventually be worth big bucks, the people who know it aren't telling.

Most collectors don't collect because the thing they collect will eventually be worth money, but simply because they enjoy the thing they are collecting. Niche markets of collecting exist because the items in question either take on an importance all their own, or because some previously collectible item becomes licensed in a new arena.

Take Barbie dolls for instance. Many people collect them to remind them of their youth. Yet Mattel, the company that owns the copyrights and trademarks on Barbie, has opened up whole new vistas by cross-pollinating Barbie with other genres. To wit, there are now Star Trek and X-File Barbies and Kens. Little Debbies (the snack cake manufacturer) regularly issues Special Edition Barbies dressed up in clothes sporting the Lit-

tle Debbie logo. In the same fashion there are special edition Levi, Pizza Hut, and other licensed Barbie tie-ins. Fast-food leader McDonald's has for several years issued miniature Barbies with its Happy Meals.

There are people who collect the McDonald's Barbies, but collect no other Happy Meal toys, simply because they are Barbies. Others collect them because they come in Happy Meals, but collect no other type of Barbies. The same can be said for any other type of licensed product. On a personal note, the author of this book got into the fast-food toy collectible market after comic book superhero items kept popping up as giveaways.

As for the nature of collectors themselves, there are those who will collect but never open up their toys, leaving them sealed in the original packaging thus rendering them mint in package (MIP). Now, while these toys will command a higher resale price, this practice denies the owner the pure and simple pleasure of posing, displaying, and playing with their toys and collectibles. I believe, and have always professed, the radical theory that toys were meant to be opened and played with, and the heck with "eventual resale value".

As can be expected, there are clubs for collectors of not only specific types of toys (Barbies, Beanies, comic book items), but for collectors of fast-food toys (McDonald's, Burger King, etc.). In these days of the Internet, it is almost child's play to get online, type "fast-food toys" into your search engine, and come up with dozens, if not hundreds, of sites to visit, clubs to join, and e-zines to subscribe to. Some clubs and Web sites are listed at the end of the book to give you a starting point. Plus, there are always toy and collectible shows across the country where many of these premiums wind up.

Most of the fast-food franchises have their own corporate Web sites as well (listed at the end of this book) which can steer you toward clubs that support their toys, or to people that will provide lists or toys for sale.

Whatever you collect — Barbies, superheroes, Garfield, movie tie-ins, or even more esoteric premiums — remember: Collectibility, like beauty, is in the eye of the beholder. All you need do is convince the person selling the toy of your dreams that you could live without it, even though it is the Holy Grail you covet so dearly.

A Brief Word about Fast-Food Premiums and Tie-ins

Even before compiling this compendium of fast-food toys and collectibles, it became apparent (to those of us who actually pay attention to these sorts of things) that not only do certain types of toys continue to pop up as fast-food collectibles year after year, but so do certain licenses. Some of the reasons are obvious: 1) all of the various franchises are essentially drawing from the same potential pool of consumers and 2) upon seeing what works for the competition, it only makes sense to implement a similar type of promotion program in your own chain, so as to tap into an existing market.

Popular licenses involve TV shows, movies, respected and recognizable icons, and other items of this ilk. It is at least partially for this reason that when McDonald's initially passed on licensing any of the non-classic Disney characters (Mickey & Co., etc.), Burger King snapped them up, giving Burger King access to killer promotions with *The Lion King, Toy Story,* and *The Hunchback of Notre Dame.* Burned by this misstep, McDonald's worked aggressively to lock up the rest of the Disney pantheon, which it ultimately did in 1997. When it lost Disney to McDonald's, Burger King went right out and acquired the other major player in the kid enter-

A&W Christmas ornament of the Great A&W Root Bear, 1998 edition.

tainment industry as a partner — Nickelodeon. Thus, when McDonald's was pushing *A Bug's Life,* Burger King was hyping DreamWorks S.K.G.'s *Antz.*

While McDonald's has Barbies, Hot Wheels, Beanie Babies and now Furbys, Burger King has acquired Britain's Teletubbies; KFC nabbed the very hot Japanese video-game characters from Pokémon; and Taco Bell not only has Matchbox cars, but also seems to have an ongoing deal with Fox TV, giving it access to *The Mask,* Marvel's *Spider-Man* and the *X-Men* cartoon shows, *DC Comics' Batman Adventures,* and several other popular kid cartoons. Meanwhile, both Marvel and DC continue to license out the same characters to other chains — in 1998 Spider-Man and Co. appeared at KFC, while Superman and his pals showed up in Subways during 1999.

Among the cool cats, Garfield has popped up at Subway, while Felix shows up regularly at Wendy's. Denny's appears to have a lock on those stone-age folks, the Flintstones; while the denizens of Jellystone Park continue to appear at Arby's. Those silly Warner Bros. Looney Tunes have appeared virtually everywhere.

Given that the number of McDonald's outlets is nearly double the number of Burger Kings, with

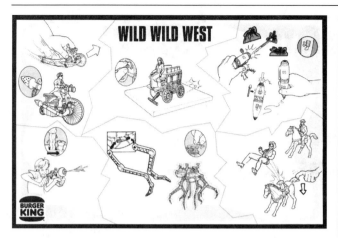

In 1999, Burger King had a toy tie-in with the film, Wild Wild West, starring Will Smith.

everyone else a distant third, it is easily understandable that most people think of the "fast-food wars" existing solely between these two. Still, with the advent and aggressive marketing of the licensed tie-in, this is not necessarily the case. Especially when you stop to consider what franchise has inked deals with what products. Tricon (KFC, Pizza Hut, and Taco Bell) is a strong contender with its powerful partnership with George Lucas. In 1997 Taco Bell issued a set of Star Wars toys for the release of the special edition of George Lucas' classic trilogy.

This partnership obviously continued with the onslaught of *Episode I: The Phantom Menace*. Part of the hype of the movie was Lucasfilms' deal with Pepsi and its former restaurant division, the newly spun-off Tricon. The deal had a single set of some 28-plus toys spanning the three franchises

Still, licensed characters aren't the only way to go. Burger King, McDonald's and numerous other chains have a set of their own company-specific characters that appear as toys and giveaways from time to time. Further, non-licensed/generic toys are always popular, both among the big boys and the rest of the pack. What company hasn't issued a summer fun, Halloween, or year-end holiday package?

In December of 1998 we became aware that McDonald's was test marketing breakfast Happy Meals (yes, complete with the toy!). Apparently, this was done as a way to cater to customers who would come in for breakfast and ask for the toy. One McDonald's employee we spoke to indicated that a nationwide rollout was imminent, while another felt that it wouldn't catch on nationally, but might become a location-specific choice that franchise owners could make. In July of 1999 Burger King rolled out their Big Kid's Meal featuring two extra pieces of chicken tenders or a double hamburger, larger fries and larger soda. This move was obviously done to appeal to slightly older kids with larger appetites who will often want more than a standard kid meal, but are still interested in the toy.

Given all of this, there will never be a dearth of licenses, genres, or generic items from which to choose. To which we can only say:

"Bring 'em on. We'll collect 'em all!"

And the Winner is...

A Quick and Thoroughly Subjective News Flash from the Front Lines of the Burger and Toy Wars:

Anyone who doesn't think that there is an on-going knockdown, drag-out battle going on in the fast-food franchise business hasn't been paying attention. Sure, McDonald's, Burger King, and the rest of the gang have all been vying for your stomachs (and bucks), for years, but these days there is a new weapon they are bringing to bear on us all: our children. That's right, while there will always be a battle royal between the Big Mac and the Whopper, the newest battleground is between the McDonald's Happy Meal and Burger King's Kid's Meal.

Ever since the advent of the Happy Meal some 20 years ago, there has been an ever-escalating battle for our bucks that is waged through our children. If there is any doubt of this, all anyone needs do is to turn the clock back a few years, and revisit the first McDonald's Teeny Beanie Baby promotion. That was the year that many of us scoured our respective counties looking for those stuffed beasties.

Personally, that came a few years earlier in this household, with the 15th-year promotion of McDonald's Happy Meal in 1995. That year, Ronald's employer issued a 15-car train set with individual cars sporting several of the most popular characters that had graced their burger meals over the years. There were Disney characters and Barbie, of course. My wife and I thought that it would be fun to get the whole set for our son. Well, we did, but not until we visited nearly every McDonald's in a 40-mile radius — and some more than once.

Virtually the same thing occurred during the first Teeny Beanie Baby promotion. Our son had been passively collecting regular Beanies — they had just come into vogue — and we thought that it would be fun to get him an entire set of the Teenie Beanies. Well, we did, as well as a second MIP set. It didn't occur to us that as the first set proved to be so popular, a second larger set would follow. Acquiring that set was a veritable freak show. By then our daughter was old enough to want a set as well, requiring the purchase of three complete sets – one for each kid, plus the requisite MIP set.

In spite of the frenzy of collecting full sets, it is not often that the members of this household go full-bore crazy over acquiring all the characters. Still, this is not to say that the fast-food merchandisers don't try to get our attention.

In the early 1990s McDonald's passed on the right to bid on some of Disney's non-tested movies. At the time, McDonald's was more interested in tie-ins with the classics, that is to say the Mickey Mouse family (Donald, Goofy, et. al.), as well as the established movies (Cinderella, etc.). McDonald's passed on the newer, untested films, like *Lion King, Toy Story,* and *Beauty and the Beast.* Burger King jumped into the fray and snapped up the rights.

As it turned out, the King struck gold. *Lion King* was a runaway smash hit, as was *Toy Story.* In fact, the Lion King promotion proved to be so successful that Burger King actually ran out of toys, extended its promotion, and began including special five-packs of trading cards produced by the fledgling Impel/SkyBox trading card company. Impel had made its mark in the collectibles industry with its popular Marvel Universe and DC Cosmos cards. It was, however, the Lion King cards that brought it to the attention of the mass market. As things turned out, it was Impel/SkyBox's Lion King/Disney association that helped boost it from just another trading

Hardee's®

card house to a major player. SkyBox was so successful that it was later acquired by Marvel Comics.

Toy Story proved to be another hit, and resulted in a pair of toy sets from Burger King — one when the movie first came out, and a second when the video hit. Burger King had not only issued a couple of *Lion King* sets, but actually re-issued the first set because of the initial shortfall. Burger King's runaway success with the string of hit Disney films caused McDonald's to re-think its strategy and resulted in the chain bringing its full weight to bear on the licensing agreement, swiping it away from its main rival. Thus it proved to be an interesting turn of events that when the *Toy Story* video hit the shelves, and the toys hit Burger King's Kid's Meals, that a likeness of Buzz was simultaneously issued by Ronald's folks as a part of a "video hits" selection.

While McDonald's wound up with the *Toy Story* follow-up A Bug's Life, Burger King delivered Antz. While McDonald's has Disney, Burger King has Nickelodeon, giving it Rugrats, Hey Arnold, Action League Now! and a host of other kid-friendly tie-ins. So the war goes on. Still, one can't help wonder so long as the Ty-guys are popular (and Beanies are a license to print money), when the Teeny critters come around once more, do Burger King and the rest of the competition simply give up the ghost and close up or offer up an "also-ran" toy, or will they actually attempt to line up some big guns to try and put a dent in the clown's armor?

If this battle was only between the king and the clown, it might be an even race to call. But, as this book attests, there are many other players. While not nearly as widespread as either of the leaders, Taco Bell does have a couple of nice licensing arrangements going for it. The first is with the Fox-TV network, from which it has issued quite a number of very cool sets, including superheroes, the Tick

and the Mask, and the X-Men, off the strength of their animated cartoon, not the Marvel Comic. Taco Bell also has had ties to Warner Bros. — issuing at least one set of Batman toys off the movies.

Still the biggest and best tie-in for the little Chihuahua is with Mr. Lucas himself. In 1997, Taco Bell issued a set of toys that tied in with the release of the special edition Star Wars trilogy. With *Episode I: The Phantom Menace,* the company, along with KFC and Pizza Hut, sprung a new set of Star Wars toys on us.

If only as an aside, we are required by a sense of whimsy combined with a heaping helping of irony to mention the Sylvester Stallone/Wesley Snipes 1993 film *Demolition Man.* Not only did Taco Bell issue a plastic cup as a tie-in to the movie, but during the course of the sci-fi movie the character Stallone played, — officer John Spartan, who had been revived in 2032 from a 1993 cryogenic sleep — was taken out to a plush dinner at a Taco Bell and told that Taco Bell had won the fast-food wars of the late Twentieth Century, and apparently was the only restaurant still in business.

Happy B-Day Mickey D! This train set was issued in 1994 to celebrate 15 years of Happy Meals!

As if the Teenie Beanie promotion wasn't enough; McDonald's added Furbys to its arsenal of Happy Meal toys, and if that wasn't enough, the promotion (which ran in the spring of 1999), offered 10 alternate versions of eight different Furbys for a total of 80 unique pieces! Holy colorful critter invasion Batman!

Okay, okay, We'll see your pair of (bendable) Jacks (from Jack In The Box) and raise you a (Dairy) Queen. Sorry, we couldn't resist. From 1999.

As for the rest of the pack, none of them seem to have forged tie-ins with as much mass-market appeal as these. Sure, each of them have scored well with one-shot tie-ins. Marvel Comics has been all over the fast-food map with toys at Burger King, McDonald's, Pizza Hut, Hardee's, Subway, Taco Bell, KFC, Roy Rogers, and (long ago) at White Castle, and 7-Eleven. DC Comics has issued toys with McDonald's, Taco Bell, and Subway. Felix the Cat has appeared at Wendy's. Archie Andrews and his pals were once at Hardee's. Pokémon popped up at KFC and Burger King. Yogi Bear and his Jellystone buddies have shown up at Roy Rogers. Garfield took a cat nap at Subway. And Star Trek has journeyed to Dairy Queen.

Still, with McDonald's and Burger King leading the pack and Taco Bell coming up fast on the inside track, it will have to be a surprise up-and-comer to hook up with one of the other franchises to really crack the market as far as fast-food toy promotions go. The way fads and "hot" properties arrive full-

This sticker was part of a 1997 Halloween Burger King promotion. The promotion included classic monster PVCs that popped up out of various containers (a coffin, a box, etc.).

blown on the scene these days, it's almost a sure bet that such a licensing deal is only a handshake, a TV or movie deal, and kid's meal away.

Stay tuned.

A Burger King Kid from the 1996 glow-in-the-dark set.

It's Jim West and Artimus Gordon to the rescue! A pair of Wild Wild West toys from Burger King's 1999 series.

On the Front Lines

One Franchise Owner's Perspective

Floyd Scholz is the former owner of three McDonald's restaurants in Westchester County, New York. During his time in the fast-food business, Scholtz took a unique approach to decorating his stores, using Happy Meal toys and vintage posters. In addition to setting up glass display cases of Happy Meal toys in each of his three locations, he hung vintage ads, posters, and McDonald items on the walls. Always promoting in-house products, the posters tended to be of classic Coca-Cola ads pulled from old magazines and framed. Floyd rotated the toys in the display cases a few times a year, always keeping them two or three years behind the current promotions and enhancing the feeling of old-fashioned nostalgia prevalent in his stores.

Authors Bob Sodaro and Alex Malloy sat down with Scholz and asked him to recall some of his experiences in the fast-food promotion business.

Alex: When did you start collecting fast-food toys?

Floyd: Probably '72 or '73.

Alex: So it was with the store that you really got into it.

Floyd: (We had) Happy Meals back then, but they weren't as routine. They used to have them, then not have them. For a while they would bring one in, then not have one, then bring it back. Eventually, we were doing it every 4 to 5 weeks.

Alex: I've noticed that on eBay that some of the display stand-ups are going for $5-, 6-, $700 or more. Do you save those?

Floyd: Yeah, I save those.

Bob: I notice that McDonald's hasn't done any superhero tie-ins in quite a while.

Floyd: We did a good Batman. We did Batman glasses. We did a Spider-Man thing for the TV show and the comic book. It did work, but that was more our generation. This generation is a different animal. There's the Power Rangers, we did them.

Bob: About Beanies, when they first came out, did you have any idea that they would prove to be as popular as they turned out to be?

Floyd: No, not a clue. That opened up a lot of eyes, because we didn't have any color cards. The color cards came out after Beanie Baby #1.

Bob: That was two years ago.

Floyd: That killed us. The Beanie craze killed us. These cards came out shortly thereafter so we could see and feel whatever it was.

Alex: What was it like? Do you remember your first thoughts when you got them in?

Floyd: I was on vacation and my phone didn't stop ringing because people knew where I was. I don't go on vacation unless I have to. The phone was ringing and I had no clue what was going on. I came back a couple of days early. It was a madhouse, a madhouse.

Bob: Before the Beanies hit, was there ever anything of this nature and/or intensity surrounding the Happy Meal toys?

Floyd: No.

Bob: We're convinced that when McDonald's runs the Beanie Baby promotion that everyone else should just close for a couple of weeks. Who's gonna go someplace else? It's like a license to print money.

Floyd: Let me tell you, when we knew about this, (the Beanie Baby promotion), McDonald's changed its whole philosophy. We stop meetings, we stop schooling, we stop conventions. They put all their efforts into Beanie Babies. It is just amazing to me how the world changes, and people know what is going to happen and they are here. It's probably the craziest four weeks that you ever went through.

Bob: Before the Beanie Babies, what was your best promotion?

Floyd: Good question. The first Barbie/Hot Wheel was good. That was the first boy or girl toy we did and we couldn't say boy or girl, because it was a discriminatory thing. God forbid if you had a girl, but she wanted a Hot Wheel, or if we gave you a Barbie that's a big deal, so it's "which one do you want?" (Laughter) We don't ask for a boy or a girl, we ask "a Barbie or a Hot Wheel."

Bob: That didn't even occur to me, but you're right, my son isn't a car kid, but my daughter is, but she'd still rather have the Barbie.

Alex: As you said, you have to order six months in advance; so you ordered "X", maybe 2X"

Bob: because they told you that this is going to be hot. How many "X" did you order?

Floyd: They give you an idea of how many units per thousand you are going to sell and usually it's like 200 per thousand, or 150 per thousand.

Bob: So you have 1,000 customers, 200 of them are going to be ordering Happy Meals?

Floyd: Right, and (with the Beanies) we were selling 700 to 800 per thousand. We were selling a week's supply in a day.

Alex: Where do the Beanies come from? I understand that there was a million of each Beanie and each store was supposed to get one of each and it was what, a six-week promotion and everybody was out of it.

Bob: Now, when you have something like that and you know that you are going to run out of supplies, do you have back-up supplies of previous promotions?

Floyd: Absolutely, we do. What they are are dogs or ones that didn't sell well.

Alex: What about a couple of years ago you did the 101 Dalmatians, how was that?

Floyd: Yes, which was a great promotion. That was, without a doubt, our second best promotion.

Bob: I had no idea that they were actually issuing 101 Dalmatians until after it was all over.

Alex: You could have written in to get the set, but I'm sure that very few people did because it was $99.

Floyd: It was $99 for the whole set. You couldn't buy individuals, you had to buy the whole set. I still get calls from people looking for certain ones, and they had the place mat and you could check off on the place mat to see what ones they were getting. The bags were polystyrene bags you couldn't see in. But if you felt them to see which one was in them you could get a pretty close idea. It wasn't numbered; you got what you got. However it didn't take the stores long to realize that the boxes were labeled, 101 Dalmatians "A" 101 Dalmatians "B". So case "A" had "X" amount of toys, and case "B" had "X" amount of toys. It didn't take the stores long to realize that A, B, C, D were different toys. We got the word out to the people that "Our "B" toys were starting tomorrow." Usually they start on Friday. People come in and would buy the "B" toy, which were different toys.

The Dalmatians were great. We had swap nights in the stores and people would come in and swap them. That really worked out great.

Bob: Would you do that with the Beanies?

Floyd: You don't have to worry about swap nights with Beanies, those people are doing it on their own.

Bob: That's true.

Floyd: We did it in our stores, to try and help the customers. We also didn't have any extra Beanies to sell them. We had extra Dalmatians to sell. It went very well and they were really able to produce them easier. Ty has a hard time making them (Beanies). The Dalmatians were easier.

Alex: What about the promotions where you sell toys separately like Snowball; how do those sell?

Floyd: Yes, those are really collectibles. They were dated, it was about Christmas time, they were stocking stuffers, and we sold them very well.

Bob: What about the audiotapes and CDs and the videos and other stuff?

Floyd: Yes, it all sold well.

Bob: Then there were the Mermaid toys.

Floyd: Yes, we did Mermaid I and II, that was the gold set. They were done in styrene packs and they had a complete set in gold.

Bob: Were people coming back in to see which ones you had?

Floyd: Yes. They were also something you could buy (as a complete set). I don't recall what the price was for them but you could send in for a set of them as well. We got a little tear-off card and you could buy a gold set.

Alex: When the first Beanies first came out the prices for Happy Meals ranged from $1.99, $2.99, as much as $3.49 depending what part of the country you were in. I figured that at $1.99 you could buy all of them and have a big party with the food.

Floyd: Again, which has to do with demographics what the market will bear. What the store is up against for sales, a big competitor down the street, the whole nine yards, and as you know, we can't price fix. Anytime we do a promotion on TV there is a price point it's a vote. The company votes for it. If they all vote for it, it goes, if they all don't vote for it, it doesn't go. So for price pointing for Happy Meal toys it's whatever the traffic will bear. If we can get 5 bucks for a Happy Meal we'll do it. But you can't price yourself out.

Bob: This may be very subjective, but what was the worst toy, one that you feel that you just couldn't give away?

Floyd: There was one that was pretty disappointing, and it was pretty recently. It was the Tamagotchi. We did a Tamagotchi, and it looked the same, but it wasn't really close, we were getting these things back in droves, it was so, I mean we shouldn't have done it. It was just so cheesy.

Bob: Oh we got a couple of those, and I thought they were kind of cool.

Floyd: Customers were looking for real Tamagotchi's and you don't advertise it as a full Tamagotchi, you just advertise it as a Tamagotchi. They should have named it Tamagoochi or something, but they didn't and that was a real bust.

Alex: Do you feel that the competition is getting greater with other toys?

Floyd: Absolutely, there are tie-ins, and that's the deal.

Alex: What do you see as the future of fast foods with McDonald's as far as toys go?

Floyd: I think they are going to tie in as much as possible to things like *A Bugs Life*. I think the tie-in is very important because it gives us another vehicle to promote, I think that tie-ins are key, and anything current, and hot. Some things are current but not hot.

Alex: What age group do you find that the kids with the Happy Meals pull them in the strongest?

Floyd: Well it depends on the toy, the age group that is brought in the most, 4 to 8 'cause they know and that they can collect them. But look at teens, it's amazing sometimes.

Bob: Are there many licensed products that jump from place to place? Or do they tend to stay. Bobby's World for instance, I know that both you and Taco Bell did that one.

Floyd: There's always somebody coming out and going around. McDonald's likes to tie in and have a tie-in, they don't like to tie in with someone who's going with three or four different people. That's not how it goes. If you tie in with us, you tie in with us only. If we dump you or they dump us, then they go somewhere else.

A Hero Sandwich, A Side of Fries... (And An Action Figure To Go!)

Faster than the line at the drive-up window; stronger than steaming-hot coffee; tastier than a flame-broiled burger; able to get full-grown adults to order children's meals; and now appearing at your local fast-food restaurant — your favorite comic-book superheroes! Given the growing popularity of comic books, and their increased incursions into the mainstream consciousness over the past decade or so, it's probably inevitable that four-color heroes began popping up at fast-food chains all over the country. Only, instead of stopping in for a burger and fries, they were going home with the patrons as toys packed in with the kids' meals.

While cartoon characters themselves are perennially popular as kid meal giveaways, this discussion is specifically about comic-book superheroes — those ultra-muscled, over-testosteroned, longjohn-wearing, four-color icons of our misspent youth.

Since their initial appearances in 1975, more and more comic-book heroes have been making the sojourn to the halls of fast-foodom. As of this writing there have been some 20 or so sets of mostly Marvel and DC characters kicking around the secondary collectibles market. Interestingly, many of the entries in this field are tied not so much to the comics themselves but to events in the mainstream world (i.e., the release of a movie, the appearance of a TV version of the character, etc.).

The earliest group of heroes that popped up in association with a fast-food/food store[1] were from the hip, underdog Marvel Comics at 7-Eleven. In 1975 and again in 1977, the quickie-mart chain issued sets of plastic Slurpee cups emblazoned with the images of numerous Marvel superheroes. There were only about a dozen characters in the first group of cups,

while the second set had closer to 30. These sets of cups are very rare. Rarer still is the collection that includes all of them. Part of the reason for this is that they were very limited in distribution. 7-Eleven was only a small, mostly southern East Coast chain.

Hardee's was next up with a set of four buckets of, again, Marvel characters. The Hardee's group was followed by a character set from McDonald's that not only has proven to be the coolest group of characters, but perhaps served as precursor of melded comic-book universes to come. This particular set from the early 1990s, called JLA/Looney Tunes, married the Looney Tunes characters with the DC Superheroes (both are owned by Time Warner). Though not superheroes, even though they were briefly portrayed as such, Archie and his pals wound up snubbing Pop Tate's Chock'lit shop to make an appearance at the modern version of the burger drive-in.

For the most part, these characters have been available in groups of four or five — one available each week during a month-long promotion — and mostly the toys have been PVC figures. In recent years, McDonald's has tended to issue toys in groups of eight, with four being figurines, and four being vehicles. Many of the smaller chains have favored a toy

Proving that superheroes are still in, Carl's Jr. issued a new set of Spider-Man toys in May, 1999.

---

[1] Superheroes actually have a long association with food products going all the way back to the '40s. This article deals specifically with superheroes and fast-food chains.

that is neither a figure or a vehicle, but some other sort of toy that taps into the imagery of the license in question (flying things, tops, water squirters, etc.).

For a time, McDonald's was the only chain that offered an additional, usually non-advertised, toy specifically developed for children under 3. These toys have no removable and/or moving parts. To acquire these toys, it is necessary to not only know that they exist, but to actually inquire if they are available. As a rule, most chains force the patron to actually purchase the meal to acquire the toy. Again, McDonald's is generally the exception. When stores allow the toy to be sold separately, it is usually available for a reduced price of around a dollar.

For fans of comic-book heroes, a trip to the local fast-food eatery is a small price to pay to acquire the latest representation of their favorite character. Following is a comprehensive rundown of characters, years, and eateries of the various incarnations of the toys. For the sake of organization, the sets will be grouped alpabetically by the fast-food chain that released them.

Burger King

In 1984, BK issued a set of DC superhero cup holders that consisted of Superman, Batman, Robin, and Wonder Woman. This was followed in 1987 by two Superpowers sets tied into the Saturday morning cartoon. The first one consisted of a Superman birthday coin, a Batman toothbrush holder, an Aquaman tub toy, and a Superpowers stick-on door shield. The second set, another set of cup holders, featured Wonder Woman, Batman, and Superman, as well as the villainous Darkseid.

In 1996, Burger King finally gave Krypton's last surviving son his due with a set that celebrated the Man of Steel without combining him with the other DC superheroes. The Superman set included five items: A caped Superman figure, standing; a Superman pop-up that was launched from a base bearing his famous logo; balancing Superman soaring over the Daily Planet building; a spinning phone booth (Clark Kent is painted on the outside of the phone booth, and when it is operated, the phone booth sides drop to reveal Superman inside); and finally, ace reporter Lois Lane driving a drop-top red roadster. All in all, a very cool set.

An honorable mention goes to the wacky heroes of Nickelodeon's *Kablam! Action League Now!*, although they were not based on a comic book. These so-called heroes appear in two (way too) brief segments in an intentionally badly done pseudo stop-motion animation. The heroes are always fighting the evil mayor, and usually wind up tripping over themselves and each other. In 1998, Burger King issued a Nickelodeon set that included a pack of four of these misfits. The Action League Now! figures were Flesh (a totally nude, non-anatomically correct male doll), Thunder Girl, Stinky

Diver, and Meltman, a half-melted frogman. The series is hysterical, and the figures are a must for anyone collecting fast-food superheroes.

Carl's Jr.

In 1999, Carl's Jr. and sister company Hardee's issued a new set of four Spider-Man toys. These toys included a Spidey web flyer, a Spidey disc launcher, a Spidey web spinner, and a Spidey web hovercraft. Which goes to prove that just when you think the long underwear set is down and out, someone, somewhere will remember those four-color heroes from their youth, and bring them back once more to battle for truth, justice, and fast food.

Jack in the Box

In August of 1999, Jack in the Box issued a set of toys based on DC characters. The figures included Wonder Woman, Batman in the Batcar, Superman and Clark Kent, Aquaman, Green Lantern, The Flash, and the villain Darkseid.

Hardee's

In 1990, Hardee's kicked open the door to superhero kid toys with a group of four characters: Spider-Man, Captain America, The Hulk and Thor. The four characters were merely the tops of the characters melded to a vehicle, with their individual logos emblazoned on them. As this group is perhaps the oldest recorded group that was part of a national chain, finding all four of them is a very tough chore indeed.

The following year, Hardee's repeated this formula (characters stuck in cars), with four Archie characters (Archie, Veronica, Betty, and Jughead). Interestingly enough, this marked the only appearance of the Archie kids in kid meals. It wasn't until 1996 that Hardee's, which essentially began the fast-food superhero craze, unveiled its next entry.

Holy Web Heads kids! The Fearsome Doc Ock is flanked by two Spideys (the under-3 Spidey is on the left), from 1993. The under-3 Spidey was a slightly lighter color than the standard one.

17

The cover of one of the four 1994 Real Heroes comics issued by Marvel Comics through Pizza Hut.

That year, Hardee's, along with Roy Rogers, issued perhaps the most ambitious group of toys. Instead of combo character/vehicles that looked like they hailed from the dollar mart, the chain delivered an interlocking diorama and eight-figure set of characters. A ninth figure was also available as the "under-3" toy. The diorama consisted of two PVCs (an X-Man and a villain), plus a plastic base on which the characters could stand. Each of the eight characters had a hole in one foot that fit over a corresponding peg on each base allowing them to stand, and the four bases fit together to form a larger display.

The characters were Wolverine vs. Blob; Rogue vs. Avalanche; Storm vs. Phantazia; and Cyclops vs. Commando. The ninth character was the Beast and was attached to a "Time Transporter" device that served as the vehicle of the set. Each set of figures and diorama came with a comic book especially prepared by Marvel for the twin chains, along with a set of trading cards — one to each pair of characters — and "certificates of authenticity" for each set.

KFC

With virtually no advanced fanfare, KFC introduced a set of Marvel toys in June of 1997. The six-toy set consisted of a Spidey wall-walker; a Hulk pencil twirler (the Hulk, when stuck over a pencil eraser would twirl around); a Spider-Man symbol clip (a Spider emblem belt clip where the front could attach over a standard flashlight to project a Spider-Signal); a Wolverine press 'n go cycle; a Fantastic Four terra craft (Invisible Woman and Thing in a wind-up craft that could propel through the water or roll on the ground); and an Invisible Woman escape launcher (Invisible Woman was inserted into a launch tube and when released, would jump into the air via a spring-release mechanism).

Not the best mix of toys, but certainly eclectic in nature. Each toy was also packed with a 12-page mini-comic that gave one- and two-page origins of the various characters represented in the set. The comic also contained a $10-off coupon for a Brighter Child Interactive CD-ROM (Amazing Math, featuring the Marvel characters), as well as two pages of puzzles and descriptions of the six toys.

McDonald's

Ray Crock's baby is not only far and away the largest fast-food chain, but also the chain with the most toys under its corporate belt. McDonald's wasn't the first to tap into the comic-book market, but it certainly made up for it by kicking off a string of offerings in 1988 with a set of Archie characters riding in their own little cars. In 1991, they delivered what has to be the coolest set of comic-book related figures. This Super Looney Tunes set melded the best Looney Tune characters (Bugs, Daffy, Taz, and Petunia Pig), with the most popular DC heroes (Superman, Batman, Flash, and Wonder Woman), respectively. Each of the four had a two-piece plastic costume that snapped over them, transforming them into Super-Bugs, Batduck, Taz-Flash, and Wonder Pig. The under-3 toy was Daffy in a Batduckmobile.

This set was followed up later on that year with a set of four Batman vehicles that tied into the second Tim Burton Batman movie, Batman Returns. The set consisted of a Batmobile that fired off a sleeker,

Taz-Flash, Super Bugs, Wonder Pig, and Batduck are easily some of the coolest toys to ever come with a burger and side of fries.

Hey, is that Invisible Girl (Woman) I see? From McDonald's in 1996.

Spoon! The Tick, and his pals invaded Taco Bell a couple of times, starting in 1995.

turbo-charged Batcar; Batman sticking out of a Bat-sub; the Penguin's Penguincar; and Catwoman in a Catcar. The last three vehicles were of the combo figure/vehicle toy. This set drew some fire, not due to the toys themselves, but because of the movie. Some parents were concerned with the fact that there were toys tied to a movie that was touted as being unsuitable for the very small children who would be attracted to Happy Meals in the first place.

It took Ronald and crew two more years (1995) to return to comics for a Happy Meal toy, and when they did, it was again with the "Darknight Detective," although this time around it was the animated Batman TV series that took the nod. This set of eight toys, plus one under 3, consisted of four figures and four vehicles, thus starting the company's trend to go four-and-four with toys.

The figures were Batman, Batgirl, The Riddler, and Catwoman, who came with a four-footed, lioness figure. The vehicles were Robin on a motorcycle, Poison Ivy in a "snapper" car, The Joker in a Joker-mobile complete with ramming Joker head, and Two-Face in a car that could flip between its "good" and "evil" halves. The under-3 toy resembled the standard Batman figure, except the cape did not detach. Later that year McDonald's issued its fourth comic-book related toy. This time it managed to acquire a Marvel connection with a set of Spider-Man toys that were

tied to the Fox-TV animated series. This series continued with toys that proved popular with the Bat-toys. The figures were Spider-Man; Peter Parker (whose head would change to a half Peter/half Spidey "Spider-Sense" head when you rotated his right arm); a Doc Ock figure (that was cooler than the existing Marvel PVC in comic shops); and Mary Jane Watson-Parker, Peter's supermodel wife, who came with a pair of snap-on outfits.

As an aside; whoever designed Mary Jane — fondly referred to as "MJ" — apparently either didn't realize that she was a world-class model, was color blind, fashion-impaired, or all three. MJ came dressed in a yellow top, blue jeans, red cowgirl boots, and a purple coat that fell to her knees. Accompanying her was a red v-necked mini-dress with white dickey, and black purse slung crossways over her shoulder; as well as a green top and black skirt, with a purple bag and shopping bag ensemble. The two alternate outfits could be snapped onto her frame, making her easily the worst-dressed fashion victim on the fast-food set.

The four vehicles consisted of characters again welded to their respective vehicles — never mind that none of them ever got near vehicles like these in either the TV show or in the comics. Spider-Man joined villains Hobgoblin, Scorpion, and Venom. The under-3 toy was a Spidey figure that looked essentially like the standard Spider-Man figure.

Wolverine, Spidey and the Fantastic Four's Thing take their wheels out for a spin in 1996 with McDonald's third series of toys based on Marvel Comics superheroes.

Looking very much like an earlier incarnation of the younger half of a certain Dynamic Duo, this is actually the X-Man Jubilee.

Robin has ridden on Batman's coat tails through many fast-food promotions.

The following year, in 1996, McDonald's delivered another Marvel series, this time digging deeper into its animated TV heroes. The company delivered The Hulk, The Human Torch, Invisible Woman (who was translucent/white in her "normal" mode, but gained color when she got cold), and a half Storm who was stuck in a wheeled "sparking" cloud. The vehicles were: The Thing in an opening tank-like vehicle, Spider-Man, Wolverine, and Jubilee. The under-3 toy was Spider-Man hunched over and grabbing his knees looking very much like a wobbly-ball.

Pizza Hut

In 1994, Pizza Hut teamed up with Marvel Comics to issue a set of comic books and plastic cups featuring a bevy of Marvel heroes. Each comic book spotlighted a team of four heroes and several villains duking it out. What made these comics special, however, was that each one carried a pro-social theme (substance abuse, community service, prejudice, etc.) as well as the standard fisticuffs.

Heroes who starred in the books included: Iron Man, Spider-Man, Firestar, the Human Torch, Captain America, Daredevil, Wasp, Falcon, Jubilee, Prof. X, Black Panther, the Thing, and others. These comics tend to be more interesting than the standard-issue stuff because the writers are seriously attempting to inject some semblance of social consciousness into the stories.

Subway

In 1996, Subway came out with a set of five Spider-toys. These included two vehicles (a Spider-car

Spidey and his pals (1995) show off their new sets of wheels.

and a Spider-plane); a Spidey-squirter (a Spider fist that could shoot water); a Spidey "flip face" badge (a clip-on plastic badge with Spidey printed on it, the head of which would flip between Spidey and Peter); and a Spidey web thrower (another Spidey fist from which would extend a paper "web" when flicked forward).

At the end of 1998, Subway balanced the scales with a set of four DC Comics-related backpack hangers. These four heroes — Superman, Batman, Flash, and Wonder Woman in her invisible Amazon plane — could be clipped onto a child's backpack or wherever else might suit their fancy.

Taco Bell

In 1995, Taco Bell entered the comic toy market with the first of two sets of Tick toys that tied into the Fox-TV animated show. The first set of five toys included an Arthur wall climber; a "roller" Tick — with wheels, that would crash through a cardboard

All-rightie then!, The Tick made two appearances at Taco Bell, this set is from '95.

wall — a Thrakkorzog squirter; a Tick finger puppet; and a set of three superhero "cling" sheets.

This set was followed by a group of four Mask toys, also tied into the Fox animated TV program. Toys included a Mask top (with the Mask's face on one side and Stanley Ipkiss' on the other); Ooze 'N Form with Wacky Dough; Milo with Mask (a finger puppet); and an "It's Party Time!" light switch cover. Not the best selection of toys, but serviceable.

The second Tick set came out in 1996, and consisted of four toys A "balancing" Tick who would balance on his chin on a brick wall; a Flying Arthur that could really glide; a Sewer Urchin that could go under water and rise to the surface when filled with baking soda; and Charles the Brain Child. This second group of Tick toys was much larger than the initial set, and more interesting in concept, design, and execution.

Looking for the Mask? This set of toys was at Taco Bell in 1995.

With the kickoff of the summer blockbuster *Batman and Robin* in June of 1997, Taco Bell pulled off a surprising follow-up to its *Star Wars* toys — see *May the (Fast Food), Force be with You* — by releasing a set of very cool Batman toys. This 4/1 set consisted of a Mr. Freeze squirter figure (the under-3 toy); a break-away Batmobile, the sides of the self-propelled car would pop open when it struck an object; a miniature Batsignal flashlight (no batteries required, it began operating when a cardboard tag was removed from the back, and the "on" button was depressed); and a Batman on Ice Freeze Pop (a Batman figurine on a stick that can be frozen into a juice pop).

How can someone look so good, and yet dress so badly? "Spidey-Sense" Peter Parker and supermodel wife MJ (along with her hideous wardrobe), from McDonald's 1995 set.

The most clever toy proved to be Poison Ivy's Hideout, which was a terrarium complete with an Ivy and Freeze figurine, cardboard punch-outs of Batman, Robin and Batgirl, plastic base and clear-domed top, and a tiny bag of seeds. By combining with dirt and water, you could set up an actual terrarium. In spite of the fact that doing so will probably ruin the cardboard punch-outs, this particular toy was easily the most ingenious of the set. Without a doubt, Taco Bell goes way out of its way with toys, and has definitely upped the ante on fast-food giveaways.

Following on the heels of its Batman and Robin set, Taco Bell delivered another Mask set. This one consisted of a Mask flyer (a spinning helicopter figure of the Mask), Putty Thing & Fish Guy, Pretorius Wind Up, and a Whistling Spinning Top Mask face.

White Castle

One of the earliest fast-food collectible superhero sets came from the home of the square hamburger. This set of character buckets was intended to be beach toys. The four-bucket set featured Spider-Man, She-Hulk, Captain America, and the Silver

The under-3 toy from McDonald's JLA Supertoons collection in 1991. Very rare, and very cool.

Surfer, each emblazoned on the side of the bucket. It's not known if these came with shovels.

Other Characters/Other Franchises

Some other comic-book-related items came out from the other franchises as well. Wendy's also issued a couple sets of comic books in 1993 and then again in 1994, at least one of which was produced by and partially drawn by legendary comic book artist Neal Adams. These very cool comics were produced with a special 3-D process, and came with cardboard 3-D glasses.

What the Future Holds

While superheroes and comic books aren't as popular in the new millennium as they were during the 1980s and 1990s, it is too soon to count them out as fast-food giveaways. Especially when they are still fodder for TV animation shows and movies. There are always plans for movies based on comic book characters.

The cyclical nature of the giveaway business suggests that more characters will once again pop up in fast-food chains.

Jealous of the Darknight Detective's many appearances at rival McDonald's, The Mighty Man of Steel (finally, in 1997), appeared in his own Kid Meal set, along with then-girlfriend Lois Lane, at Burger King.

Archie and his Jalopy cruised into Hardee's in 1991.

Born at Nickelodeon, the Action League Now! Heroes appeared at Burger King in 1998.

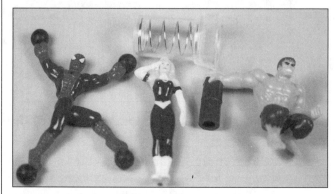

A bunch of Marvel heroes showed up at KFC in 1997 without so much as a press release.

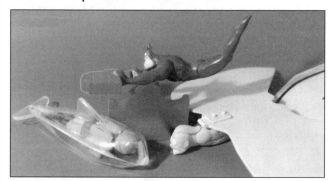

It's the Tick, and I don't want to hear any nonsense about it; from the second collection at Taco Bell in 1996.

Superheroes/Comic Book Listings

During the 1980s, superheroes and comic book characters became very visible in the mainstream press, from the highly successful Batman and Teenage Mutant Ninja Turtles movies and TV shows, to the Death of Superman plot line that ran in the comics themselves. With this increased visibility, superheroes began to show up more often as fast-food premiums and giveaways. The following list delineates comic book superheroes and characters that were translated into kid's meal premiums. Please note, this list only includes characters that began as comic book figures. Comic strip characters (Peanuts, Garfield), and characters that started in animated movies or TV that may have gone on to appear in comic books (*The Lion King*, *Toy Story*), are not included. Unlike other listings in this book, this list is strictly chronologi-

cal. An article about superhero/comic book characters appears elsewhere in this guide.

All prices are for items mint in package (MIP), unless otherwise noted.

Where applicable, the date(s) of distribution and additional information on the following premiums were provided by the individual chains.

Domino's Pizza
1975

Dick Tracy

Dick Tracy..225.00

7-Eleven

Marvel Superhero Slurpee Cups

(16-oz. plastic cup.)

Angel	4.00
Black Knight	4.00
Black Widow	4.00
Daredevil	4.00
Doc Savage	4.00
Iron Fist	4.00
Ka-Zar	4.00
Killraven	4.00
Mister Fantastic	4.00
Silver Surfer	4.00
Red Sonja	4.00
The Thing	4.00
Thundra	4.00
Yellowjacket (Hank Pym)	4.00
Warlock (Him)	4.00
The Watcher	4.00
Set of 16	185.00

7-Eleven
1977

Marvel Superhero Slurpee Cups

(15-1/2-oz. plastic cup.)

The Avengers (Scarlet Witch, Vision, Iron Man, Beast, Yellowjacket (Hank Pym), Captain America, & Thor vs. the Overlord)	9.00
Captain America & the Falcon	9.00
Captain America & the Red Skull	9.00
Captain Marvel	9.00
The Champions (Ghost Rider/Johnny Blaze, Angel, Hercules, Black Widow, & Iceman)	9.00
Conan #1	9.00
Conan #2	9.00
The Black Panther	9.00
Daredevil	9.00
Dracula	9.00
Dr. Strange & the Dread Dormammu	9.00
The Fantastic Four	9.00
The Fantastic Four & Doctor Doom	9.00
Howard the Duck #1	9.00
Howard the Duck #2	9.00
The Hulk & the Abomination	9.00

From McDonald's Marvel Comics collection, in 1996. Pictured here, are the Hulk, the Human Torch, and the Invisible Woman.

From McDonald's first go-round with DC Gotham City protector in 1991.

The Hulk & Wendigo	9.00
The Inhumans	9.00
Iron Fist	9.00
Iron Man	9.00
Ms. Marvel	9.00
Nova	9.00
Red Sonja	9.00
Silver Surfer & Mephisto	9.00
Spider-Man	9.00
Spider-Man w/Kraven & Sandman	9.00
Thor on Rainbow Bridge	9.00
Thor & Frost Giants	9.00
Thor & Loki	9.00
Set of 29	320.00

7-Eleven
1977

Marvel Superhero Glass Slurpee Cups

(15 oz. — It is not known how many of the glass Slurpee cups were produced. Only Spider-Man & Thor can be verified. It is believed to have been a local run only in the Orlando area and that perhaps as many as four different glasses were made.)

Spider-Man	10.00
Thor & Frost Giants	10.00
Slurpee cup #3	10.00
Slurpee cup #4	10.00
Set of 4	55.00

7-Eleven
1981-82

Marvel Superhero Glass Slurpee Cups

(One cup featuring four heroes — Spider-Man, Captain America, Hulk, & Spider-Woman — issued in conjunction with a contest.)

Each cup	5.00

Burger King
1984

Superhero Cup Holders

Super-Man	6.00
Batman	6.00
Robin	6.00
Wonder Woman	6.00

Burger King
1987

Super Powers

Superman birthday coin	5.00

Batman toothbrush holder......................................5.00
Aquaman tub toy..5.00
Superpowers stick-on door shield..........................5.00

Super Powers Cup Holders
Darkseid...5.00
Wonder Woman 5.00
Batman..5.00
Superman 5.00

McDonald's
1988

New Archies Figures in Cars (limited distribution)
Archie in red car..6.00
Betty in blue car 6.00
Jughead in yellow car 6.00
Moose in pink car..6.00
Reggie in green car...6.00
Veronica in purple car 6.00

White Castle
1989

Marvel Character Buckets
Spider-Man 5.00
She-Hulk 5.00
Captain America 5.00
Silver Surfer 5.00

Burger King
1990

Teenage Mutant Ninja Turtles Badges
Raphael...5.00
Leonardo...5.00
Michaelangelo...5.00
Donatello...5.00
Shredder 5.00
Heroes In A Halfshell 5.00

Hardee's

Marvel Superheroes Figures in Vehicles
Hulk in bulldozer 4.00
She-Hulk in car 4.00
Spider-Man in Spidey-car 4.00
Captain Marvel 4.00
Set of 4...27.00

Hardee's
1991

McDonald's second set of Batman toys (1988), this time based on the animated TV series.

A second Thor cup from 7-Eleven's 1977 Marvel Superhero collection.

Archies (characters in vehicles)
Archie in red car 4.00
Jughead in green car 4.00
Veronica in purple car 4.00
Betty in blue car...4.00
Set of 4 ....23.00

Burger King

Teenage Mutant Ninja Turtles Bike Gear
Water bottle 5.00
Pouch 5.00
Spoke tabs..5.00
License plate 5.00

Pizza Hut

Rocketeer
Glider 2.00
Pizza box 5.00
Beverage Container w/cap 5.00

McDonald's

Justice League of Looney Tunes
   (Looney Tune characters wearing removable JLA costumes.)
SuperBugs...4.00
BatDuck...4.00
TazFlash 4.00
Wonder Pig 4.00
BatDuck in sub (under-3).......................................4.00

Batman Movie Set
Batmobile (fired off a sleeker, turbo-charged Batcar) 4.00
Batman in Batsub 4.00
Penguin car 4.00
Catwoman in a Catcar 4.00

McDonald's
1993

Batman (animated TV series-figure/vehicle set)
Batman w/detachable cape 4.00
Batgirl figure 4.00
The Riddler figure 4.00
Catwoman figure (w/lioness figure) 4.00

Taco Bell raised the bar on super-hero tie-ins with this top-flight Batman & Robin set from the 1998 movie. The movie was sub-par, but the toys rocked!

Robin on motorcycle 4.00
Poison Ivy in "Snapper" car.. 4.00
The Joker in Ramming Head Joker-mobile..................... 4.00
Two-Face in "Flip & Twist" car 4.00
Batman w/fixed cape (under-3)....................................... 4.00

Wendy's
1994

3-D Classic Comics

Treasure Island w/pink glasses...................................... 3.00
Robin Hood w/silver glasses... 3.00
Call of the Wild w/purple glasses 3.00
King Arthur w/green glasses 3.00
Swiss Family Robinson w/blue glasses 3.00

Pizza Hut

Marvel's Real Heroes

(Comic books and plastic drink cups. Each comic book had the heroes dealing with an important social issue. The comics and cups were not bagged together, and thus can only be found loose.)
Iron Man, Spider-Man, Firestar, & Human Torch (Substance Abuse) 4.00
Captain America, Daredevil, Wasp, Falcon (Community Service) 4.00
Jubilee, Prof. X, Black Panther, Thing (Prejudice)........... 4.00
Comic Book #4... 4.00
Cup #1 (Iron Man, Spider-Man, Firestar, & the Human Torch) 4.00
Cup #2 (Captain America, Daredevil, Wasp, Falcon) 4.00
Cup #3 (Jubilee, Prof. X, Black Panther, Thing) 4.00
Cup #4 .... 4.00

McDonald's
1995

Spider-Man (figure/vehicle set)

Spider-Man figure 4.00
Spider-sense Peter Parker figure.................................... 4.00
Doc Ock figure 4.00
Mary Jane Watson-Parker figure (w/two "snap-on" outfits) 4.00
The Hobgoblin in car 4.00
Scorpion in car 4.00
Venom in car 4.00
Spider-Man in car... 4.00
Spider-Man (under-3; similar to regular figure) 4.00

Wendy's

3-D Color Classics (Produced by Continuity Comics)

20,000 Leagues Under The Sea 4.00
Gulliver's Travels 4.00
Peter Pan.. 4.00
The Time Machine 4.00
The Elephant's Child 4.00

Hardee's

X-Men Battle Figures

(PVC figures of X-Men squaring off against a supervillain. Each pair attached to a base and all four bases fit together to form a single diorama. Four different Marvel X-Men comic books and trading cards also came with this series, as well a "certificate of authenticity". A fifth figure of the Beast on wheels also came with this series and was considered the under-3 toy. Set also distributed at Roy Rogers. Toys, cards and comics were not bagged together, and thus are listed here separately.)
Cyclops vs. Commando... 5.00
Wolverine vs. The Blob.. 5.00
Storm vs. Phantasia 5.00
Rogue vs. Avalanche 5.00
Beast Time Traveler (on wheels) 5.00
Comic book #1... 5.00
Comic book #2... 5.00
Comic book #3... 5.00
Comic book #4... 5.00
Comic book #5... 5.00
Trading card #1.. 5.00
Trading card #2.. 5.00
Trading card #3.. 5.00
Trading card #4.. 5.00

Roy Rogers

X-Men Battle Figures

(PVC figures of X-Men squaring off against a supervillain. Each pair attached to a base and all four bases fit together to

One of four Marvel Comics distributed (along with plastic drinking cups) at Pizza Hut in 1994.

form a single diorama. Four different Marvel X-Men comic books and trading cards also came with this series, as well a "certificate of authenticity". A fifth figure of the Beast on Wheels also came with this series and was considered the under-3 toy. Set also distributed at Roy Rogers. Toys, cards and comics were not bagged together, and thus are listed here separately.)

Cyclops vs. Commando 5.00
Wolverine vs. The Blob 5.00
Storm vs. Phantasia.. 5.00
Rogue vs. Avalanche 5.00
Beast Time Traveler (on wheels) 5.00
Comic book #1 .... 5.00
Comic book #2 .... 5.00
Comic book #3 .... 5.00
Comic book #4 .... 5.00
Comic book #5 .... 5.00
Trading card #1 .... 5.00
Trading card #2 .... 5.00
Trading card #3 .... 5.00
Trading card #4 .... 5.00

Taco Bell

The Tick (Fox-TV animated show)
Arthur wall climber 4.00
"Roller" Tick... 4.00
Thrakkorzog squirter 4.00
Tick Finger puppet 4.00
Set of 3 Tick "cling" sheets... 4.00

The Mask (Fox-TV animated show)
Mask top 4.00
Ooze 'N Form with Wacky Dough 4.00
Milo with Mask finger puppet 4.00
"It's Party Time!" light switch cover 4.00

The Tick II
"Balancing" Tick 4.00
Flying Arthur.. 4.00
Under water Sewer Urchin 4.00
Charles the Brain Child.. 4.00

McDonald's
1996

Marvel Heroes figure/vehicle set The Hulk figure 4.00
The Human Torch figure 4.00
"Color changing" Invisible Woman figure 4.00
"Sparking" Cloud Storm 4.00
The Thing in Tank 4.00
Spider-Man in Car.. 4.00

Proving that rivals can peacefully co-exist, this set of Marvel heroes was issued from McDonald's in 1996.

One of the DC superhero cup holders issued by Burger King in 1984.

Wolverine in car... 4.00
Jubilee on motorcycle.. 4.00
Spider-Man ball (under-3)... 4.00

KFC
Casper The Friendly Ghost
Apr. – May
Each 3.50

Subway
Spider-Man (Marvel Comics)
Sept. – Oct.
Spider-car 4.00
Spider-plane 4.00
Spider-squirter..4.00
Spider-"flip face" badge 4.00
Spider-web thrower 4.00

KFC
1997

Marvel Superheroes
June – Aug.
Incredible Hulk pencil twirler...4.00
Spider-Man symbol clip 4.00
Invisible Woman escape launcher 4.00
Wolverine Press 'n Go 4.00
Spider-Man wall walker 4.00
Fantastic Four Terra Craft...4.00

Superman (DC Comics)
Superman balancing on Daily Planet Bldg. 3.00
Phone Booth: Clark Kent pictured on outside; spins open to
    reveal Superman 3.00
Standing Superman – push "S" and arms go up in flying
    position 3.00
Lois Lane in pull-back car...3.00
Base unit w/"S" symbol. Push "S" and he flies 3.00

Carl's Jr.

The Tick
May 28 – June 8
Each Premium 4.00

These Marvel heroes appeared at KFC over the summer of 1997 with little or no fanfare.

Subway
1998

DC Superheros Backpack Hanger Tags

(Included superhero collector cup.)

Oct. 26 – Nov. 29

Wonder Woman plane	4.00
Batman	4.00
Flash	4.00
Superman	4.00

Sbarro
1999

Casper and the Ghostly Trio Watches

Casper watch	3.00
Fatso watch	3.00
Stinky watch	3.00
Stretch watch	3.00

Carl's Jr.

Spider-Man

Spider-Man disc launcher	3.00
Spider-Man Web flyer	3.00
Spider-Man Web spinner	3.00
Spider-Man Web hovercraft	3.00

Jack in the Box

DC Comic Book Characters

Wonder Woman	3.00
Batman in Batcar	3.00
Superman & Clark Kent	3.00
The Flash	3.00
Aquaman	3.00
Green Lantern	3.00
Darkseid	3.00

This 7-Eleven comic book ad ran in '81 for the Slurpee cup and contest.

This is a 1994 ad for Pizza Hut's cross promotion with Marvel Comics. Included in this promotion were an X-Men comic book, and an X-Men plastic cup. The personal-size pizza was also imprinted with an X-Men image. This ad appeared in several Marvel comics.

May the (Fast-Food) Force be with You

More than Just a Movie Phenomenon, Star Wars has Become a Major Marketing Machine That is Poised to Take Over the Galaxy

It started simply enough, three lone heroes banded together to do battle with the greatest evil the galaxy had ever seen. No, we're not talking about Qui-Gon Jinn, Obi Wan Kenobi, and Queen Amidala. Nor are we speaking of Luke Skywalker, Han Solo, and Princess Leia Organa. We are speaking, of course, of KFC's Colonel Sanders, the talking Taco Bell Chihuahua, and the new Pizza Hut spokesperson, the Pizza Delivery Girl, who, more than doing battle with evil, have joined the market blitz surrounding *Star Wars Episode I*.

The joining of these three characters and franchises marks a new chapter not only in the field of advertising — it is the first time that the three franchises have been banded together for an advertising campaign — but in the seminal sci-fi saga of George Lucas' Star Wars mythos, as well. As the campaign indicates, this time out, the toys were delivered from the launching pad of a trio of fast-food chains. Each of the three franchisees carried toys relating to one of the three worlds showcased in *The Phantom Menace*, with KFC represented by Naboo, Pizza Hut by Coruscant, and Taco Bell by Tatooine.

As for the impact of *Episode I: The Phantom Menace*, we'll let history be the judge. For now, we'll address the film only as it relates to fast-food merchandising.

One of the Defeat the Dark Side game pieces from the 1999 Star Wars Episode I game.

When *Star Wars* first came out, the Lucas fast-food marketing machine began slowly with only a set of four glasses doled out to Burger King. The set continued in 1980 with *The Empire Strikes Back*, and again in 1983 with *The Return of the Jedi*. Since the pressure for high-ticket, fast-food, kid meal licensing tie-ins wasn't nearly as great, there never was a line of kid's-meal toys for the original trilogy. A second series of *Star Wars* promotional sets was issued through Burger Chef. For the first go-round, there were a number of toy and mini-games packed with Burger Chef's Funmeal promotion. With *The Empire Strikes Back*, Burger Chef issued a set of posters. It is not known if there were any items issued with the third film, as it was around that time that the chain was acquired and absorbed by Hardee's.

Nearly two decades later, with the release of the special edition in 1997, all that changed. *Star Wars* toys finally appeared at Taco Bell. The set contained seven items (six toys, plus an under-3 figure) that spanned the original three films. The set redefined the nature of kid toys as the detail and quality of construction was far above that of many of the toys then being issued for other tie-ins. (See list immediately following for specifics about each set.)

With this set, each of the three chains offered not only a line of toys, but cup toppers — large plastic cups with the heads and torso of a prominent character mounted on top as a lid — and other items. As always, the toys came with the kid's meals, while the cups and toppers were available with oversized drink purchases and came with the other meal specials. Due to the nature of the promotion and the generosity of the store managers, it was possible to

"The Force Anakin. Remember the Force!" The Skywalker clan returned as fast food premiums in 1999 with the onslaught of "Episode I, The Phantom Menace" licensing and hype.

Princess Leia Organa, The balancing Millennium Falcon, and the Spinning Death Star from the Star Wars Special Edition set of toys from Taco Bell, available back in 1997.

Another of the Defeat the Dark Side game pieces from the 1999 Star Wars Episode I game.

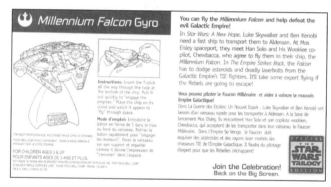

Fly the Millennium Falcon! Join the celebration of Star Wars' triumphant return as fast-food premiums for the first time in 15 years.

A Queen Amidala cup topper from the Star Wars Episode I The Phantom Menace KFC collection, 1999.

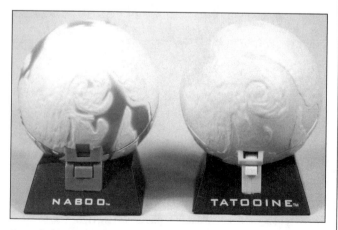

Two of the three planets featured in Star Wars Episode I: The Phantom Menace.

The schematic for the Star Wars Puzzle Cube from the 1997 Special Edition Taco Bell set.

R2-D2 from the 1999 Phantom Menace set.

acquire each of the kid meal toys and cups without actually purchasing the food. The boxes that the toys were packed in unfolded to form a diorama for each item while the backs, when stacked together, formed a special Star Wars mural.

The Commercials

The first Episode I-related Tricon spot had a wax figure of the Colonel come-to-life when he hears Princess Amidala's plea for help over a nearby radio. He rushes Batman-like into his vintage white roadster and speeds off into the night. Next to join him is the newly introduced, but nameless, Pizza Hut Delivery Girl. She, too, hears the plea, and pulls over to the side of the road, abandoning her pizza delivery vehicle on a bridge. She rushes to the edge, and takes a flying swan dive off the side, into the Colonel's roadster as it drives by. "Punch it," she calmly states as they speed off into the night. Finally, they pull up to a swinging nightclub. The door of the club opens, followed by the car door, and Taco Bell's famous talking Chihuahua enters the car and props himself up "shotgun" between the other two. "Let's do this," he deadpans, and the car takes off to adventure as the Star Wars theme swells.

The second commercial had an announcer talking about a growing evil and three legendary heroes who have taken up the mantel of protectors of the universe. The three heroes are the three from the previous commercial staged in a classic Star Wars pose. This time, the tag-out to the spot is the dog quipping, "Right after lunch."

The third and fourth spots had the trio going up against the computer-generated battle droids from the movie. The trio was actually transposed into the movie scenes via the same ILM magic that created the scenes in the first place. Again, each one ends on a one-liner from the smart-aleck dog ("You're a real Colonel?" in the third when they are confronted by hundreds of enemy droids; and "Look

What I Found?" in the fourth when he pulls up in a captured Trade Federation tank).

In all of these spots except the first, the Defeat the Dark Side game was promoted. The game had patrons collecting game tokens from each chain. The tokens were found on the tops of certain drink cup lids that were to be collected and turned in for numerous prizes, ranging from instant food winners to grand prizes worth thousands of dollars. In all of the spots, proper reverence is given for not only the Star Wars mythos and The Phantom Menace film, but to the three fast-food franchise icons as well.

KFC/Planet Naboo

The kid toys included: Jar Jar Binks squirter, Queen Amidala's Hidden Identity, Anakin Skywalker's Naboo Fighter, Trade Federation Droid Fighter, Planet Naboo, Swimming Jar Jar Binks, Opee Sea Creature Chaser, Naboo Ground Battle, and Gungan Sub Squirter. The cup toppers include Boss Nass, Captain Tarpals, Queen Amidala, and R2-D2. Other items include printed chicken buckets with scenes on the outside (Anakin Skywalker, Captain Tarpals, Battle Droid and Queen Amidala), as well as Flying Bucket Toppers (Jar Jar Binks, and Battle Droid).

Pizza Hut/Planet Coruscant

Over at Pizza Hut, Coruscant kid meal toys featured a Jar Jar Binks squishy, Lott Dodd's Walking Throne, Yoda's Jedi Destiny, Queen Amidala's Royal Starship, R2-D2, Planet Coruscant, Sith Holoprojector,

This Anakin flip bank was part of the 1999 Episode I set of toys. When "flipped" Anakin's photo was switched with Darth Vader's, and any coin placed in the slot would fall into the bank "safe" below.

A third Defeat the Dark Side game piece from the 1999 Star Wars Episode I game. Collect 'em all and win a planet.

and Darth Maul's Sith Infiltrator. Cup toppers are: Jar Jar Binks, Mace Windu, Nute Gunray, and Yoda.

Taco Bell/Tatooine

On the outlying Skywalker home world (Taco Bell/Tatooine), kid meal toys include: Anakin's Podracer, Planet Tatooine, Walking Sebulba, Darth Maul's Sith Speeder, Hovering Watto, Joking Jar Jar Binks, Sebulba's Podracer, Levitating Queen Amidala's Royal Starship, Anakin Skywalker Transforming Bank, Anakin Viewer, and Sith Probe Droid Viewer. The cup toppers are Anakin Skywalker, Darth Maul, Sebulba, and Watto. There are also four, limited-edition posters available, which, when combined, form an oversized picture of the planet Tatooine.

Toy Overview

From the initial offerings of both the toys, toppers and other material, we discovered that it was relatively easy to acquire each item. This, of course, is based upon the availability of a KFC, Pizza Hut, and/or Taco Bell location in your area. It should be noted that while all three have corporate Web sites (kfc.com, pizzahut.com, and tacobell.com) with location finders for operations near you, the Pizza Hut finder proved to be somewhat less than totally accurate.

Of the items acquired, the Joking Jar Jar (Taco Bell), was quite cool (it stuck its Gene Simmons-length tongue out when his arms were lowered), as was the Yoda's Jedi Destiny (Pizza Hut – essentially a tricked up 8-Ball), Darth Maul (Taco Bell), Mace Windu (Pizza Hut), and R2-D2 (KFC) cup toppers. The other toys

All of the Special Edition Trilogy toys gathered together in one piece.

looked quite collectible as well, but still, there didn't seem to be a "Teenie Beanie" type rush to glom up all of these toys. This was attributed to not only the older nature of the customers, but the glut of Star Wars toys and collectibles already available.

But That's Not All

If fans of the series who made a point to collect the three sets of fast-food toys relied only on the printed lists on the toys' packaging, they would have missed some toys. It is not known why, but not all of the kid toys were listed in all of the promotional materials. The "extra" toys came in boxes that duplicated another listed toy's section of the mural. So if you think that you got them all just because you completed the mural, you might actually be missing a couple.

Still, it is exactly this type of market that will ultimately make these toys more valuable than some other toys and collectibles. There are far fewer fast-food toys than standard toys, thus making them ultimately more desirable for the truly rabid fans. Further, the very presence of new fast-food *Star Wars*

A flying Boba Fett soars above the landscape searching for new prey. From the '97 Taco Bell set.

This is the game board you got at KFC, Pizza Hut, and/or Taco Bell to play the Episode I Defeat the Dark Side game.

toys is surely a sign that the older items will dramatically increase in value.

While there are few movies that are powerful enough to pull together three franchises (even three owned by the same company), one wonders if there will be future campaigns that draw on the three chains. For while none of them individually can stand up to the marketing power of a Wendy's, Burger King or McDonald's, the three together pull in a significant piece of the marketplace.

Star Wars Listings

Unlike the other lists in this volume, this one follows a chronological rather than alphabetical listing of the toys. Thus the initial trilogy items are listed first, followed by the special edition re-release (regardless of the issuing franchise, which is also noted), followed by the *Phantom Menace* items. An article about *Star Wars*, (the original trilogy, its re-release as the special edition, and the release of the new trilogy with *Episode I: The Phantom Menace*), appears elsewhere in this guide.

All prices are for items mint in package (MIP), unless otherwise noted.

Where applicable, the date(s) of distribution and additional information on the following premiums were provided by the individual chains.

Burger Chef
1977

Star Wars Posters

Chewbacca	10.00
Droids	10.00
Luke Skywalker	10.00
Darth Vader	10.00

Burger King

Star Wars Glasses

Darth Vader	12.00
Luke Skywalker	12.00
Chewbacca	12.00
R2-D2 And C-3PO	12.00
Set of 4	65.00

Burger Chef
1978

Star Wars Funmeal Trays

Darth Vader's Card Game	8.00
TIE Fighter	8.00
X-Wing Fighter	8.00
Land Speeder	8.00
R2-D2 Droid Puppet	8.00
C-3PO Droid Puppet	8.00
Flight Game	8.00

Burger Chef
1980

Star Wars Posters

(Three different posters featuring characters from *The Empire Strikes Back*.)

Each poster	9.00

Burger King

Star Wars: The Empire Strikes Back Glasses

Lando Calrissian	12.00
Luke Skywalker	12.00
Darth Vader	12.00
R2-D2 And C-3PO	12.00
Set of 4	60.00

Burger King
1983

Star Wars: Return Of The Jedi Glasses

Jabba The Hutt	8.00
Ewok Village	8.00
Luke Skywalker And Darth Vader	8.00
In The Emperor's Throne Room	8.00
Han Solo In The Tatooine Desert	8.00
Set of 4	50.00

Taco Bell
1997

Star Wars Special Edition

Millennium Falcon Gyro	4.00
3-D Puzzle Cube	4.00
Floating Cloud City	4.00
R2-D2 w/Princess Leia figurine	4.00
Flying Bobba Fett	4.00
Yoda/Darth Vader 3-D cube	4.00
Yoda Squishy (under-3)	4.00

A pair of Empire Strikes Back glasses from Burger King's 1980 set.

George Lucas took his pet project (Star Wars), to Burger King during the first trilogy of films. This set of Return of the Jedi glasses hails from 1983. As the millennium drew to a close, he moved the fast-food tie-in over to the Tricon family of restaurants.

KFC
1999

Star Wars Episode I: The Phantom Menace
(In conjunction with sister companies Pizza Hut and Taco Bell.)

Planet Naboo Toy Series

Kid Meal Toys
Queen Amidala's Hidden Identity....................................3.00
Anakin Skywalker's Naboo Fighter.................................3.00
Trade Federation Droid Fighter.......................................3.00
Planet Naboo..3.00
Swimming Jar Jar Binks..3.00
Opee Sea Creature Chaser..3.00
Naboo Ground Battle..3.00
Gungan Sub Squirter...3.00
Boss Nass Squirter (under-3)...3.00
Jar Jar Binks Squirter (under-3)......................................3.00

Cup Toppers
(Oversized, plastic cups with character tops.)
Boss Nass..4.00
Captain Tarpals..4.00
Queen Amidala...4.00
R2-D2...4.00

Chicken Buckets w/Star Wars Scenes
Anakin Skywalker..3.00

This Planet Coruscant toy from Pizza Hut was part of the Phantom Menace toys in 1999. It popped open to reveal a lightsabre battle between Qui-Gon Jinn and Darth Maul.

Captain Tarpals...3.00
Battle Droid..3.00
Queen Amidala...3.00
Flying Bucket Toppers
Jar Jar Binks..3.00
Battle Droid..3.00

Pizza Hut

Star Wars Episode I The Phantom Menace
(In conjunction with sister companies KFC and Taco Bell.)

Planet Coruscant Toy Series

Kid Meal Toys
Lott Dodd's Walking Throne 3.00
Yoda's Jedi Destiny 3.00
Queen Amidala's Royal Starship.....................................3.00
Planet Coruscant..3.00
Sith Holoprojector...3.00
Darth Maul's Sith Infiltrator 3.00
Jar Jar Binks Squishy (under-3) 3.00
R2-D2 (under-3)..3.00

Cup toppers
(Oversized, plastic cups with character tops.)
Jar Jar Binks..4.00
Mace Windu..4.00
Nute Gunray 4.00
Yoda 4.00

Taco Bell

Star Wars: The Phantom Menace
(In conjunction with sister companies KFC and Pizza Hut.)

Planet Tatooine Toy Series
Kid Meal Toys
Anakin's Podracer 3.00
Planet Tatooine...3.00
Walking Sebulba...3.00

Anakin viewer and Joking Jar Jar Binks kids meal toys, from Taco Bell's 1999 Episode I collection.

The Phantom Menace kid's meal toys from each of the three fast-food chains all came in special designer boxes which doubled as backdrops for the toys.

If you were looking for Star Wars Episode I fast-food items in 1999, then you needed to go to KFC, Pizza Hut, and/or Taco Bell for your fix.

This Jar Jar Binks flying disc doubled as the top for a bucket of the Colonel's famous chicken.

Darth Maul's Sith Speeder 3.00
Hovering Watto 3.00
Joking Jar Jar Binks 3.00
Sebulba's Podracer 3.00
Levitating Queen Amidala's Royal Starship 3.00
Anakin Skywalker Transforming Bank 3.00
Anakin Viewer (under-3) 3.00
Sith Probe Droid Viewer (under-3) 3.00

Cup Toppers
(Oversized, plastic cups with character tops.)

Anakin Skywalker 4.00
Darth Maul 4.00
Sebulba 4.00
Watto 4.00

Limited-Edition Posters
(When combined form an oversized picture of the planet Tatooine.)

Poster #1 .... 3.00
Poster #2 .... 3.00
Poster #3 .... 3.00
Poster #4 .... 3.00
All 4 .... 20.00

A&W

Company Profile

A&W lays claim to being the world's oldest fast-food franchise chain, and as it was originally founded on June 20 in 1919 by Roy Allen, it stands to reason that this claim is correct. According to the company's history, with a root beer recipe purchased from a pharmacist in Arizona, Allen opened his first hamburger and root beer stand, in Lodi, California, selling mugs of root beer for 5 cents.

Business turned out to be so brisk that he soon took on Frank Wright, an employee, as a partner. The company eventually wound up taking its name by combining the first initial of the partners' last names (Allen & Wright).

During the 80-year history of the company, it managed to achieve several other firsts, including becoming the first car-hop service restaurant in the U.S. (in 1923). By 1925, Allen began selling A&W franchises. This move established A&W as not only America's first franchised restaurant chain, but the archetype for fast-food franchises.

As A&W expanded, so did its menu, which went on to include not only burgers, fries and root beer, but hot dogs, salad bars, and its signature root beer floats.

This bean bag toy was from The Great A&W Root Bear 1997 edition.

Frosty Mugs for All

Allen and Wright expanded rapidly throughout northern California, eventually reaching to Texas and Utah. In 1924, Allen bought out Wright and began to actively pursue a franchise sales program. It was at this time that he trademarked the A&W Root Beer name and logo. By the mid-30s, Allen had over 170 franchised outlets operating in the Midwest and West. To ensure uniform quality, Allen sold A&W Root Beer concentrate exclusively to each franchise operator.

By the '50s, with well over 450 A&Ws nationwide as well as in Canada, Allen retired, selling the business to Gene Hurtz, who formed The A&W Root Beer Company. During the post-war era, with the booming economy and growing automobile sales, drive-ins were becoming increasingly popular. A&W was in the right place at the right time, and, as it was one of the few nationally established drive-in restaurant chains, the company grew by leaps and bounds. By 1960, over 2,000 A&Ws were in operation.

In 1963, the company changed hands again. Taking over was the J. Hungerford Smith Company, which had been manufacturing the A&W Root Beer concentrate since 1921. It was in that same year that the first overseas A&W Restaurant opened its doors — on the island of Guam. Quick expansion led the international division to the Philippines.

Another Year, Another Sale

In 1964, both A&W and J. Hungerford Smith Company were acquired by United Fruit Company of Boston. In 1970, United Fruit was bought out by The AMK Corporation, which then formed United Brands Company. At this time, A&W adopted both a new trademark and a new name, becoming A&W International, Inc.

A Great A&W Root Bear straw, 1999 edition, was available in various colors.

In 1971, United Brands formed a wholly owned subsidiary, A&W Beverages, Inc., for the purpose of making and distributing A&W Root Beer to grocery stores. Cans and bottles of the new product were initially introduced in Arizona and California. Retailers across the country were soon carrying the product.

The 1980s & More Changes

In 1982, Alfred Taubman, a developer of shopping centers and real estate, purchased A&W Restaurants, Inc. It was then that new menu concepts and management techniques were implemented through the chain. Franchising efforts were halted while a new store prototype was developed. By 1986 the international division had expanded its operations into seven Southeast Asian countries with a corporate office located in Malaysia that serves as A&W's international operations headquarters.

Moving Towards the Millennium

In 1994, Sagittarius Acquisitions, Inc., purchased A&W Restaurants, Inc., from the Taubman interests. The new ownership intends to move A&W Restaurants into a new era of growth and prosperity in the new century.

A&W Toy Listing

All prices are for items mint in package (MIP), unless otherwise noted.

Where applicable, the date(s) of distribution and additional information on the following premiums were provided by the individual chains.

1980s

Root Bear Mini Flying Disc: Each 5.00

1990

Hanging A&W Bear: Each.. 5.00

1993

The Great Root Bear's Custom Coloring Books: Each.... 5.00
The Great Root Bear's Nursery Rhyme Kid's Cup:
    Each 5.00
The Great Root Bear's Magic Garden Seeds: Each 5.00
The Great Root Bear's Flying Saucer: Each.................... 5.00
The Great Root Bear's Treasure Island Treasure Map Puzzle:
    Each 5.00
The Great Root Bear's Traffic Safety Rulers: Each 5.00
The Great Root Bear's Custom Growth Chart: Each....... 5.00
The Great Root Bear's Root Beer Police Badge: Each ... 5.00
The Great Root Bear's Teddy Bear Ears: Each 5.00

1994

The Great Root Bear's 75th Anniversary Kid's Cup:
    Each 5.00

A bean bag bear from The Great A&W Root Bear 1998 collection.

Another A&W bear; this one from 1990.

The front and back of an A&W glass that was issued in 1992.

Custom Molded Chocolate Great Root Bear: Each 5.00
The Great Root Bear's Fossil Flyer: Each 5.00
The Great Root Bear's Frontier Flyer: Each 5.00
The Great Root Bear's Beach Bucket: Each 5.00
The Great Root Bear's Secret Wrist Wallets: Each 5.00
A&W Mini Mugs: Each 8.00
The Great Root Bear's Magic Color Change Kid's Cup:
    Each 5.00
The Great Root Bear's Adventure Activity Stickers:
    Each 5.00

1995

A&W Root Bear Jelly Belly Beans: Each 5.00
A&W Die-Cast Pull-Back Wheelie Racers: Each 8.00
A&W Mini Mugs: Each 8.00
The Great Root Bear's Floatin' Flyer: Each 5.00
The Great Root Bear's Re-Stix Stickers: Each 5.00
The Great Root Bear's Monster Cups: Each 6.00
A&W Halloween Weepuls: Each 5.00
A&W Holiday Weepuls: Each 5.00

1996

The Great Root Bear's Cruisin' Kid's Cup: Each 5.00
A&W Cruisin' Car Chocolate Bars: Each 8.00
The Great Root Bear's Figurines: Each 5.00
The Great Root Bear's Cruisin' Flyers: Each 5.00
A&W Mini Mugs: Each 5.00
A&W Weepuls: Each 5.00
The Great Root Bear's Monster Kid's Cup: Each 6.00

1997

The Great Root Bear's Rockin' A&W Kid's Cup: Each 6.00
The Great Root Bear's A&W Kid's Stickers: Each 5.00
The Great Root Bear's Custom Weepuls: Each 7.00
A&W Mini Basketballs: Each... 5.00
Cruisin' A&W Kid's Playmats: Each 5.00
A&W Cruisin' Convertibles Die-Cast Cars: Each 8.00
A&W Formula Racers Die-Cast Cars: Each 8.00
A&W Dinosaurs: Each 5.00

The Great Root Bear's Cruisin' Car Flyers: Each.............5.00
The Great Root Bear's Drinking Straw Characters:
    Each..5.00
A&W Mini Mugs: Each..5.00
A&W Anti-Gravity Vertical Cruisiers: Each 5.00
Cruisin' A&W Kid's Activity Playset Stickers: Each...........5.00
The Great Root Bear's Rockin' Monster Kid's Cup:
    Each..5.00

1998

The Great Root Bear's Cruisin' Neon Balls: Each 5.00
The A&W All-American Food Dude Straw Characters:
    Each..8.00
The Great Root Bear's Star Cruiser Kid's Cup: Each.......5.00
A&W Die-Cast Cruisin' Cars: Each..................................8.00
A&W Die-Cast Formula Racers: Each..............................8.00

An A&W throwing disc from the 1980s.

A bag from an **A&W** kid's meal, circa 1999.

A&W Glow-in-the-Dark Dinosaurs: Each 5.00
A&W Starship Cruisers/Vertical Wall-Racers: Each 8.00
A&W Cool Kid's Card Game: Each 5.00
A&W Magic Rainbow Springs: Each 7.00
A&W Mini Mugs: Each 7.00
The Great Root Bear's Sliding Starship Puzzles: Each....8.00
A&W Root Bear Mug Straw Sippers: Each......................7.00
A&W Cool Zoo Animals: Each......................................5.00
A&W Halloween Weepuls: Each 5.00
A&W Holiday Weepuls: Each 5.00

1999

A&W All-American Food Mini Mugs: Each 7.00
The Great Root Bear's Puffy Fun Stickers: Each 5.00
A&W/Garfield Coloring Books: Each 5.00
The Great Root Bear's Custom Crayons: Each...............5.00
The Great Root Bear's Magic Garden Seeds: Each........5.00
A&W Retro Mini-Basketballs: Each 7.00
The Great Root Bear's Custom Molded Kid Straws:
   Each..5.00
A&W Retro Magic Springs: Each...................................7.00
A&W Soft Vinyl Basketballs: Each..................................7.00
A&W Mini-Mugs: Each..7.00
The Great Root Bear & the All-American Food Dude Flyers:
   Each..5.00
A&W Bump Bump Bumper Cars: Each 8.00
A&W Creepy Crawlers: Each 7.00
A&W Dinosaurs: Each 5.00
The Great Root Bear Figurines: Each 5.00
A&W Coney Ponies: Each..5.00
A&W Classic Fairytale Story Books: Each 5.00
A&W Cool Anniversary Weepuls: Each...........................5.00
A&W/Garfield Holiday Coloring Books: Each 5.00
Great Root Bear Magic Springs: Each 7.00

Arby's

Company Profile

Founded in 1964, Arby's — along with T.J. Cinnamons Bakery — is a part of the Triarc Restaurant Group (Atlanta, Georgia). Forrest and Leroy Raffel started out in the restaurant business in the 1950s when they purchased their uncle's restaurant equipment business. Their fledgling food service consulting firm rapidly grew to national scale.

An Arby's adventure meal bag from its Cosmix Creatures promotion in 1999.

According to the company's history, it was a late-night excursion by the brothers to a small Boston sandwich shop for a 79-cent roast beef sandwich that served as their inspiration. Apparently it kick-started an idea that the time had come for a fast-food franchise that specialized in serving roast beef rather than hamburgers. Believing that they could make a go of it, they attempted to purchase the name Big Tex, but were unable to convince an Akron businessman who was already using the name to sell it to them. Eventually they settled on Arby's, which is meant to stand for R.B., short for Raffel Brothers, not roast beef.

The first Arby's opened in Boardman, Ohio, on July 23, 1964. The restaurant's menu consisted of roast beef sandwiches, potato chips, and a beverage. The brothers took a year to refine their opera-

tion before attempting to open the operation up for franchise opportunities. The second Arby's debuted a year later in Akron, Ohio. By 1998, there were some 500 licensees operating over 3,000 restaurants worldwide.

In 1997, the Arby's Foundation board of directors adopted a new charter reflecting a "dedication to the support and nurturing of families in need and their children." Part of this new attitude is reflected in the company's Adventure Meal program. Through this partnership the Adventure Meal program helps generate funds for an organization designed to improve the lives of children and families in need. One result of this partnership is that every time an Adventure Meal is purchased, 1 cent is donated to the Arby's Foundation. In 1997, the foundation raised nearly $175,700 from the sale of Adventure Meals.

Arby's Adventure Meal program is designed to take children on a multitude of adventures, ranging from educational to intellectual to exploratory. Needless to say, some are simply action-oriented.

According to an Arby's spokes-person, there exists no official archive of premiums for the Arby's Adventure Meal program. Programs have included jungle adventures, dinosaur adventures, and circus adventures. There was apparently a "Mr. Men/Little Miss" series of toys some years back, as well as a Babar series, which lasted for a year, and a Looney Tunes program that also lasted for several months. Since the mid-90s, Arby's has concentrated on developing non-licensed toys for its Adventure Meal program.

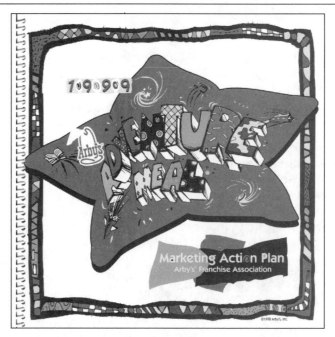

The cover of Arby's marketing action plan book for 1999.

Arby's Toy Listing

All prices are for items mint in package (MIP), unless otherwise noted.

Where applicable, the date(s) of distribution and additional information on the following premiums were provided by the individual chains.

1981

Adventures of Mr. Men and Little Miss Figurines

Little Miss Giggles	5.00
Little Miss Late	5.00
Little Miss Naughty	5.00
Little Miss Shy	5.00
Little Miss Splendid	5.00
Little Miss Star	5.00
Little Miss Sunshine	5.00
Little Miss Helpful	5.00
Little Miss Lucky	5.00
Mr. Bump	5.00
Mr. Clever	5.00
Mr. Daydream	5.00
Mr. Funny	5.00
Mr. Greedy	5.00
Mr. Grumpy	5.00
Mr. Happy	5.00
Mr. Lazy	5.00
Mr. Noisy	5.00
Mr. Nosey	5.00
Mr. Rush	5.00
Mr. Strong	5.00
Mr. Tickle	5.00
Mr. Bounce	5.00
Mr. Mischief	5.00

1987

Looney Tunes Figurines w/oval base

Bugs Bunny	5.00
Pepe Le Pew	5.00
Daffy Duck	5.00

Elmer Fudd	5.00
Roadrunner	5.00
Porky Pig	5.00
Tazmanian Devil	5.00
Tweety Bird	5.00
Yosemite Sam	5.00

Polar Swirl Penguins PVC Figurines

Penguin in tuxedo w/green loafers	6.00
Penguin in red shorts	6.00
Penguin in mask and snorkel	6.00
Penguin with yellow surfboard	6.00

Scooby Doo Dough

Scooby Doo (purple)	5.00
Shaggy (orange)	5.00
Scrappy Doo (blue)	5.00

1988

Looney Tunes Stiff-legged Figures

Bugs Bunny	5.00
Daffy Duck	5.00
Elmer Fudd	5.00
Roadrunner	5.00
Tazmanian Devil	5.00
Wile E. Coyote	5.00

Looney Tunes Character Pencil Toppers

Bugs Bunny	3.00
Daffy Duck	3.00
Porky Pig	3.00
Sylvester	3.00
Tazmanian Devil	3.00

★ ARBY'S ADVENTURE MEAL ★

A header card for Arby's Adventure Meal program used during 1999.

Tweety Bird 3.00
Yosemite Sam 3.00

Looney Tunes World of Fun Stuff Packs
Arby's Restaurant (Pack #1) 6.00
Bugs Pit Stop & Gaseteria (Pack #2) 6.00
Drive-In Movie Theater (Pack #3) 6.00
Firehouse (Pack #4) 6.00

Looney Tunes Car-Tunes
Bugs Bunny Buggy 5.00
Daffy Duck Dragster... 5.00
Sam Rackin' Frackin' Wagon 5.00
Roadrunner Racer... 5.00
Sylvester Cat-Illac 5.00
Tazmanian Devil Slush Musher.......................... 5.00

1989

Looney Tunes PVC Figurines
Bugs Bunny.. 5.00
Elmer Fudd 5.00
Road Runner... 5.00
Sylvester 5.00
Tazmanian Devil... 5.00
Wile E. Coyote 5.00

Looney Tunes Christmas Ornaments
Bugs as Santa.. 6.00
Porky the Toy Soldier... 6.00
Tweety the Elf 6.00

Looney Tunes PVC Fun Figures
Daffy Duck as schoolboy 4.00
Sylvester as fireman 4.00

One of Arby's Cosmix creatures from 1999.

Tazmanian Devil with scarf 4.00
Set of three 14.00

1990

Babar The Elephant Finger Puppets
(All 4 characters are rotoform molded in durable PVC plastic.)
Barbar 5.00
Pom 5.00
Arthur w/Zephir 5.00
Celeste 5.00

Babar The Elephant License Plates
(Each plate is 5-1/2" x 2-1/2" and molded in PVC plastic
with full-color laminated decal.)
Paris 5.00
Brazil..5.00
USA 5.00
North Pole..5.00
Set of 4 ....20.00

Babar The Elephant Jigsaw Puzzlebooks
Cousin Arthur's New Camera 3.00
Babar's Gondola Ride 3.00
Barbar and the Haunted Castle 3.00
Babar's Trip to Greece 3.00
Set of 4 ....11.00

Babar The Elephant Vehicles
Arthur in car boat 4.00
Flora on tricycle 4.00
Babar in helicopter..4.00

Babar The Elephant World Tour Racers
Babar in red car 4.00
Arthur in yellow car 4.00
Celeste in green car 4.00

1991

Babar The Elephant Storybooks
Read and Get Ready, Set, Go Calendar 4.00
Read and Have Fun 4.00
Read and Grow and Grow 4.00
Set of 3 ....13.00

Babar The Elephant Stampers
Flora 4.00
Babar 4.00
Arthur 4.00
Zephir 4.00
Rataxes 4.00
Set of 5 ....20.00

Babar The Elephant Summer Sippers
Purple top 4.00
Yellow top 4.00
Orange top...4.00

1992

Babar The Elephant World Tour Squirters
Babar 4.00
Alexander 4.00
Celeste 4.00

1993

Yogi & Friends Mini Throwing Discs
Ranger Smith (blue) 4.00
Yogi (orange) 4.00
Cindy (green)...4.00

How To Merchandise Your Adventure Meal Program

Adventure Meal Program
1. Translite - Calendar Program
2. Translite - Calendar Program
3. Translite - 8 Combo
4. Translite - Generic Other
5. Indoor Banner - Calendar Program
6. Register Insert - Calendar Program
7. Display Poster - Calendar Program
8. Window Banner - Calendar Program
9. Horizontal Hanging Banner - Store Decor
10. Vertical Hanging Banner - Calendar Program
11. Table Tents - Calendar Program
12. Premium Display - Adventure Meal
13. Mobile - Adventure Meal

How to best display your wares; direct from the 1998 Arby's marketing action plan booklet.

1994

Hanna-Barbera's Crazy Cruisers
Yogi 4.00
Snagglepuss 4.00
Cindy 4.00

Yogi & Friends Squirters
Yogi in basket... 4.00
Boo Boo w/ice cream 4.00
Cindy w/camera 4.00

1995

Yogi & Friends
Yogi 3.00
Quick Draw McGraw 3.00
Item #3 .... 3.00
Item #4 .... 3.00

1996

Doodle Top Jr.
Blue Huckleberry..................................... 2.00
Pink Yogi 2.00
Top #3 .... 2.00
Top #4 .... 2.00

Yogi & Friends Puzzle
Ranger Smith 4.00
Huckleberry Hound 4.00
Yogi 4.00
Item #4 .... 4.00

Yogi Spirograms
Yogi 2.50
Boo Boo 2.50
Cindy 2.50
Item #4 .... 2.50

Yogi Snow Domes
Snagglepuss 5.00
Cindy 5.00

Yogi 5.00
Item #4 .... 5.00

1997

Jungle Adventure Transformers
Dec. 1996 – mid-Jan.1997
Each transformer 3.00

Dinosaur Adventure
Mid-Jan. – Feb.
Dino Dough.. 3.00
Spinner/viewer 3.00

Adventures in Outer Space
March – mid-April
Spaceships 3.00
Kaleidoscope 3.00
Stamper 3.00

Adventures in Construction
Mid-April – May
Each building block set............................ 3.00

Summer Fun Adventures
June
Each Micro Super Soaker......................... 3.00

Adventures in Sports
July
Finger puppet cup.................................... 3.00

Back to School Adventures
August
Fake out.. 3.00
Puzzle pen 3.00
Pullback car 3.00
School tools 3.00

Circus Adventures
September
Elephant squirter 3.00
Clown car.. 3.00
Human cannonball................................... 3.00

Monster Adventures (4 figures)
October
Each monster dough figure 3.50

Adventures in Magic
November
Got your number...................................... 3.00
Squirting chocolate 3.00
Vanishing coin 3.00

Mountain Rescue Adventures
December
Snowboarder 2.50
Power skier 2.50
Jet pak 2.50
ATV rider... 2.50

Jungle Zoids
Tigazoid 2.50
Turtlazoid 2.50
Gorillazoid 2.50
Rhinozoid.. 2.50

1998

Adventures in Music
(Five musical instruments.)
Jan. to Mid-Feb.
Flute.. 2.50

Tambourine 2.50
Sax 2.50
Harmonica 2.50
Microphone 2.50

Adventures in Art
Mid-Feb. – March
Rocket squirter 2.50
"Color Me" Fish 2.50
Coloring scroll 2.50

Pirate Adventures
April
Rowboat 2.50
Pirate Popper 2.50
Candy-filled sword 2.50
Chest 2.50

Animal Adventures
(Five different bean bag animals.)
May
Each animal 3.00

Space Adventures
(Four different space crafts.)
June
Each space craft 3.00

Summer Adventures
July
Beach ball 2.50
Inflatable frisbee 2.50
Sand pail/shovel 2.50
Swoosh ball 2.50
Collapsible cup 2.50
Sand toys 2.50

A mobile utilized by Arby's to promote its current food special. And no, the food isn't really free, this is just an illustration from Arby's 1998 marketing action plan booklet.

Island Adventures
August
Treasure map puzzle 2.50
Squirty boat toy 2.50
Pull-back car 2.50
Monkey game 2.50

Computer Adventures
September
Pull-back mouse 2.50
Mouse maze game 2.50
Pinball game 2.50
Stickers 2.50

Glow-in-the-Dark Adventures
October
Chalkboard 2.50
Dracula top and car 2.50
Frankenstein bank 2.50

Adventures with Elmo
(Cups with finger puppets.)
Nov. – Dec.
Elmo 3.50
Ernie 3.50
Cookie Monster 3.50

1999

Spy Adventures
January
Secret decoder watch 2.50
Backpack hanger 2.50
Secret puzzle map 2.50
Secret compartment pencil case 2.50

Adventures In Sports
(Includes subscription offer for *Sports Illustrated for Kids* plus one of four sports balls.)
February
Softball 2.00
Basketball 2.00
Soccer ball 2.00
Football 2.00

Dinosaur Adventures
(Four different funky dinosaurs with accessories (sunglasses, shorts, vests), and interchangeable parts.)
March
Each premium 2.00

Science Adventures
("Mad Cy" and his female sidekick.)
April
Mad Cy pull-back car 2.00
Rolling yoy 2.00
Laboratory puzzle map 2.00
Mad Cy flashlight 2.00

Adventures In Travel
(Four Crayon Carz made out of Crayon pieces.)
May
Car 2.00
Train 2.00
Plane 2.00
Boat 2.00

Adventures Under the Sea
(Four water Olympics toys.)
June
Eel basketball 2.00

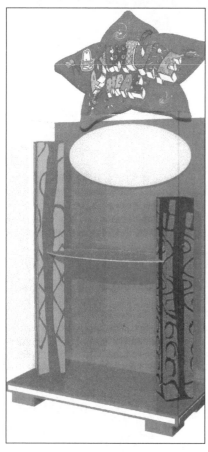

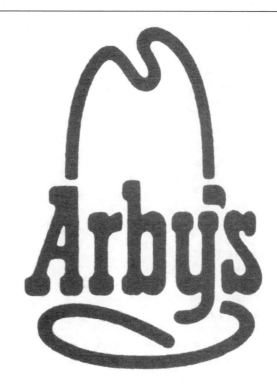

A point of purchase display stand from Arby's 1998 adventure meal promotional campaigns.

Manta Ray ring toss 2.00
Octopus tentacle toss 2.00
Arby's deep sea diving 2.00

Space Adventures
(Cosmix the Space Creature, plus a chance to win a trip to NASA's Space Camp.)
July
Cosmix planet popper 2.00
Moon pull-back car 2.00
Moon holder 2.00
Moon puzzle map 2.00

Dinosaur Adventures (Dino Buddies)
Buddy 2.00

Ziggy 2.00
Spots 2.00
Bubbles 2.00

Crayon Travelers
(Set of 4, vehicles and crayons. Each one comes with three color Crayons and postcards to color and send out.)
Purple train 2.00
Orange boat 2.00
Green car 2.00
Blue truck 2.00

2000

Animal Viewers
Each item 2.00

Burger King

Company Profile

Co-founded in 1954 by James W. McLamore and David Edgerton, the first Burger King restaurant is still operating at 3090 NW 36th Street, Miami, Florida. That first menu included 18-cent broiled hamburgers, 18-cent milkshakes, 12-ounce regular and 16-ounce large sodas. In 1957, the company's trademark Whopper sandwich was first introduced and sold for 37 cents. The following year the company kicked off its "Burger King, Home of the Whopper" campaign.

In 1961, the company began both national and international franchising programs, with the first international location opening in 1963 in Puerto Rico. The Pillsbury Company acquired all 274 restaurants Burger King Corp. owned and operated and established it as a subsidiary in 1967. In 1974, the "Have It Your Way" campaign was launched. Burger King went European in 1975 by opening a location in Madrid, Spain. Drive-thru service was also introduced that year. It wasn't until 1977 that Burger King finally established locations in all 50 states with the opening of its 2,000th location, in Hawaii.

By 1982 the drive-thru proved to be so popular that Burger King expanded its hours to include late-night service. Always looking to improve its menu, Burger King debuted a salad bar in 1983. It introduced both the croissan'wich and self-serve drinks nationally in 1985.

The company was doing so well that in 1986 it opened a record 546 new restaurants worldwide. That year there were 4,743 restaurants in operation, including 402 international restaurants in 25 coun-

tries. Two more items were added to the national menu; chicken tenders and french toast sticks. In 1987 it introduced the bagel sandwich to the menu.

Ownership of the company changed hands again in 1988, when PLC acquired The Pillsbury Company and all of its subsidiaries, including Burger King. That year, yet another new menu appeared with the regional rollout of chicken international sandwiches. In 1989 there was another major expansion as Burger King, Europe took off with the acquisition and conversion of nearly 100 Wimpy counter service restaurants in the United Kingdom. Grand Metropolitan acquired Wimpy restaurants that August, and a total of 200 restaurants were converted by the summer of 1990.

The year 1990 proved to be a pivotal year in the burger wars, as Burger King nationally launched its Kids Club program. This proved very successful, as approximately 1 million children registered in the

BK's collection of toys from Disney's Hunchback of Notre Dame.

If you are a kid under age 8, or can pass for one, you can join the Burger King Kids Club.

45

In 1999, Burker King was visited by four classic monster PVC figures. This was a sticker that came with the Creature from the Black Lagoon figure.

Rosie, the Queen of Nice, is a kid's meal toy, thanks to Nickelodeon. From the 1999 Kid's Choice Awards.

During the Teletubby promotion in 1999, strawberry Tubby custard briefly became a part of BK's kid meal.

program's first two months. By 1998 there were over 5 million kids registered. The company also introduced the BK broiler — a flame-broiled chicken sandwich, and switched to 100-percent vegetable oil for its french fries. In 1992, Burger King made its initial partnership with Disney (the first of nine promotional theatrically released tie-ins). This first pairing included tie-ins for the animated films *Beauty and the Beast* and *Pinocchio*.

The Kid Meal program proved so successful that in 1993 Burger King Corporation became the largest single circulation publisher of children's magazines with the release of three new magazines, distributed to more than 3 million members of its Kids Club program. In 1994, the Disney/Burger King association went through the roof with the release of *The Lion King*, much to the ire of McDonald's, which had a prior relationship with Disney, but had chosen to pass on non-classic properties. This was followed by the success of *Toy Story* in 1995 and *The Hunchback of Notre Dame* in 1996. *Toy Story* proved to be such an overwhelming success that more than 43 million premiums and 15 million trading cards from SkyBox were distributed in 5-1/2 weeks.

Burger King went on to announce a promotional partnership in 1996 with Universal Studios for the Steven Spielberg, Michael Crichton film *The Lost World*, the sequel to the blockbuster film *Jurassic Park*.

A second set of *Toy Story* toys were issued with the release of *Toy Story* on video the following year. McDonald's chose this time to take action, and after being stung with a string of Disney/Burger King successes, signed an exclusive contract to create and distribute fast-food toy tie-ins with Disney. When *Toy Story 2* debuted in 1999, it was McDonald's and not Burger King that carried Buzz, Woody, and Company.

Burger King Toy Listing

All prices are for items mint in package (MIP), unless otherwise noted.

Where applicable, the date(s) of distribution and additional information on the following premiums were provided by the individual chains.

1972
Doll, Cloth Cartoon King 16" 35.00

1977
Star Wars Glasses
Darth Vader... 15.00
Luke Skywalker.. 15.00

Chewbacca..15.00
R2-D2 and C-3PO 15.00
Set of 4 ....75.00

Miscellaneous
Cloth Doll (dressed as King on TV) 30.00

1979
Burger King Glasses
Burger Thing..9.00
Duke of Doubt...9.00
Marvelous Magical Burger King.......................9.00
Sir Shake A Lot...9.00
Wizard of Fries 9.00

The cartoon CatDog was so popular with kids that Burger King added a CatDog set to its lineup in 1999.

Set of 5 .... 50.00
Burger King Pencil Topper 5.00
Burger King Mini Flying Disc.................... 5.00

1980

Star Wars: The Empire Strikes Back Glasses
Lando Calrissian 12.00
Luke Skywalker 12.00
Darth Vader 12.00
R2-D2 and C-3PO 12.00
Set of 4 .... 60.00

1983

Star Wars: Return of the Jedi Glasses
Jabba The Hutt 8.00
Ewok Village 8.00
Luke Skywalker and Darth Vader In The Emperor's Throne Room 8.00
Han Solo In The Tatooine Desert 8.00
Set of 4 .... 50.00

1984

Super Hero Cup Holders
Superman 10.00
Batman 10.00
Robin 10.00
Wonder Woman 10.00

1985

Mark Twain Country Series Glasses
Mark Twain 12.50
Tom Sawyer 12.50
Huck Finn 12.50
Octagonal Study 12.50
Set of 4, in box 60.00

Masters Of The Universe Plastic Cups
Thunder Punch He-Man Saves The Day 4.00
He-Man & Roboto To The Rescue 4.00
Spydor Stalking Enemies of Skeletor 4.00
He-Man Takes on the Evil Horde 4.00

Critter Carton Punch-Out Paper Masks
Bird 4.00
Chicken 4.00
Tiger 4.00

Rabbit 4.00
Dog 4.00
Panda 4.00
Duck 4.00
Turtle 4.00

This is a Burger King Town Punch-Out Buildings
Barn, Horse Whirl and Wheel Game 4.00
Fire Station, Engine and Fireman 4.00
Restaurant 4.00
Apartment 4.00

1986

Mealbots (paper masks with 3-D lenses)
Broil Master (red box) 4.00
Burger Beta (gray box) 4.00
Winter Wizard (blue box) 4.00
Galactic Guardian (yellow box) 4.00

Thundercats
Snarf Straw Holder 5.00
Plastic Cup-Bank 5.00
Secret Message Ring 5.00
Light Switch Plate 5.00

Christmas Crayola Bears (plush toys)
Red 5.00
Yellow 5.00
Red 5.00
Purple 5.00

Animal Boxes (activity booklets)
Hippo 3.00
Bear 3.00
Lion 3.00

Rodney and Friends Plush Toy w/Holiday Fun Booklet
Rodney (Holiday Fun & Games box) 6.00
Rhonda (Holiday Decorating box) 6.00
Randy (Holiday Fun At The Toy Store box) 6.00
Ramona (Holiday Sweets and Treats) 6.00

1987

Dino Meal Punch-Out Sheets
Triceratops 4.00

Glow-in-the-dark Burger King kids (Glo-Force) arrived in stores outfitted with all sorts of uniform toys in 1996.

Men in Black proved to be so popular that BK brought it back for a second set of toys when the movie was turned into a WB animated TV show. This loop-the-loop car toy was from the second 1998 collection.

Wooly Mammoth	4.00
Tyrannosaurus Rex	4.00
Stegosaurs	4.00

Super Powers
Superman Birthday Coin	15.00
Batman Toothbrush Holder	15.00
Aquaman Tub Toy	20.00
Superpowers Stick-On Door Shield	15.00

Super Powers Cup Holders
Darkseid	15.00
Wonder Woman	15.00
Batman	15.00
Superman	15.00

Silver Hawks
Silver Sticker-Mirror	6.00
3-D Name Plate	6.00
Special Days Calendar	6.00
Pencil Topper	6.00

Masters of the Universe II Toys
Decoder Ring	6.00
Other premiums in series	6.00

Chipmunk Adventure
Alvin Pencil Topper	4.00
Bicycle License Plate	4.00
Other premiums in series	4.00

Haunted Mansion Plastic Cup
Glow-In-The-Dark Plastic Cup	4.00

Cruisin' Rules Fun Booklet
Bicycle Safety	4.00

ALF
Joke and Riddle Disc	3.00
Door Knob Card	3.00
Sand Mold	3.00
Refrigerator Magnet	3.00

Many Faces of ALF (puppet w/record)
Surfin' With ALF	7.00
Rockin' With ALF	7.00
Cookin' With ALF	7.00
Sportin' With ALF	7.00

Christmas Purrtenders (plush toys)
Dog-Romp-Purr	4.00
Bunny-Hop-Purr	4.00
Duck-Flop-Purr	4.00
Mouse-Scamp-Purr	4.00

Trak-Pak
Golden Junior Classic Books:
Train To Timbuktu	4.00
Roundabout Train	4.00
My Little Book of Trains	4.00
The Circus	4.00

Pilot Pak Styrofoam Airplanes
Two-Seater Plane	4.00
Sunburst Pattern on Wings	4.00
Lightning Pattern on Wings	4.00

Mickey's Toontown vehicles
Mickey & Minnie in red car	4.00
Goofy in green car	4.00
Donald in white tug boat	4.00
Chip 'n' Dale in red trolley car	4.00

1988

Purrtenders
Free Wheeling Cheese Rider	8.00
Flip-Top Car	8.00
Radio Bank	8.00
Storybook	8.00

Trak-Pak (Golden Jr. Classic books)
Train to Timbuktu	3.00
Roundabout Train	3.00
My Little Book of Trains	3.00
The Circus	3.00

Pilot Pak (foam airplanes)
Two-Seater	3.00
Sunburst pattern on wings	3.00

"To infinity and beyond" was the catch phrase from this Buzz Lightyear figure that was available in the second BK promotion in 1996.

Lightning pattern on wings 3.00
Plane #4 .... 3.00

Captain Power Containers (space ships)
Powerbird XT-7 .... 5.00
Biodread Patroller 5.00
Powerbase 5.00
Premium #4 .... 5.00

1989

Nerfuls Rubber Characters (interchangeable):
Officer Bob 5.00
Bitsy Ball 5.00
Fetch 5.00
Scratch 5.00

Bone-Age Skeleton Kits
Similodon 5.00
Mastodon 5.00
Dimetrodon 5.00
Tyrannosaurus Rex 5.00

Spacebase Racers Plastic Vehicles
Super Shuttle 8.00
Moon Rover 8.00
Starship Viking 8.00
Cosmic Copter 8.00

Sea Creatures Terry Cloth Wash Mitts
Dolly Dolphin 4.00
Stella Starfish 4.00
Sammy Seahorse 4.00
Ozzie Octopus 4.00

Tricky Treaters PVC Figurines
Zelda Zoombroom 5.00
Frankie Steen 5.00
Gourdy Goblin 5.00

Matchbox Cars
Red Ferrari 5.00
Yellow Corvette 5.00
Blue 4 X 4 .... 5.00
White Police Car 5.00

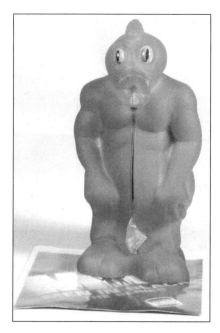

Another MIB toy from BK's 1998 animated set.

Talk show hostess and part-time Kmart pitchwoman Rosie O'Donnell spent so much time on her show raving over toys that Burger King gave her the ultimate honor, they turned her into a BK toy in 1999. The set tied into the Nickelodean Kid's Choice award show. Rosie is shown here about to get slimed.

Fairy Tales Cassette Tapes
Goldilocks and The Three Bears 4.00
Jack & The Beanstalk 4.00
Hansel and Gretel 4.00
Three Little Pigs 4.00

Christmas Sing-A-Long Cassette Tapes
We Three Kings/O Holy Night 4.00
Deck The Halls/Night Before Christmas 4.00
Joy To The World/Silent Night 4.00

Miscellaneous
Burger King Stuffed Doll 30.00
Good Goblins Figures, each 7.00

1990

Kids Club Action Figures
I.Q. 4.00
Jaws 4.00
Kid Vid 4.00
Boomer 4.00

Teenage Mutant Ninja Turtles Badges
Raphael 5.00
Leonardo 5.00
Michaelangelo 5.00
Donatello 5.00
Shredder 5.00
Heroes In A Halfshell 5.00

Simpsons Statues and Scenes
Bart 6.00
Lisa 6.00
Homer 6.00
Marge 6.00
Maggie 6.00

Dolls
Bart 10.00
Lisa 10.00
Homer 10.00

In 1996, Burger King had its last hurrah with Disney movies. This over-the-counter Hunchback of Notre Dame is from that promotion.

Marge.. 10.00
Maggie... 10.00

Beetlejuice 2-sided Figures
Unholy Chair 5.00
Peek-a-Boo-Do 5.00
The Ghost Post 5.00
The Charmer 5.00
Head Over Heels 5.00
Ghost-to-Ghost TV 5.00

Kid-Transporters
Boomer w/Super Shoe... 5.00
Kid Vid w/SEGA Video Gamester 5.00
Snaps w/Camera Car.. 5.00
I.Q. w/World Book Mobile 5.00
Jaws w/Burger Racer.. 5.00
Wheels w/Turbo Wheelchair 5.00
Set of 6... 35.00

Mini Record Breakers Race Cars
Dominator 5.00
Shockwave 5.00

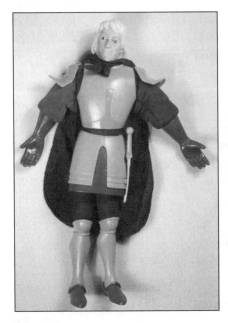

This over-the-counter puppet was also part of BK's Disney/Hunchback tie-in.

Accelerator 5.00
Indy 5.00
Fastlane... 5.00
Aero Afterburner 5.00

Lickety Splits Plastic Wheeled Food Items
Flame Broiler Buggy 4.00
Spry Fries 4.00
Carbo Cooler 4.00
French Toast Sticks 4.00
Croissant 4.00
Chicken Tenders 4.00
Apple Pie 4.00

Beetlejuice Rubber Figurine
Uneasy Chair 6.00
Peek-A-Boo-Do 6.00
The Ghost Post 6.00
The Charmer 6.00
Head Over Heels 6.00
Ghost to Ghost TV 6.00

Crayola Coloring Sets: Coloring Books and Crayons
Kid Vid's Video Vision 4.00
Snap's Photo Power 4.00
Jaw's Colorful Clue 4.00
Boomer's Color Chase 4.00
I.Q.'s Computer Code 4.00
Kid's Club Concert.. 4.00

1991

Beauty and the Beast Action Figures/Pull-backs/ Wind-Ups
Belle.. 5.00
The Beast 5.00
Chip 5.00
Cogsworth 5.00

Barnyard Commandos Commando Cuffs PVC Character/Bracelets:
Sergeant Wooly Pullover 5.00
Sergeant Shoat 'N Sweet 5.00
Private Side O' Bacon 5.00
Major Legger Mutton 5.00
Set of 4 .... 22.00

Kids Club (action figures & comic insert)
I.Q. 4.00
Boomer 4.00
Kid Vid 4.00
Jaws 4.00

Captain Planet (vehicles with two different characters)
Wheeler and Duke Nukem 5.00
Linka and Ma-Ti and Dr. Blight 5.00
Verminous Skumm and Kwame 5.00
Captain and Hoggish Greedily................................ 5.00
Set of 4 .... 22.00

Kids Club Water Mates
(BK Kids – These came in two different colors.)
Snaps In Rowboat 4.00
I.Q. on Dolphin (blue or pink shirt)........................ 4.00
Jaws on Jet Ski (green or pink jet ski) 4.00
Wheels in Hovercraft (blue and orange or brown and orange raft) 4.00

Inspector Gadget (action figure toys)
Copter Gadget 5.00

Teletubbie Tinky Winkey poses with a bunny. Both were part of a 1999 BK promotion.

Inflated Gadget	5.00
Scuba Gadget	5.00
Surfer Gadget	5.00

Life Saver Freaky Fellas
Red	4.00
Yellow	4.00

Blue	4.00
Green	4.00

Teenage Mutant Ninja Turtles bike gear
Water bottle	5.00
Pouch	5.00
Spoke tabs	5.00
License plate	5.00

1992

Disney's Aladdin PVC figures
Aladdin on Magic Carpet	6.00
Princess Jasmine on Raja the Tiger	6.00
Jafar the Sorcerer w/parrot	6.00
Genie in Lamp	6.00
Abu the Monkey	6.00

Disney's Beauty & the Beast PVC figures
Beast	6.00
Belle	6.00
Chip	6.00
Cogsworth	6.00

It's Magic
Snap's Magic Frame	4.00
Jaws Disappearing Food	4.00
I.Q.'s Magic Trunk	4.00
Kid Vid's Disappearing Act	4.00

Goofy Troop Bowlers
Wheeled figures w/bowling balls.
Goofy	5.00
Pete	5.00
PJ	5.00
Max	5.00

1993

Bonkers Fall-Apart Cars
Rabbit	4.00

These Toy Story items are from BK's first collection from the blockbuster computer-animated film in 1995.

These 1996 Toy Story items are from the second series that BK issued off the Disney/Pixar movie.

Dipsy, Po and La La arrived in Burger Kings across the country in 1999.

Jitters 4.00
Toots 4.00
Piquel 4.00
Bonkers 4.00

Glow-in-the-Dark Trolls
I.Q. Troll (orange hair)..................................... 4.00
Kid Vid Troll (pink hair).................................... 4.00
Snapps Troll (yellow hair) 4.00
Jaws Troll (green hair) 4.00

Pranks Set
Lingo's Snake 4.00
Jaws' Giant Spider 4.00
Boomer's Puzzle 4.00
I.Q.'s Woopee Cushion 4.00
Kid Vid's RC Squirter 4.00

Top Kids
Kid Vid.. 4.00

Scooby Doo, where are you? He was at Burger King in the fall of 1996 with the rest of his pals.

Burger King was big on Superman toys in the 1990s.

Wheelie.. 4.00
Jaws 4.00
Boomer 4.00

Capital Critters
Muggle in Lincoln's chair 4.00
Jammet Jams at White House............................ 4.00
Max at Jefferson Memorial 4.00
Presidential Cat at Capital Building 4.00

Dino Rollers
Blue 5.00
Red 5.00
Green.. 5.00
Purple 5.00
Yellow 5.00

Little Mermaid Splash Collection
Ariel on wind-up sea turtle 5.00
Flounder squirter 5.00
Sebastian wind-up 5.00
Urchin squirt toy.. 5.00

Mini Sports-Games Set
2 catch mitts w/ball 4.00
Mini football 4.00
Mini basketball w/hoop 4.00
Inflatable 8" soccer ball.................................... 4.00

Nightmare Before Christmas watches
Christmastown.. 6.00
Pumpkins.. 6.00
Bats & Cats.. 6.00
Halloweentown 6.00

Walt Disney World characters in vehicles
Mickey on pink stage 5.00
Minnie on yellow stage 5.00
Donald Duck on green house 5.00
Roger Rabbit on purple castle 5.00

1994

Burger King All-Stars Sports Kids Action Figures
Jaws w/football 4.00
Boomer w/hockey puck 4.00
Kid Vid w/basketball 4.00
I.Q. w/throwing disc 4.00
Snapps w/soccer ball... 4.00

Will Smith's buddies from Men in Black were available at BK in 1998.

Fast Food Miniatures

Ice-Cold Pepsi cup 3.00
Large Fries 3.00
Small Fries 3.00
Hot Dog 3.00
Whopper 3.00

Musical Fruit

Whistle Pickle 3.00

Lion King

(Movie set of PVC figures. The set was so popular not only was it issued twice in 1994, but during the first run when figures became scarce, packs of *Lion King* trading cards (SkyBox), were substituted. These cards were identical to the retail pack, except the Burger King packs came in see-thru, plastic packs. There was no Burger King identifying logo on the individual cards. The cards looked the same as the standard-issue retail cards.)
Mufasa 6.00

Love 'em or hate 'em, the Teletubbies landed at BK in the spring of 1999. Here's Tinky Winky and two of his friends.

These toys were some of the 12 Men in Black toys available in the 1998 animation set.

Young Nala 6.00
Young Simba 6.00
Scar 6.00
Rafiki 6.00
Ed, the Hyena 6.00
Pumbaa & Timon 6.00
Lion King card set (MIP only) 6.00

Z-Bots (tiny robot figures)

Buzzsaw 4.00
Jawbreaker 4.00
Turbine 4.00
Skyviper 4.00
Bugeye 4.00

1995

Gargoyles

Feb. 6 – Mar. 5
Color Mutation Broadway 4.00
Spin-to-Life Goliath 4.00
Gargoyles Pop-up Book 4.00
Glow-in-the-dark Plastic Cup 4.00
Other premiums in series 4.00

These spooky toys appeared in 1998 around "Eve of all Hallows."

Kay, Jay and a trio of slimy aliens were part of the 1998 Men in Black promotion.

Lion King Finger Puppets

Mar. 6 – Apr. 9

Pumbaa... 5.00
Rafiki 5.00
Simba 5.00
Ed, the Hyena 5.00
Scar.. 5.00

Disney's *Goofy Movie* figures

Apr. 10 – May 28

Goofy & Max in water raft squirter 4.00
Goofy & Max on water skis 4.00
Goofy on bucking bronco 4.00
Goofy & Max in fishing boat 4.00
Goofy & Max in car 4.00

Disney's Pocahontas PVC figures

June 19 – Aug. 3

John Smith 5.00
Meeko 5.00
Pocahontas 5.00
Grandmother Willow (3-piece tree)..................... 5.00
Governor Ratcliffe 5.00
Chief Powhatan (w/detachable cape) 5.00

Pocahontas Acrylic Glasses

July 5 (over-the-counter)

Meeko & Flit 5.00
Governor Ratcliffe & Percy 5.00
Chief Powhatan & Kocoum 5.00
Pocahontas & John Smith................................. 5.00

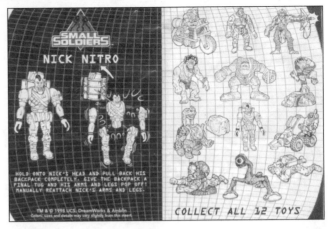

Nick Nitro was one of the vicious Small Soldiers that invaded BK during the summer of 1998.

Kid's Club Coolers

Aug. 14 – Sept. 24

Boomer 3.00
I.Q. 3.00
Kid Vid 3.00
Snaps 3.00
Jaws 3.00

Gargoyles II

Oct. 2 – Nov. 5

Spectroscope..4.00
Sparkling Spinner 4.00
Mini-Viewer 4.00
Spin-Attack Broadway 4.00
Bronx Launcher 4.00

Disney/Pixar's *Toy Story*

Nov. 13 – Dec. 18

Woody 5.00
Squash & Go Rex..5.00
Rev-Up-Racer...5.00
Buzz Lightyear..5.00
Mr. Potato Head..5.00
Army Guys...5.00

These Small Soldiers figures were born from the movie of the same name and appeared at BK in 1998.

Although it looks like another Halloween toy from BK, this over-the-counter bat is from the Fox film Anastasia.

Mr. Potatohead was so popular during his run in the Toy Story kid meal set that he spun off into a couple of his own series. This set was from the second in 1999.

Slamfist was one of the Gorgonite figures from the 1998 Small Soldiers set.

Disney/Pixar's Toy Story Hand Puppets
Over-the-counter Nov. 12 – Dec. 18
Woody... 5.00
Rex.. 5.00
Hamm 5.00
Buzz Lightyear 5.00

1996

BK Kids Glo-Force
Jan. 15 – Feb. 25
Boomer 3.00
I.Q. 3.00
Kid Vid 3.00
Snaps 3.00
Jaws 3.00

Disney's Pocahontas Hide 'n' Seek Finger Puppets
Feb. 26 – Mar. 31
Pampered Percy 4.00
John Smith's Lookout... 4.00
Busy Body Flit 4.00
Meeko's Hideout 4.00
Ruthless Ratcliffe 4.00
Peek-A-Boo Pocahontas...................................... 4.00

Disney's Oliver and Company I
For movie re-release Apr.1 – May 5
Chomping Dodger.. 4.00

Pop-Up Roscoe and Desoto.................................4.00
Scampering Tito..4.00
Floating Jenny and Oliver.....................................4.00
Speeding Scooter..4.00

Disney's Timon and Pumbaa
TV cartoon figures, May 6 – June 2
Timon...3.50
Pumbaa 3.50
Bug Munchin' Pumba 3.50
Super Secret Compass 3.50

Disney's Hunchback of Notre Dame
June 17 – Aug. 11
Laverne...4.00
Clopin 4.00
Hugo 4.00
Frollo...4.00
Phoebus..4.00
Victor 4.00
Quasimodo 4.00
Esmeralda and Djali the Goat...............................4.00

Disney's Hunchback of Notre Dame Hand Puppets
Over-the-counter, July 1 – Aug. 18
Hugo 5.00
Phoebus 5.00
Quasimodo 5.00

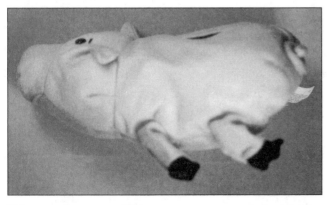

This over-the-counter Hamm puppet was part of the initial Toy Story BK promotion in 1996.

Big hair was in among the glow-in-the-dark BK Kid Trolls from 1993.

Aladdin balloons were distributed by Burger King when it still had the Disney license.

Esmeralda..5.00

Scooby-Doo
Aug. 19 – Sept. 15
Scrappy-Doo..3.00
Scooby and Shaggy...3.00
Scooby Coffin..3.00
Scooby-Doo..3.00
Mystery Machine..3.00

Disney's Oliver and Company II
For re-release of movie Oct. 1 – Oct. 29
Sneak-a-Peak Oliver..4.00
Surprise Attack Desoto...4.00
Dashing Dodger..4.00
Skateaway Tito...4.00

Disney/Pixar's Toy Story II
Oct. 30 – Dec.
Round 'em Up Woody...3.00
Spin-top Bo Peep...3.00
Stroll 'n Scope Lenny..3.00
Blast Away Buzz...3.00
Jawbreaker Scud..3.00
Spaces Out Alien..3.00
Speedy Deposit Hamm..3.00
Stretch and Roll Slinky Dog...................................3.00

Disney/Pixar's Toy Story II
Talking Woody...3.00

Good enough to eat. These M&M characters popped up at BK in 1997.

After years of sharing the spotlight with other DC characters, the Man of Steel finally rated a solo set of toys in 1997.

Talking Buzz Lightyear..3.00
Revvin' RC Racer...3.00

1997

M&M's Toys
January
Red M&M in a rolling inner tube 2.00
Orange M&M in a Dump Truck, tilt the bin to dump..........2.00
Blue M&M playing a Sax 2.00
Green M&M in a convertible.....................................2.00
Yellow M&M and his lunch box.................................2.00

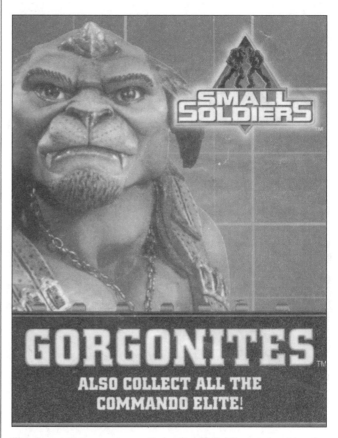

The Gorgonites were part of the Small Soldiers promotion in 1998.

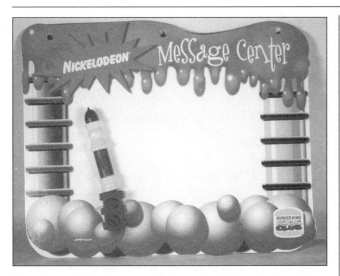

Friends could leave messages for each other with the 1999 Nickelodeon back to school message center.

Cartoon Network Wacky Racing
Feb. – Mar.

Wacky Racing Team Car 3.00
Speeding Bomber - Speed Buggy 3.00
Stone Age Rocker - Fred and Dino's foot-powered prehistoric
    racer 3.00
Burger King Race Team.. 3.00
Jeff Gordon's DuPont Race Car 3.00

Planet Patrol
Apr. – May

"All right you gold bricks, head 'em up and move 'em out!"
More Small Soldiers from 1998.

J.D.'s Shuttle Launch..2.50
Space Commander Jaws 2.50
I.Q.'s Planet Pacer..2.50
Boomer's Lightspeed Spacetop.......................................2.50
Kid Vid's Glo Chopper 2.50

The Land Before Time
May – June

Lumbering Littlefoot 3.00
Run-around Cera 3.00
Tumbling Ducky 3.00
Mealtime Spike 3.00
Squirting Petrie 3.00
Chomp, Chomp, Chomper..3.00
Jurassic Park over-the-counter watch (4 different watches):
    Each watch 4.00

M&M's Minis
July – Aug.

Secret Swarm Squirter 2.50
Chomping Teeth Swarm 2.50
Crazy Pull-Back Swarm 2.50
Scoop & Shoot Buggy 2.50

Superman
September

Superman balancing on Daily Planet Bldg. 3.00
Phone Booth: Clark Kent pictured on outside; spins open to
    reveal Superman 3.00
Standing Superman – push 'S' and arms go up in flying
    position 3.00
Lois Lane in pull back car 3.00
Base unit w/'S' symbol. Push 'S' and he flies 3.00

Scare Up Some Fun Action Toys
(includes glow-in-the-dark sticker) Oct. 6 – Nov. 2

Frankenstein...3.00
Count Dracula...3.00

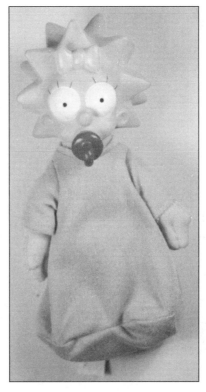

The Simpsons popped up at BK as over-the-counter dolls in 1990.

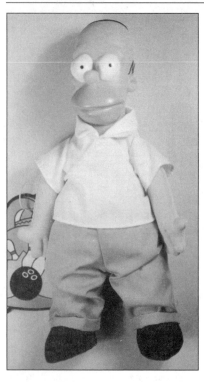

D'oh! Homer was a BK guy in the 1990s.

The Wolf Man 3.00
Scaly Squirter/The Creature from the Black Lagoon 3.00

Anastasia
Nov. 17 – Dec. 28
Anya 3.00
Fall-Apart Rasputin 3.00
Fiendish Flyer: 3.00
Bouncing Bartok 3.00
Beanie Bat 3.00
Collision Course Dimitri..................................... 3.00

Anastasia (over-the-counter items)
Rags to Riches Anastasia: An 8-1/2" doll 5.00
Runaway Train: A 12" long, motorized battery (battery included)
   includes 4 separate cars and a track to run on 5.00
Whining Bartok: An 8" plush/plastic toy 5.00
Cuddly Pooka: An adorable 6" plush dog 5.00

1998

Mr. Potato Head
Jan. 5 – Feb. 8
Mr. Potato Head Speedster 4.00
Hat's Off; Fry Flyer...4.00
Spinning Spud 4.00
Basket Shoot 4.00

Rugrats
Feb. 23 – Mar. 29
   (Includes a 12-page mini *Nickelodeon Magazine* that has some Rugrats puzzles, a coupon for Oral-B Rugrats products, and tells that the *Rugrats* movie will be in theaters in November.)
Crawling Tommy 2.50
Wind-up Chuckie 2.50
Angelica, in car 2.50
Sparking Reptar..2.50
Phil & Lil pull back 2.50

Kids Club Bug Riders
Kid Vid Scorpion 2.50
Boomer Dragonfly...2.50
I.Q. Caterpillar Crawler 2.50
Lingo Spider Flyer 2.50
Snaps Cricket Cruiser...2.50

Men in Black
Squishy Worm Guy..3.00
Squirting Worm Guy 3.00
Building Space Spinner 3.00
Globe Space Spinner 3.00

Marge looked a little like Frankenstein's bride in the Universal Monster set.

Lisa Simpson seems to have inherited her mother's hair care sense.

What would Halloween be without a set of scary figures from your favorite fast-food eatery? This Toonsylvania set came from BK in 1998.

MIB Neuralyzer 3.00
MIB Alien Detector 3.00
Slimed-Out Kay 3.00
Slimed-Out Jay 3.00
Split apart rotating Zed 3.00
Split apart light up Zed 3.00
Red Button Loop Blaster 3.00
Red Button Building Buster 3.00

Small Soldiers
Morning Brake Brick Bazooka 2.50
Boulder Blasting Punch-It Scratch It. 2.50
Nick Nitro 2.50
Soft 'N' Cuddly Slamfist 2.50
Rip Roarin' Kip Killigan 2.50
Bobbling Insaniac 2.50
Butch's Battle 2.50
Freedom Firing Archer 2.50
Crawling Link Static 2.50
Laughing Insaniac 2.50
Chip Hazard 2.50
Levitating Lens Ocula 2.50

Nickel-O-Zone
Hey Arnold Football 2.50
The Wild Thornberry's Commvee 2.50
Journey of Allen Strange 2.50
Cruising Cousin Skeeter 2.50
Action League Now! 2.50

Toonsylvania
Gurney Getaway 2.50
Screaming Screetch 2.50
Monster Maker 2.50
Phil's Teddy Crusher 2.50
Vic's Walkaway Bride 2.50

Rugrats
Okeydokey Tommy 2.50
Reptar Wagon 2.50
Aqua Reptar 2.50
Clip on Tommy with Baby Dil 2.50
Chuckie's Treasure Hunt 2.50
Phil & Lil: My Reptar 2.50
Monkey Mayhem 2.50
Shirley Lock Holmes Angelica 2.50
Dactar Glider 2.50
Scotting Susie 2.50
Baby Dil Awakens 2.50
Spike to the Rescue 2.50

1999

Mr Potato Head
Fry Fighter 2.00
Fry Jumper 2.00
Gotta Get' Em Mr. Potato Head 2.00
Smashed Potato — makes a funny sound 2.00
Light Up Mr. Potato Head — nose lights up ... 2.00

Cat & Dog
Feb. 22
Crazy Catch-Up 2.00
Gourmet Garbage Chaser 2.00
Key-Catching Clock 2.00
Souped-Up Skateboard 2.00
Wacky Waker-Upper 2.00

Nickelodeon Kids Choice Awards Toys
Apr. 12 – May 11
Slimed Again — watch green slime ooze over Rosie
    O'Donnell 2.00
Big Bold Blimp — wind it and it moves forward 2.00
Pop Goes The Rosie — Rosie pops out of a globe 2.00
Winning Wiggle Writer — the pen shakes as you try to
    write 2.00
Give The Winner A Hand inflatable hand 2.00
Heeere's Rosie—Rosie comes out from behind curtains 2.00

Teletubbies
May 10 – June 20 (clip-on bean bag finger puppets)
Tinky Winky 2.50
Dipsy... 2.50
Laa-Laa 2.50
Po 2.50
Noo-Noo 2.50
Bunny 2.50

New York Yankees Trading Card Sheets
(Three over-the-counter sheets, each with 9 players on punch-out cards, plus a coupon for a BK burger.)
Sheet #1 .... 2.00
Sheet #2 .... 2.00
Sheet #3 .... 2.00

Wild, Wild West
Movie set, July
Secret Spy Pen... 2.50

These two friendly Gorgonites arrived on Earth during BK's Toy Soldier promotion in 1998. They are flanking one of the mean Commando Elite soldiers.

Mr. Potato Head acquired a new lease on life after his appearance in Toy Story. This figure was from the first BK Toy Story set in 1995.

The Tarantula 2.50
Rita's Wild Ride 2.50
Rocket Rider 2.50
Rapid Repeating Squirter 2.50
James West Saddle Vault 2.50
Secret Spy Pen 2.50

Shades of the Wild West
(Wire rim sunglasses w/glass case — over-the-counter item.)
James West 3.00
Artemus Gordon 3.00

Back to School
Splat Calculator 2.50
Cargo Plane Pencil Case 2.50
Light-Up Rocket Pen 2.50
Light-Up Planet Pencil Topper 2.50
Nickelodeon Message Cente 2.50

Halloween Silly Slammers (Clip-ons)
October
Boo Hoo 2.50
Batty 2.50
Li' Jackie & Mo 2.50
Witchazel 2.50
Redeye 2.50

Pokémon
(Nov. 8. from *The First Movie*. Set includes 57 Pokémon characters (not including three different talking Pikachu mini-plush dolls), 151 movie scene trading cards, and six over-the-counter gold-plated cards in over-sized Pokéballs). A number of a limited edition full-color Pokémon collectible posters were produced, to address temporary spot shortages of toys. There was an exterior packaging number on each opaque plastic bag identifying the toys, however there was no correlation between the packaging number, and the Pokémon's number.)

#	Name	Type	
01	Bulbasaur	Launcher	3.50
03	Venusaur	Launcher	3.50
04	Charmander	Light-Up	3.50
07	Squirtle	Squirter	3.50
09	Blastoise	Squirter	3.50
12	Butterfree	Mini-Plush	3.50
25 A	Pikachu	Mini-Talking Plush	5.50
25 B	Pika-Chu	Mini-Talking Plush	5.50
25 C	Pika! Pika! Pika!	Mini-Talking Plush	5.50
26	Raichu	Light-Up	3.50
27	Sandshrew	Key Chain	3.50
28	Sandslash	Key Chain	3.50
31	Nidoqueen	Key Chain	3.50
32	Nidoran	Launcher	3.50
33	Nidorino	Key Chain	3.50
34	Nidoking	Key Chain	3.50
35	Clefairy	Rev-Top	3.50
39	Jigglypuff	Rev-Top	3.50
42	Golbat	Mini-Plush	3.50
43	Oddish	Mini-Plush	3.50
45	Vileplume	Key Chain	3.50
48	Venonat	Rev-Top	3.50
50	Diglett	Rev-Top	3.50
52	Meowth	Mini-Plush	3.50
54	Psyduck	Squirter	3.50
59	Arcanine	Launcher	3.50
60	Poliwag	Squirter	3.50
61	Poliwhirl	Mini-Plush	3.50
62	Poliwrath	Squirter	3.50
73	Tentacruel	Squirter	3.50
74	Geodude	Key Chain	3.50
75	Graveler	Rev-Top	3.50
76	Golem	Rev-Top	3.50
78	Rapidash	Launcher	3.50
79	Slowpoke	Launcher	3.50
81	Magnemite	Rev-Top	3.50
89	Muk	Key Chain	3.50
90	Shellder	Squirter	3.50
94	Gengar	Light-Up	3.50
100	Voltorb	Rev-Top	3.50
104	Cubone	Key Chain	3.50
106	Hitmonlee	Key Chain	3.50
109	Koffing	Rev-Top	3.50
111	Rhyhorn	Launcher	3.50
113	Chansey	Rev-Top	3.50
114	Tangela	Rev-Top	3.50
115	Kangaskhan	Key Chain	3.50
117	Seadra	Squirter	3.50
125	Electrabuzz	Key Chain	3.50
128	Tauros	Launcher	3.50
130	Gyarados	Mini-Plush	3.50
131	Lapras	Launcher	3.50
132	Ditto	Rev-Top	3.50
140	Kabuto	Squirter	3.50
143	Snorlax	Mini-Plush	3.50
149	Dragonite	Key Chain	3.50
150	Mewtwo	Light-Up	3.50
151	Mew	Light-Up	3.50
??	Togepi	Mini-Plush	3.50

Complete Set (with Pokéballs including all 3
   Pikachus) 175.00

A T-Rex hand puppet was part of the 1996 over-the-counter promotion during the first BK Toy Story series.

Over-the-counter Gold-plated cards
#25 .... Pikachu 10.00
#151 ..... Mewtwo 10.00
#39 .... Jigglypuff 10.00
#61 .... Poliwhirl 10.00
#06 .... Charizard 10.00
#?? .... Togepi 10.00

2000

Batman Beyond
Jan. 2
Action Wing Batman 2.50
J-Man Getaway 2.50
Indelible Inque... 2.50
Batarang Batman 2.50
Enemy Blight on the Glow............................... 2.50
Bat-Signal Spinner 2.50
Voice of Justice Batman.................................. 2.50
Batmobile Blast-Off. 2.50

The Wild Thornberrys
February
Thornberrys Traveling Trio 2.50
Commvee Commotion 2.50
Himalayan Mountain Climber........................... 2.50
Donnie's Wild Ride... 2.50

Pokémon
March 13 – March 26.
   (Reissue of original set of 57 toys, and/or 20 trading card sheets. The only difference is that the toys do not include the Pokéball, and that the exterior packaging numbering is completely different from the package numbering on the first set of toys. Included this time around was a coupon for $2 off *Pokémon: The First Movie* on VHS and DVD from Warner Home Video. Customers could also enter a Pokémon giveaway to win a complete set of all 57 toys (without Pokéballs), and a copy of movie. Two winners from each participating restaurant were randomly selected at the end of the promotion. Only restaurants in the U.S. participated in the giveaway. See previous listing for set details.)
2nd Set of Pokémon (except for three Pikachus) sans Pokéballs,
   each 2.00
2nd Set of Mini-Talking Plush Pikachus (A, B, C) sans Pokéballs,
   each 3.00

Complete 2nd Set (sans Pokéballs, including all three
   Pikachus) 135.00

The Road to El Dorado
   (Each Kids Meal contained 2 toys.)
Apr. 3 – Apr. 30
Swashbuckling Miguel and Prancing Altivo 2.50
Sabor Rattling Tulio and Headbutting Bull.......................2.50
Tzekel-Kan and Pouncing Jaguar 2.50
Bibo on the Go with Chel..2.50

Flintstones In Viva Rock Vegas
May 1
Puppy Dino Breaks Out (Dino walking out of his shell) 2.50
The Great Gazoo's Close Encounter...............................2.50
Fred's Two-Heel Drive (wind-up car) 2.50
Bronto King Dine & Drive (drive-thru w/Fred & Barney in
   wind-up car) 2.50

DragonballZ
   (Characters and exclusive trading cards from the collectible card game, plus an offer for a free video. Each toy has a sliver pewter-like finish except Super Saiyan Goku which has a gold tone pewter finish. They also have a light-up base w/card holder.)
May 29
Goku 2.50
Gohan 2.50
Vegeta 2.50
Frieza 2.50
Krillin 2.50
Piccolo 2.50
Super Saiyan Goku 2.50

Chicken Run
   (When all four toys are assembled together they can be used to build a 15" plane.)
June 19 – July 16
Mac's Highwire Act (plane's tail)...................................2.50
Ginger's Eggstreme Eggscape (plane's cockpit).............2.50
Rocky's Rooster Booster (plane's bottom) 2.50
Bunty Breaks Out (body and wings of plane) 2.50

Rugrats in Paris
November
Each toy..2.00

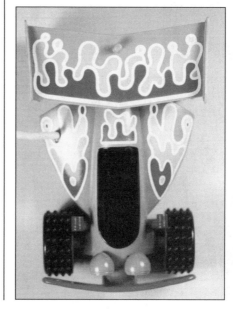

This over-the-counter vehicle was part of BK's 1995 Toy Story series.

Another over-the-counter Buzz Lightyear, this one from the 1995 series of BK Toy Story toys.

Bart the underachiever, and the rest of the Simpson clan, showed up at BK as over-the-counter dolls in 1990.

Over-the-counter Backstreet Boys exclusive CD
  (BK was a sponsor of their fall tour)
Each CD..5.00

The Big Help
Each item..2.00

NASCAR Racers
Each car...2.00

Kids Choice Awards
Each item..2.00

Pokémon 2000
  (Tie-in with the new movie — featuring cards in different shapes, sizes and colors.)
Each item..2.50

Rogue aliens beware, the Men in Black were prowling Burger Kings in 1998.

This MIP Woody from Toy Story is from the second series in 1996.

Together for the first time, Superman and Clark Kent (in spinning phone booth), from Burger King in 1997.

Carl's Jr.

Company Profile

Having left the family farm in Ohio, Carl Karcher moved to California with dreams of someday starting his own business. He did that in 1941 with his wife, Margaret, when they purchased a hot dog cart to operate at the corner of Florance and Central in southcentral Los Angeles. They borrowed $311 on their Plymouth and added $15 of their own to buy that initial cart. A few carts later they moved to Anaheim and opened their first full-service restaurant, Carl's Drive-In Barbecue, on January 16, 1945. In 1946, Karcher introduced burgers to the menu for the first time. In 1950, two more restaurants were opened. These new locations were so called "Carl's Jr." because they were smaller versions of the original drive-in barbecue.

For a brief time in 1992, the ever-elusive Waldo hung out at Carl's Jr.

Unlike most other restaurants at the time, the business had customers pay for their food when they placed their orders. By the end of the 1950s, there were four Carl's Jr. restaurants; in 1966, there were 24. By the time 1968 rolled around, the company had launched a full-scale expansion program. These new restaurants introduced carpeted dining rooms and cushioned seats — innovations in the fast-food industry. The company eventually sped up service by introducing a streamlined menu, consisting of only hamburgers, hot dogs, fries, malts and beverages.

To offset this the restaurant offered music and partial waitress service for dining room guests. The new concept became very popular and Carl's Jr. surged forward, adding 15 to 20 new restaurants a year. In 1974, it had built its first modern drive-thru. The 100th Carl's Jr. restaurant was opened in 1975. A soup and salad bar was introduced in 1976. It wasn't until 1979 that the company opened its first out-of-state location in Las Vegas. By the end of the year, the company's sales exceeded $100 million.

In 1981, the 300th location opened, and CKE went public. A year later the chain entered Arizona, but it wasn't until 1984 that Carl's Jr. was franchised for the first time. Over the next few years, numerous popular items were added to the menu, including the western bacon cheeseburger, charbroiler chicken sandwich, chicken club sandwich, breakfast platters, and the "all you want" beverage bars.

In the 1990s, Carl's Jr. continued to grow and expand with the opening of international restaurants in the Pacific Rim and Mexico. This growth continued and Carl's Jr. is recognized as an industry leader in the

Looking for a puddy tat? Well, if you stopped at Carl's Jr. in 1998, you would have found Sylvester and Tweety.

area of dual-brand concepts. It has successfully opened several dozen Carl's Jr./Green Burrito restaurants, offering its customers even greater choices. This co-branding is also reflected in CKE acquisition (in 1991) of the Hardee's fast-food franchise chain.

Not a kid's meal promotion, but worth noting nonetheless, was a Carl's Jr. contest run in 1993 that

Jim Hensen's Muppets also seem to get around. This poster promoted a 1993 set.

tied into Universal Studios Back to the Future ride. The contest featured a prize list that included a trip to the studio's theme park.

Carl's Jr. Toy Listing

All prices are for items mint in package (MIP), unless otherwise noted.

Where applicable, the date(s) of distribution and additional information on the following premiums were provided by the individual chains.

1986

Starfari
Feb. – Mar.
Each Premium 5.00

Sandcastle
June – July
Each Premium 5.00

Star Riders
Aug. – Sept.
Each Premium 6.00

Merry Meal
Nov. – Dec.
Each Premium 5.00

1987

Disneyland Circus Fantasy
Feb. – Apr.
Each Premium 6.00

December 30, 1998 through February 8, 1999

Dot Pull-back   Wakko, Yakko and Dot Freewheel   Yakko Bendable Figurine   Wakko Launcher

These wacky guys showed up at Carl's Jr. in 1999.

This sports figure skated onto the scene at Carl's Jr. in 1996.

Dinostar
May – June
Each Premium 5.00

Kool-Aid Summer Ice Pops
July – Aug.
Each Premium 5.00

School is a Jungle of Fun
Sept. – Oct.
Each Premium 5.00

Starnaments
Nov. – Dec.
Each Premium 4.00

1988

Barnyard
January
Each Premium 4.00

Dragon Kids
March – Apr.
Each Premium 4.00

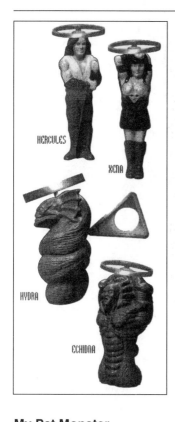

Hercules and Xena muscled in on the action at Carl's Jr. in 1996.

My Pet Monster
June – July
Each Premium 5.00

Lifesavers
July – Aug.
Each Premium 4.00

Stationery Kit
Sept. – Oct.
Each Premium 4.00

Starnaments
Nov. – Dec.
Each Premium 4.00

1989

Sea Star – Generic
January
Each Premium 4.00

Just Me and My Family
Jan. – Feb.
Each Premium 3.00

Springtime Bunny Tales
Mar. – Apr.
Each Premium 3.00

Camp Carl's Jr.
May – July
Each Premium 3.00

Star of the Class
Aug. – Sept.
Each Premium 3.00

Halloween
October
Each Premium 4.00

1990

Solar Star – Generic
January
Each Premium 3.00

Young Executive
Jan. – Feb.
Each Premium 3.00

Soccer Star
Mar. – Apr.
Each Premium 3.00

Beach Creatures
May – June
Each Premium 3.00

Zoo Crew
Aug. – Sept.
Each Premium 3.00

Fun House Facts Finger Puppets
Oct. – Nov.
Rudy Rabbit..4.00
Barney Bear..4.00
Petey Pumpkin 4.00
Glenda Ghost 4.00
Franklin...4.00
Tina Tiger...4.00

Frosty the Snowman
Nov.– Dec.
Each Premium 3.00

1991

Jellystone Fender Bender 500
  (Similar set distributed by Hardee's.)
Jan. – Mar.
Yogi & Boo Boo in Jellystone Jammer.............................6.00

Fat cat Garfield was a popular fellow with the fast-food chains. He was available at Carl's Jr. in 1997.

Hey surf doggies! This Lil' Bro merchandise hit the beach at Carl's Jr. over the summer of 1999.

Magilla Gorilla & Wally Gator in Swamp Stomper 6.00
Huckleberry Hound & Snagglepuss in Luckey Trucky 6.00
Quick Draw McGraw & Baba Looey in Texas Twister 6.00
Dick Dasterdly & Muttley in Dirty Truckster 6.00

Camping with Woody Woodpecker & Pals
Mar. – Apr.
Each Premium 5.00

Play Ball with Cracker Jacks
May – June
Each Premium 3.00

50 Nifty Years
June 26 – Aug. 6
Each Premium 3.00

PCH Back-to-School
Aug. – Sept.
Each Premium 3.00

Real Ghostbusters/Halloween
October
Each Premium 4.00

Starnaments
December
Anniversary Star 3.00
Twinkle Star 3.00
Holly Star 3.00
Moose Star... 3.00

1992

Mini Push 'n Go
Jan. – Feb.
Each Premium 3.00

Where's Waldo
Feb. – Mar.
Pencil Watcher 5.00
Incredible Activity Kit... 5.00

Glow-in-the-Dark Switch Sticker 5.00
Straw Buddy 5.00

Star Rookies
Apr. – May
Inflatable Bat... 4.00
Inflatable Ball 4.00
Baseball Card Frame w/Sticker Sheet.............................. 4.00
Baseball Card Holder w/Baseball Cards 4.00

Camp California
   (Similar set distributed by Hardee's.)
June – July
Bear Squirter 4.00
Lil' Bro Disc... 4.00
Mini Volleyball... 4.00
Suction Cup Spinner.. 4.00

Soccer Stars
Aug. – Sept.
Each Premium 3.00

Spooky Pails
October
Spider Pail & Sticker Sheet 3.00
Blob Pail & Sticker Sheet.. 3.00

Mix-and-Match Dinosaurs
   (Also distributed by Dairy Queen and White Castle)
November
Purple Apatosaurus 4.00
Blue Pteranodon 4.00
Tyranosaurus Rex 4.00
Stegosaurus 4.00

Silly Putty Silliness
Dec. – Feb. ('93)
Each Premium 3.00

1993

The Addams Family

Spooky pails are a traditional Halloween giveaway for Carl's Jr.

Happy Star Christmas tree ornaments are a mainstay at Carl's Jr. during the holiday season.

Feb. – Mar.
Each Premium 6.00

Hair Dudes
Mar. 31 – May
Each Premium 3.00

Rollerblades
May 19 – June
Rollerblade Chase Game Book 3.00
Rollerblade Snap to it 3.00
Roller Cube Game 3.00
Safe Skatin' Happy 3.00

Shark
July 7 – Aug.
Wrist Grabber 3.00
Shark Cup & Lid 3.00
Shark Bubblemaker 3.00
Shark Coin Case & Sticker Sheet 3.00

Back to School with Happy
Aug. 25 – Sept.
Magnet Frame 3.00
Bendy Pen 3.00
Pencil Case 3.00
Folder, Sticker Sheet, & Bookmark/Ruler 3.00

Spooky Pails
Oct. 6 – Oct. 31
Each Premium 3.00

Muppet Parade of Stars
Nov. 24 – Dec. 24
Miss Piggy in purple car 5.00
Gonzo in orange car 5.00
Kermit in red car 5.00
Fozzie in blue car 5.00

1994

Crazy Doodlers
Jan. 5 – Feb.15
Crazy Tip Marker 3.00
Crazy Doodler Top 3.00
Spiral Wheel Doodler 3.00
Duo Doodler w/Crayons 3.00

Happy's Hockey League
Feb. 16 – Mar. 29
Each Premium 3.50

Bone-a-Fide Friends
Apr. 6 – May 10
Steggly 3.00
Donny 3.00
Ty 3.00
Topsy 3.00

Wildballs
May 18 – June 21
Each Premium 3.00

Key Racers
June 29 – Aug. 2
Each Premium 3.00

Beakman's World
Aug. 17 – Sept. 27
Each Premium 3.00

Raging Reptiles PVC figures w/bathing suits and sunglasses
October
Brown w/yellow striped top 3.00
Green w/purple trunks 3.00
Tan w/pink & blue striped suit 3.00
Green w/yellow & red polka-dot suit 3.00

Chipmunks
Nov. 23 – Dec. 27
Each Premium 4.00

1995

EEK! The Cat
Mar. 31 – May 10
Each Premium 2.50

Cool Water Drenchers
June 7 – July 25
Each Premium 2.50

This mummy head coin holder was from the 1998 Eerie, Indiana set.

It was OK to cry "shark" at your local Carl's Jr. during this 1993 promotion.

Two Cool Cows
July 28 – Sept. 26
Each Premium 2.50

Spooky Pails
Sept. 20 – Oct. 31
Each Premium 2.50

Cups & Crazy Wavy Straws
October
Each Premium 2.50

Life Savers
Nov. 22 – Dec. 31
Each Premium 2.50

1996

Bobby's World
Jan. 15 – Feb. 26
Bobby's Double Duty Dozer 2.50
Rollin' Roger 2.50
Wacky Weebly 2.50
Bobby's Silly Scrambler 2.50

Bendable Buddies
Mar. 20 – Apr. 30
Each Premium 2.50

Swan Kats
May 8 – June 18
Each Premium 2.50

Racers
June 26 – Aug. 6
Each Premium 2.50

Bump in the Night
Aug. 14 – Sept. 17
Each Premium 2.50

Spooky Pails
Sept. 25 – Oct. 31
Each Premium 2.50

Tootsie Roll's 100th Anniversary Train Set
Nov. 20 – Dec. 25
Engine 2.50
Freight Car 2.50
Passenger Car 2.50
Caboose 2.50

1997

Scared Guy
Jan. 2 – Feb. 11
Each Premium 2.50

Sonic the Hedgehog
Feb. 19 – Apr. 1
Each Premium 2.50

Life with Louie
Apr. 23 – May 27
Each Premium 2.50

The Tick
May 28 – June 8
Each Premium 4.00

Hercules & Xena
July 15 – Aug. 26
Hercules Launcher 4.00
Xena Launcher 4.00
Hydra Launcher 4.00
Echidna Launcher 4.00

Earthworm Jim
Sept. 3 – Nov. 18
Snott Squirter 2.50
Earthworm Jim Plasma Blaster 2.50

Crazy Doodlers were all the rage at Carl's Jr. in 1993.

68

Woody Woodpecker bike accessories were big at Carl's Jr. in 1999.

Princess What's Her Name Spinner 2.50
Monster Dog Peter Puppy 2.50

Munsters Cool Combo Buckets
Sept. 24 – Oct. 30
Each of 4 Buckets 5.00

Garfield Christmas Racers
Nov.19 – Dec. 25
Clearing the Way 5.00
Snowmobile 5.00
Slippin' & Sliding 5.00
Downhill Racer 5.00

1998

Where is Carmen Sandiego
Spy Camera 2.50
Vanishing Landmark Viewer 2.50
Map Airplane Magnifier 2.50
Locator Game 2.50

Bad Atti-Toads
Charga-Toad 2.50
Dunka-Toad 2.50
Goalie-Toad 2.50
Socca-Toad 2.50

Beetle Borgs Metallix
Feb. 25 – Apr. 7
Each of 4 toys 3.00

Woody Woodpecker Bike Gear
Apr. 15 – May 26
Water Bottle 3.00
Wheel Clacker 3.00
Bike Spinner 3.00
License Plate 3.00

Weird Eerie Indiana
June 3 – July 14
Werewolf Milk Truck Stamp Dispenser 2.50
Mummy Head Coin Holder 2.50
ATM Money Grabbing Bank 2.50
Rolling Alley-gator Action Toy 2.50

Sylvester and Tweety Mysteries
July 22 – Sept. 15
Spinning toy w/Sylvester and Tweety inside 3.50
Sylvester and Tweety Pull-back Roller 3.50
Sylvester and Tweety Runaway Chair 3.50
Sylvester Water Squirter 3.50
Tweety's the Chase is on Viewer 3.50

Casper
Sept. 23 – Oct. 27
Each Premium 3.50

Space Goofs
Sept. 19 – Dec.22
Each Premium 3.00

1999

Animaniacs
Dec. 30 – Feb. 9
Wakko, Yakko, & Dot free wheel racer 3.50
Dot Pull-back 3.50
Yakko Bendable Figure 3.50
Wakko Spring Loaded Launcher 3.50

Felix the Cat
Felix Magic Yo-Yo 2.00
Puzzle Block (Felix's magic bag of tricks) 2.00
Felix Binoculars 2.00
Felix Zipper Pull (watch his face change) 2.00

Spider-Man
May
Spider-Man Disc Launcher 3.00
Spider-Man Web Flyer 3.00

Kids could be star baseball players in 1999.

A walking robot wandered into Carl's Jr. and walked out with a kids meal.

Spider-Man Web Spinner	3.00
Spider-Man Hover Craft	3.00
Carl's Jr. Antenna Star	4.00

Pinky & the Brain
The Brain Box with temporary tattoos	2.00
Pinky in the Cheese Spinning Top	2.00
Elmyra Mouse Launcher	2.00
Pinky and The Brain Rocket Ship	2.00

Pink Panther
Jet Groover — Pink Panther in a Jet	2.00
Magnificent Magnifier	2.00
Clouseau Sticker Dispenser (holds a roll of U.S. stamps)	2.00
Jet Ski Jammer	2.00

Spy Dogs
Ralph Hydrant Squirter	2.00
Cat Astrophe and Mitzy Chase Game	2.00
Scribble's Motor 'n' Mail Box	2.00

Angus Periscope	2.00

Addam's Family Halloween Pails
Each of 4 buckets	2.50

Blazing Bugs
Bug Shooter	2.00
Electric Firefly	2.00
Hopper's 'Copter	2.00
Flyswatter Follies	2.00

2000

The Nuttiest Nutcracker
(Toys from the video)
Each toy	1.50

The Jetsons
George's Joyride	2.00
Elroy's Sky Surfer	2.00
Astro's Crazy for Cats	2.00
Galactic Gazer	2.00

Cartoon Network Cow & Chicken
Evil Cownevil	1.50
Just the Tube of Us	1.50
Watch Out for that Chicken	1.50
Take Along T.V.	1.50

Big Guy & Rusty the Boy Robot
(Based on the Dark Horse comic-book series.)
Rusty's Alien Equalizer Pull-ring Flyer	2.00
Big Guy Stomper Wind-up Walker	2.00
Airborne Alien Flying Disc	2.00
Big Guy Blast-off Spring Jumper	2.00

Tom and Jerry
June
Charging Cheddar Jerry	2.00
Speeding Spike	2.00
Squirter Tom	2.00
Tom and Jerry Show Viewer	2.00

"Super Secret" Promotion
July
Each toy	1.50

Dairy Queen

Company Profile

Founded in 1940, International Dairy Queen (IDQ) has been a part of American neighborhoods for generations. As the world's largest dessert chain, the IDQ Companies (which include Orange Julius and Karmelkorn) are a major player in the international fast-food arena. The Dairy Queen tradition that many Americans grew up with now exists in more than 25 countries, and is continuously growing.

DQ was the brainchild of J.F. McCullough who, in 1938, was experimenting with a new type of frozen dessert in his Green River, Illinois, ice cream company (The Home Made Ice Cream Company). He discovered that his dessert stayed better if it was kept soft and was dispensed fresh from the freezer rather than hard, and scooped out of a container. In order to test his theory, he approached Sherb Noble, a customer of his in Kankakee, Illinois, to see if he was interested in carrying the new product.

The response proved overwhelming. With the addition of a brand-new type of freezer that was capable of not only dispensing the proper serving amount, but could keep the ice cream at the proper temperature, the new dessert treat was well on its way. An agreement was signed for the freezer/dispenser in 1939, and by 1940 the first of many stores was ready to open for business.

It was in the 1950s that DQs began adding hot food to the menu. Again, it was an idea whose time had come. By the 1960s, there were over 3,000 DQs in the US. At this time the current logo was designed, and the company added "International" to its name.

In the 1980s DQ added both Orange Julius and Karmelkorn to its family of food groups, expanding not only its reach, but product lineup.

The Dairy Queen/Brazier concept features the Dairy Queen treat line of soft-serve dairy products and Brazier fast-food menu. These stores are designed to include indoor dining, restroom facilities and a drive-thru window unit. Some of the locations include outdoor dining areas and children's playgrounds.

Dairy Queen/Limited Brazier stores are often in urban markets in highly visible, strip-type shopping centers. The stores are placed where they are easily accessible to large numbers of pedestrians and/or motorists. This concept features soft-serve dairy

Karmelkorn, like Orange Julius, is a Dairy Queen company.

Orange Julius is owned and operated by International Dairy Queen.

Portly Garfield PVCs showed up at the right place, Dairy Queen, during a 1999 promotion.

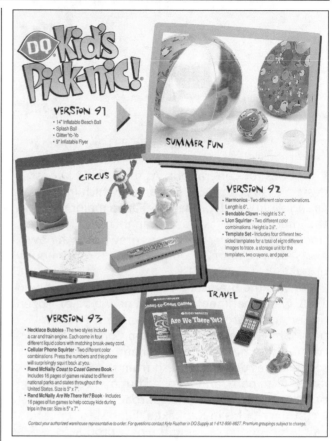

Here is a sampling of some of the Kid's Meal toys that DQ distributed in 1998.

This Cartoon Factory Kid's Meal set (#99) gave kids a chance to be cartoonists in 1998.

Eat at DQ and see the world, or at least the world as it was presented in this world travel set in 1994.

Dairy Queen's sport set provided kids with some indoor fun during the winter of 1999.

We don't know where Wishbone came from, but he wound up at DQ in '99.

products, frozen cakes and logs, frozen yogurt and Brazier hot dogs and barbecue sandwiches.

Treat Center franchise units combine the Dairy Queen soft-serve product line, Karmelkorn caramel coated popcorn and/or the Orange Julius creamy fruit beverages. The mix of unique concepts and product lines make it a popular choice in major shopping malls across the US.

On January 7, 1998, IDQ, Inc. became a wholly owned subsidiary of Berkshire Hathaway Inc. Currently, IDQ develops, licenses and services a system of more than 5,790 Dairy Queen stores in the U.S., Canada and other countries. The main menu features hamburgers, hot dogs, beverages, and various dairy desserts. There are around 410 Orange Julius locations in the U.S., Canada and abroad. These operations feature blended drinks made from orange juice, fruits, and other fruit flavors, along with various snack items. There are some 45 Karmelkorn stores featuring popcorn and other treat items. Almost 90 percent of the outlets are in the US; the rest are scattered in more than 20 other countries

In 1996, in cooperation with the U.S. Consumer Product Safety Commission (CPSC), IDQ voluntarily recalled some 150,000 toy water batons that were distributed with Kid's Meals. This was done after it was discovered that if a child sucked or chewed on the baton's end cap, it was possible that the cap could come off, releasing small, plastic balls from inside the baton. It was determined that the end-

cap and the balls presented a possible choking hazard to young children.

IDQ received as many as eight reports of the baton's end cap coming off. No injuries were ever reported. The toy water baton, distributed with Kid's Meals at Dairy Queen stores nationwide from June through October 1996, was a clear plastic rod, measuring 9 inches long, with glitter and blue, purple, and green balls floating in water inside of the baton. The ends were adorned with purple caps with Dairy Queen printed on the rod itself.

At the time of the announcement, consumers were asked to take the batons away from young children and return them to their local Dairy Queen store. DQ offered consumers returning the batons a free Kid's Meal or ice cream sundae for each baton returned.

As it is assumed that most of these batons were returned to DQ and/or disposed of, any remaining in the secondary, collectible market are naturally harder to find, and thus worth more as a collectible item.

IDQ currently has two separate promotional programs in place to disseminate products. One is media-supported, and the other is its warehouse program.

In the list that follows, the media-supported promotions are identified as either Treatmeal or, as it eventually became called, Kid's Meal. The warehouse program items proceed the Treat/Kid's Meal items for each year that the two programs have been in place. The following list contains only the items that are DQ-specific. Orange Julius items are listed separately. As of this writing, Karmelkorn does not have any collectible or promotional program in place.

Like most fast-food chains, DQ loves to brand toys that it issues, as these 1998 DQ trucks proved.

Dairy Queen Toy Listing

All prices are for items mint in package (MIP), unless otherwise noted.

Where applicable, the date(s) of distribution and additional information on the following premiums were provided by the individual chains.

1991
Pictionary (three different games)
Each game... 4.00

DQ Ice Cream Whistles
Single Ice Cream Cone 3.00
Double Ice Cream Cone 3.00
Radio Flyer
Red Wagon...3.00
Treatmeal #1
Flavor Friend Characters
Strawberry Bear...4.00

DS9's starship, the USS Defiant, warped into Dairy Queens across the country in 1977. This set of Star Trek toys is the only known fast-food set.

Marshmallow Moose	4.00
Butterscotch Beaver	4.00
Chocolate Chimp	4.00
Drinking Straw	4.00
Color Change Tumbler	4.00
Magnet –3 versions	4.00
Mini Squeeze Bottle – 3 versions	4.00

1992

Rock-a-Doodle Figurines
Chanticleer	4.00
Grand Duke	4.00
Patou	4.00
Snipes	4.00
Peppers & Edmond	4.00

Silly Putty
Marshmallow Moose	3.00
Chocolate Chimp	3.00
Strawberry Bear	3.00

DQ Suction Cup Spinners
Strawberry Bear	3.00
Butterscotch Beaver	3.00
Chocolate Chimp	3.00
Marshmallow Moose	3.00

Treatmeal #2
Pictionary – 3 versions	4.00
Scented Marker – 2 versions	3.00
Flavor Friend Characters Sidewalk Chalk – 3 versions	3.00
Crayon Package and Coloring Sheet	3.00

Treatmeal #3
Pictionary – 3 versions	4.00
Klick Stix	3.00
Pop Rocket – 3 versions	3.00

Treatmeal #4
Beatrix Potter Books	4.00
Flavor Friend Magnets – 3 styles	3.00
Pop Rocket – 3 versions	3.00
Klick Stix	3.00

Treatmeal #5
Sand Pail & Shovel	3.00
Seek & Find Book	3.00
Scented Marker – 3 styles	3.00
Zap Disc – 3 versions	3.00

Treatmeal #6
Mini Flyer – 2 versions	3.00
Color Change Tumbler	3.00
Pictionary	4.00

Treatmeal #7
Pull-Back Racer – 6 versions	3.00
Shoe Laces w/Bracelet – 4 versions	3.00
Flavor Friends Poster	3.00
Radio Flyer Wagon	3.00
Flavor Friends Magnet	3.00
Wrist Pack	3.00
Pictionary	4.00

Treatmeal #8
Silly Putty – 3 versions	3.00
Zap Stick – 3 versions	3.00
Prisimscope – 4 versions	3.00
Troll Sticker Sheet – 4 versions	3.00
Pictionary	4.00

Treatmeal #9
Travel Tumbler	3.00
Troll – 8 versions	3.00
Squeeze Bottle – 3 versions	3.00
Pop Rocket	3.00
Klick Stix	3.00
Pictionary	3.00

1993

Dennis the Menace Cool Heads
Dennis the Menace 3-D topper & cup	6.00
Margaret 3-D topper & cup	6.00
Joey 3-D topper & cup	6.00
Ruff 3-D topper & cup	6.00

Tom 'n' Jerry
Jerry Sizzling Stamper	3.00
Tom Sizzling Stamper	3.00
Jerry Squirter	3.00
Tom Squirter	3.00
Jerry Rolling Car	3.00
Tom Rolling Car	3.00

Bear Water Color Set
Plastic bear with paint pallet and small brush	4.00

Starts December, 1997

Dennis the Menace is a DQ kid, as this 1997 set proved.

These Pound Jungle characters showed up at DQ in 1998.

Creative Child Card Set
ABC Flash cards 5.00
Crazy Eights 5.00
Go Fish 5.00
Old Maid 5.00

Dinosaur Bubbles
Different dinosaurs on bubble containers.
Each 4.00
Yo-Yo 4.00

Holiday Train
(Four-car set with company logo and Dr. Pepper decals on the cars; also distributed by Sonic Drive-In & White Castle.)
Engine 3.00
Coal car 3.00
Box car 3.00
Caboose 3.00

Treatmeal #10
Monster w/trading card 3.00
Scented Marker 3.00
Tattoo Sheet 3.00
Beatrix Potter Book – 6 new versions 3.00
Magnet – 3 versions 3.00
Pictionary 4.00

Treatmeal #11
Groan Tube – 4 colors 3.00
Pop Rocket
   Space Shuttle vehicles
Pink 3.50
White 3.50
Gray 3.50
Yellow 3.50
Modeling Clay Pack 3.00
Water Squirter – 7 versions 3.00
Pictionary 4.00

Treatmeal #12
Accordion Mini Squeeze Bottle – 2 versions 3.00
Dino Sticker – 4 versions 3.00
Paint Set 3.00
Zap Disk – 3 versions 3.00
Scented Marker 3.00
Pictionary 4.00

Treatmeal #13
Wall Walker – 4 versions 3.00
Wagon 3.00

Surprise Magazine 3.00
Sidewalk Chalk – 3 versions 3.00
Snicker Card 3.00
Pictionary 4.00

Treatmeal #14
Transformer – 10 versions (#s 0-1) 4.00
Beach Ball 3.00
Flip Flop – assorted colors 3.00
Troll 3.00
Pictionary 4.00

Treatmeal #15
Prisimscope – 4 versions 3.00
Ecology Activity Book w/Crayons – 3 versions 3.00
Sunglasses (neon) 3.00
Accordion Squeeze Bottle 3.00
Pictionary 4.00

Treatmeal #16
Scented Marker 3.00
Pull-back Race Cars (each car was different color, and had a
   decal on hood).
Green w/bee 3.00
Red w/doves 3.00
White w/tire 3.00
Blue w/Chevy logo & stars 3.00
Orange w/flame 3.00
Car #6 .... 3.00
Crazy Straw 3.00
Transformer 3.00
Shoelaces 3.00
Pictionary 4.00

Treatmeal #17
Dino Static Cling 4.00
Trading Card 3.00
Magnet 3.00
Dino Pull-Apart 3.00

Treatmeal #18
Dino Pull-Apart – 3 versions 4.00
Dino Finger Puppet – 3 versions 4.00
Floppy Flyer 4.00
Straw Connector – 4 versions 4.00

DQ kids could become Junior Astronauts in 1998.

Dairy Queen seemed to be an appropriate venue for a promotion called "Extreme Arctic."

Curious George Book – 4 versions 3.00
Pictionary 4.00

Treatmeal #19
Glow-in-the-Dark Tumbler – 2 versions 3.00
High Bounce Ball – 2 versions 3.00
Dino Pull-Apart
   Mix-and-Match Dinosaurs (also distributed by Carl's Jr. and White Castle)
Purple Apatosaurus 4.00
Blue Pterodactyl... 4.00
Tyrannosaurus Rex.. 4.00
Stegosaurus... 4.00
Sweatband – 3 versions.. 3.00

Treatmeal #20
Animal Sipper – 2 versions 3.00
Playing Card – 3 versions 3.00
Dino Trading Card (5/pk) 3.00
High Bounce Ball – 2 versions 3.00

Treatmeal #21
Surprise Magazine.. 3.00
Dennis the Menace Sticker (2/set)................................. 3.00
Utensil – 4 versions.. 3.00
Magic Spring 3.00

Treatmeal #22
Ocean Static Cling – 2 versions..................................... 3.00
Hoadley Book – 2 versions 3.00
Dino Trolls (set of 4, each troll came with 4 different color hair – pink, yellow, blue, and 4th color)
Boy (green w/blue coveralls)... 4.00
Girl (tan w/pink dress) 4.00
Other 2 trolls 4.00

1994

Dennis the Menace Make Believes
April
Dennis the Menace Fire Engine Pullback 6.00
Joey Hot Rod Pullback.. 6.00
Margaret Figurine w/Snap-on Astronaut Suit................. 6.00
Ruff Figurine w/Snap-on Dragon Costume 6.00

Baby's Day Out (movie set)
July
Baby Bink's Activity Book.. 3.00

Baby Bink's Pop-up Diary Book...................................... 3.00
Baby Bink's Sticker Book.. 3.00
Baby Bink's Confusing Crooks Pop-up Book 3.00

Alvin & the Chipmunks Music Makers
August
Simon's Maraca... 4.00
Theodore's Kazoo 4.00
Alvin's Pan Flute 4.00
Chipmunk's Tambourine 4.00

Balance Buddies Stacking Figures
Red.. 3.00
Light blue 3.00
Yellow.. 3.00
Pink.. 3.00
Dark Blue... 3.00

Suckerball
Plastic ball with suction cups 2.50

Circus Train
Engine 6.00
Red car/cage 6.00
Yellow car/cage... 6.00
Caboose 6.00

Dennis the Menace Christmas Ornaments
Denis & Joey in stocking 5.00
Dennis w/candy cane 5.00
Dennis w/wreath 5.00
Dennis wrapping gift 5.00

Treatmeal #23
Softball – 3 versions (packed in assortment of all 3).. 3.00
Flexi Block 3.00
Dennis the Menace Color Your Own Puzzle – 4 versions... 5.00
Dino Sticker Puzzle – 4 versions 4.00

Treatmeal #24
Press n' Go Car – assortment of 5 program versions.......... 34.00
Bendable Dino Triceratops 3.00
Velociraptor.. 3.00
Brachiosaurus.. 3.00
Three others 3.00
Dennis the Menace Glow Cup w/Straw & Lid.................. 4.00
Crazy Bouncer – 4 assorted colors 3.00

Looking for superheroes? These tough guys showed up at DQ in 1997.

This group of stuffed barnyard animals took up residence at DQ in 1998.

Kid's Meal #25
Baby Barbell Cup 3.00
Bloom Ball 3.00
Under Sea Static Cling Activity Book 3.00
Funny Racer Pull-back – 12 styles 3.00

Kid's Meal #26
Mini Bubble Water Game – 4 different games 3.00
Sport Bear Crayon Set w/paper – 4 styles 3.00
3-D Tattoo w/3-D Glasses – 8 tattoos 3.00
Dennis the Dragon Book 4.00

Kid's Meal #27
Press N' Go Space Shuttle – 4 styles 3.00
Africa & Australia Search Activity Book – 25 of each 3.00
Deep Sea Activity 3.00
Space Shuttle Hologram Puzzle 3.00
Balance Builder – 5 per pack 3.00
Sand Pail Set 3.00

Kid's Meal #28
Mini Puzzles – assorted styles of clowns 7 frogs 3.00
My Favorite Story Cassette
    Beauty and the Beast 3.00
    Jack & the Beanstalk 3.00
12 oz. Sport Sipper – 4-color/1 style 3.00
Race Car 3.00

Kid's Meal #29
Space Cruiser Pull-back Vehicle – 6 styles 3.00
Baby Dino Troll 3.00
Embroidered Character Sweatband
    Dennis the Menace 4.00
    Margaret 4.00
Travel Bingo Game 3.00

Kid's Meal #30
Sand Pail w/shovel – 2 colors 3.00
Inflatable Frisbee – 1 style/4-color imprint 3.00
Accordion Squeeze Bottle – 2 designs 3.00
Beach ball – 4-color imprint 3.00

Kid's Meal #31
Triangular Slinkee 3.00
Custom Yo Yo – 2 styles 3.00
Dino Bubbler – 6 styles/assorted colors 3.00
Custom Dennis the Menace Activity Book 4.00

Circus Train – 4 styles 3.00
Goof Ball – 2 colors of balls...............................3.00
Puzzle Maze 3.00
Dino Paint Set...3.00

Kid's Meal #32
DQ Super Ball..3.00
Color Transfer – 2 versions 3.00
Barney Figurine – 3 versions..............................3.00
Baby's Day Out Book – 4 styles 3.00

Kid's Meal #33
G.I. Joe Jeep 4.00
Kitty Surprise 3.00
Puppy in my Pocket...3.00
Transformer 3.00

Kid's Meal #34
Dennis the Menace Twisty Block...........................5.00
German Shepherd & Dalmatian Book/Dog.....................3.00
Dennis the Menace Dig Zig-Zag Card 6.00
Silly Putty...3.00

1995

Dennis the Menace Music Makers
January
Dennis the Menace 3-D Sipper 5.00
Margaret 3-D Sipper 5.00
Joey 3-D Sipper 5.00
Ruff 3-D Sipper 5.00

The Jetsons
April
George & Jane's Space Sphere Inflatable 5.00
Astro's Treadmill Workout Pull-back.......................5.00
Elroy's Intergalactic Twirler 5.00
Rolling Rosie's Pull-back 5.00

Bobby's World
July
Globe Trotter Viewer..2.00
Twister Adventure 2.00
Bobby's Bulldozer 2.00
Suction Webbly..2.00

Muppets
October
Kermit Finger Puppet Topper & Cup........................5.00
Miss Piggy Finger Puppet Topper & Cup....................5.00

Don't call the exterminator. These DQ bugs were supposed to come with your Kid's Meals back in 1998.

What better place to play than a "Kidsville" that came with its own DQ? This was available in 1997.

Gonzo Finger Puppet Topper & Cup 5.00
Fozzie Finger Puppet Topper & Cup 5.00

Dogs (PVC figures)
German Shepherd 3.00
Dalmatian 3.00
Others in set... 3.00

Kid's Pick-nici (various Mattel toys)
Puppy in My Pocket 4.00
G.I. Joe in Jeep 4.00
Transformer 4.00
Kitty Surprise.. 4.00

Kid's Meal #35
Duck Whistle 3.00
Collapsible Cup – 2 colors 3.00
Dennis the Menace Velcro Paddle Ball Game 5.00
Dennis the Menace Dragon Book 5.00
Dennis the Menace Activity Book 5.00
Dennis the Menace Sticker Book.................................... 5.00
Dennis the Menace Fun Book... 5.00

Kid's Meal #36
Play Doh & 3-D Dennis the Menace Face 3.00
Play Doh & Ruff Figure 3.00
Play Doh & Margaret Cut-out... 3.00
Play Doh & Rolling Pin... 3.00

Kid's Meal #37
Frame Magnet.. 3.00
Color on Transfer 3.00
Dennis the Menace Face & Ruff Straw 5.00
Moon Squeesh Ball.. 4.00

Kid's Meal #38
Alvin & the Chipmunks.. 4.00
Color on Transfer 3.00
Dennis the Menace Face & Ruff Figure 4.00

Kid's Meal #39 (repeat of Kid's Meal #30)
Sand Pail w/shovel – 2 colors 3.00
Inflatable Frisbee – 1 style/4-color imprint 3.00
Accordion Squeeze Bottle – 2 designs 3.00
Beachball – 4-color imprint 3.00

Kid's Meal #40
Kite.. 3.00

Superball 3.00
Barney Colorform Set.. 4.00
Dennis the Menace Milk Caps.. 4.00

Kid's Meal #41
Crazy Bouncer Ball.. 3.00
Knuckle Squirter 3.00
Bike Kit, Collapsible Cup, or Sunglasses 3.00
Heart and Star Slinky... 3.00

Kid's Meal #42
Custom Pencil Case 3.00
3-D Apple Eraser 3.00
Hour Glass & Liquid-Filled Ruler 3.00
Water Color Paint Set 3.00

Kid's Meal #43
Dennis the Menace Dart Game 4.00
Dennis the Menace Punching Bag – 2 styles 4.00
Dennis the Menace Sport Sipper Cup 4.00
Bendable Spider – 4 styles.. 3.00

Kid's Meal #44
Dennis the Menace & Ruff Yo-Yo – 2 styles 4.00
Race Car – 12 assorted styles 3.00
Mini Vinyl Bag – 3 styles... 3.00
Clean-up – several past items used 3.00

Kid's Meal #45
Yo-Yo Squeeze Ball – assorted colors............................ 5.00
Bendable Jungle Animal – 5 styles................................. 3.00
Tattoo Sheet – 2 versions 3.00
Dennis the Menace & Joey Pinball Game – 2 versions 4.00

Kid's Meal #46
Coloring Kit – 3 different colors 3.00
Dennis the Menace & Ruff Toy Flashlight – 2 styles 4.00
Puzzle Block – 2 versions.. 3.00
Bendable Frog – 4 styles... 3.00

Kid's Meal #47
Magic Wrist Slate.. 3.00
Periscope – 2 different colors 3.00
Misc. Item (Dennis/Ruff Pinball Game, Jungle Animal, Dipper
    Straw) 4.00
Bump 'n Go Racer 3.00

The folks at DQ seem to like dinosaurs. This set was from 1998.

1996

Dennis the Menace Games

January

Dennis the Menace Maze Game 5.00
Dennis the Menace Playing Baseball Wristband Game 5.00
Ruff Doghouse Wristband Game 5.00
Dennis the Menace Vanishing Coin Game 5.00

Beethoven (movie set)

April

Squeeze and Pounce Caesar 4.00
Drool & Slobber Squirter 4.00
Beggin' Beethoven 4.00
Sparky Figurine 4.00
See Spot Go Rolling Dog 4.00

The Busy World of Richard Scarry

June

Lowly Worm Finger Puppet & Apple Car 4.00
Hilda Hippo Finger Puppet and Hippomobile 4.00
Bananas Gorilla Finger Puppet and Banana Mobile 4.00
Huckle Cat Finger Puppet & Shark Car 4.00

The Magic School Bus

Aug.

9 piece Pik-a-Part Bus 3.00
Bus Blaster Bus 3.00
5-in-1 Music Maker 3.00
Vinyl Activity Pouch w/Stickers, Eraser, & Crayon 3.00

Dennis the Menace Blow Carts

December

Dennis the Menace in Blow Car Blow Cart 4.00
Margaret Pushing Buggy Blow Cart 4.00
Joey in Fire Engine Blow Cart 4.00
Ruff in Wagon Blow Cart 4.00

Kid's Meal #48

Wiggle Wobbler – 2 styles 3.00
Animal Popper – 2 styles 3.00
Polar Roller – 2 styles 3.00
Dino Track – 2 styles 3.00

Kid's Meal #49

Pull-back Airplane – 4 colors 4.00
Dennis the Menace Floppy Flyer 4.00
Dennis the Menace & Ruff Paddle Drum Game –
    2 styles 4.00

Another DQ dinosaur set arrived in stores nationwide in 1997.

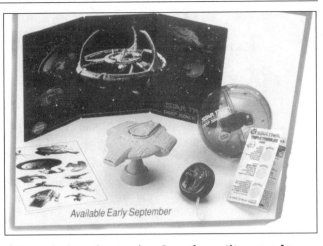

Available Early September

Here's a look at the complete *Deep Space Nine* set of toys issued by DQ in 1997.

Dennis the Menace Bowling Game 4.00
Dennis the Menace Ping Pong Set 4.00
Dennis the Menace Spinning Top 4.00

Kid's Meal #50

Lion King Bubble Cup w/Wand, Powder, & Lid 4.00
Lion King Paper Yo-Yo 4.00
Simba & Hyena Figuring Straw 4.00
Lion King Activity Book 4.00

Kid's Meal #51

Pound Puppy Pencil w/Topper – 2 styles 3.00
Pound Puppy Pinball Game – 2 styles 3.00
Pound Puppy Puzzle – 2 styles 3.00
Pound Puppy Case 3.00

Kid's Meal #52

Sip-A-Mug – 4 assorted colors 3.00
Balance Butterfly – 3 assorted colors 3.00
Lizard – 12 assorted styles 3.00
Video Camera Teleidoscope – 2 colors 3.00

Kid's Meal #53

Dennis the Menace Color Changing Spoon 4.00
Children's Sunglasses – 4 colors 3.00
Fish Squeesh – 3 styles 4.00
Wind-up Robot – 2 colors 3.00

Kid's Meal #54

Ice Cream Bowl w/Spoon – 3 colors 3.00
Sand Art 3.00
Musical Flute 3.00
Soccer Game Set 4.00

Kid's Meal #55

Dennis the Menace Cone Container – 4 different
    colors 4.00
Dennis the Menace Jump Rope 4.00
Water Baton 4.00
Dennis the Menace Cone Container – 4 different
    colors 4.00

Kid's Meal #56

Dog & Cat Flyer 3.00
Dog Parachute 3.00
Cat Kite 3.00
Sand Castle Squirter 3.00

It may not always involve a DS9, or even Star Trek, but outer space is a recurring theme at DQ. This set was from '99

Kid's Meal #57

Mini Mold pack of five 3.00
Hunchback Coloring Book 4.00
Milkcap Wrist Pack... 3.00
Misc. items from previous National Premiums Dennis the
    Menace games & Beethoven 3.00

Kid's Meal #58

Fish Vinyl Pencil Pouch 3.00
Fish Eraser & Pencil 3.00
Fish Paint Set.. 3.00
Glitter & Maze Ruler – 25 of each................... 3.00

Kid's Meal #59

Dolphin Activity Clip 3.00
Dolphin Sticker Dispenser............................. 3.00
Dolphin Template/Bookmark w/Crayon........... 3.00
Dolphin Embosser w/modeling clay 3.00

Kid's Meal #60

(skipped this version #)

Kid's Meal #61 (Circus Version)

Big Top Chalk Board w/pack of chalk.............. 3.00
Window Walker – 2 styles................................ 3.00
Circus Stacker (5 per pack) 3.00
Circus Flipper Game Set................................. 3.00

Kid's Meal #62 (Freeky Friends Version)

Tumbling Spider — 2 styles 3.00
Inflate an Alien.. 3.00
Tumbling Spider 3.00
Light Blob 3.00

Kid's Meal #63

Echo Mic. 3.00
Block Cup w/lid & straw
Sports Trivia Book... 3.00
Wrist Yo-Yo 3.00

Kid's Meal #64

3-1/2" Pullback Racer – 4 styles & colors 3.00
Alpha Robot – 24 characters 3.00
Collapsible Cup – 2 different colors 3.00
Frosty the Snowman Coloring Book – 2 styles 3.00

1997

National Wildlife Federation Figurine (each item comes
with a continent stand & collector's card)

February

Emperor Penguin w/Antarctica Stand & Card 3.00
Jaguar w/S. American Stand & Card............................... 3.00
Giant Panda w/Asia Stand & Card 3.00
Koala w/Australia Stand & Card 3.00
Wolverine w/Europe Stand & Card................................. 3.00
African Elephant w/Africa Stand & Card......................... 3.00
Grizzly Bear w/N. American Stand & Card 3.00
    Tiny Toons (each item includes figuring, cup & topper, April)
Babs Bunny Cup Topper.. 3.00
Dizzy Devil Cup Topper... 3.00
Plucky Duck Cup Topper... 3.00
Buster Bunny Cup Topper... 3.00

Nickelodeon

Hey Arnold Beach Gear Holder 3.00
Aaaah!!! Real Monsters Squirters 3.00
Rocko's Modern Life Ring Toss 3.00
Rugrats Inflatable Wobble Ball 3.00

The Flintstones Figurines

August

Wilma on Keyboards 3.50
Dino playing Tambourine 3.50
Fred on Vocals 3.50
Barney on Bongos 3.50

Felix the Cat

October

Felix and Mice Dustbin Roller... 3.50
Felix the Cat Mobile 3.50
Felix & Sheba Phone Book.. 3.50
First Bank of Felix Coin Bank.. 3.50

Dennis the Menace Train Set

    (Each car came w/cardboard track.)

December

Rolling Dennis the Menace Engine 3.50
Rolling Joey Train Car 3.50
Rolling Ruff Train Car 3.50
Rolling Margaret Caboose... 3.50

Kid's Meal #65

Dogs 'n Katz Version

Pull String Pet – 2 styles.. 3.00
Animobile – 2 styles... 3.00
Card Car (w/three pictures) – 2 styles/bus & taxi 3.00
Rip Cord Racer – 4 styles & colors................................. 3.00

The Mighty Knights brought DQ kids back to the land of dragons and castles in 1999.

Kid's Meal #66

Repeat of 46a (Coloring Kit – 3 different colors) 3.00
Magic Wrist Slate 3.00
Periscope – 2 different colors 3.00
Puzzle Maze – 2 different colors 3.00
Bump 'n Go Racer – 6 styles 3.00

Kid's Meal #67

Space Version
Balancing Space Shuttle 3.00
Glow Earth Bounce Ball 3.00
Prismatic Sticker Sheet – 2 styles 3.00
Space Trivia Book 3.00

Kid's Meal #68

Kidsville Version
Girl Doll – 2 styles 4.00
Boy Doll – 2 styles 4.00
Punch Out DQ Store w/Playmat 4.00
Punch Out SchoolHouse w/Playmat 4.00

Kid's Meal #69

Pound Puppy Version
Color Change Board – 2 styles 3.00
Puppy Figurine – 4 styles 3.00
Dart Ball Game 3.00
Goof Ball 3.00

Kid's Meal #70

Dinosaur Version
Dino Bubbler – 6 styles 3.00
Dino Squirter – 4 styles 3.00
Dino Bendable – 4 styles 3.00
Dino Finger Puppet – 4 styles 3.00

Kid's Meal #71

Ocean Stuffed Animal Version
Walrus 3.00
Penguin 3.00
Whale 3.00
Lobster 3.00
Polar Bear 3.00

Kid's Meal #72

Summer Sports Version
Golf Set (2 clubs, 1 ball, & green) 3.00
Crazy Knob Ball 3.00
Flyer – 4 different colors 3.00
Badminton Set (2 paddles, 1 birdie) 3.00

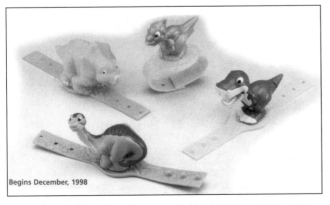

Begins December, 1998

These DQ Land Before Time watches could help kids tell what time it is, or was, back in 1998.

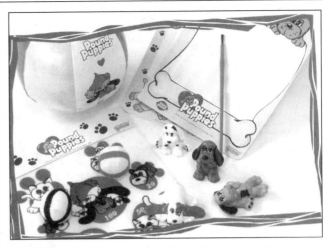

Pooch lovers had to like the DQ Pound Puppies set from 1997.

Kid's Meal #73

Dennis the Menace
Dennis the Menace Blow Chart 3.50
Dennis the Menace & Margaret Bendable 3.50
Dennis the Menace Color Change Spoon 3.50

Kid's Meal #74

Double Agent Version
Cellular Phone/Periscope 3.00
Camera/Telescope 3.00
Coin/Secret Decoder 3.00
Beeper/Magnifier 3.00

Kid's Meal #75

Mighty Mouse Version
Heckle/Jeckle Pencil w/Topper 3.50
Mighty Mouse Twisty Straw 3.50
Mighty Mouse Spinning Top – 2 styles 3.50
Mighty Mouse Pocket Puzzle 3.50

Kid's Meal #76

Insect/Nature Version
3-D Puzzle – 4 styles 3.00
Lady Bug Magnifier – 2 styles 3.00
Frog Squirter – 4 styles 3.00
Bubbler – 4 styles 3.00

Kid's Meal #77

World Traveler Version
Wrist Compas 3.00
Vacation Viewer 3.00
Atlas Travel Pack 3.00
Passport Pack 3.00

Kid's Meal #78

3" Round Magic Spring 3.00
Soft Ball Sport Squeesh – 4 styles 4.00
Knuckle Squirter – 2 colors 3.00
10-piece Building Block Set 4.00

Kid's Meal #79

Deep Space Nine Version
Balancing USS Defiant Space Ship 3.50
Inflatable Space Ball 3.50
Lenticular Tribble Yo-Yo 3.50
Cling On Pack 3.50

This group of ocean stuffed animals was shipped to DQs around the country back in 1997.

Kid's Meal #80

Jungle Bean Filled Animals Version

Lion 3.00
Tiger 3.00
Elephant 3.00
Monkey 3.00
Zebra 3.00

Kid's Meal #81

Star Fairies & Micro Machines Version

Star Fairies Finger Puppets 3.00
Star Fairies Twisty Figurine Straw 3.00
Micro Machine Collapsible Cup 3.00
Micro Machines Color Change Board 3.00

Kid's Meal #82

Puzzle & Game Version

Rubicks Cube 3.50
Card Game – 4 custom styles 3.50
Tic Tac Toe Game 3.50
Challenge Puzzle – 2 styles 3.50

Kid's Meal #83

Mighty Heroes Version

Mini Bob Bag 4.00
Fun Flyer – 2 different shapes 3.00
Yo-Yo – 4 styles 3.50
Dart Ball Game – 2 colors 3.00

Kid's Meal #84

Alien Version

Alien Squish Man – 3 different colors 3.00
Alien Flip Cubes 3.00
Star Ship Container w/Sticker – 2 styles 3.00
Alien Glow Sticker 3.00

1998

The Land Before Time Cups

January

Cera Cup 3.00
Ducky Cup 3.00
Spike Cup 3.00
Littlefoot Cup 3.00

Puzzle Place

April

Kiki & Jody Swinging Puzzle Piece 2.50

Ben Kicking Soccer Ball Puzzle Piece 2.50
Leon & Julie Teeter-totter Puzzle Piece 2.50
Skye Dribbling Basketball Puzzle Piece 2.50

DQ Treats

June

Rolling DQ Sandwich Water Ball 2.50
DQ Mix-n-Match Cone 2.50
Banana Split Pullback Racer 2.50
Wind-up Sundae 2.50
Bendable Blizzard 2.50

Carmen Sandiego

July

Locator Game 3.00
Spy Camera Right-Angle Viewer 3.00
Secret Decoder Game 3.00
Crime Stopper Map Game w/Airplane Magnifier ... 3.00

The Busy World of Richard Scarry

June

Huckle Cat Rotocast Floating Boat Squirter 3.00
Lowly Worm Rotocast Floating Boat Squirter 3.00
Mr. Fumble Rotocast Floating Boat Squirter 3.00
Sergeant Murphy Rotocast Floating Boat Squirter ... 3.00

The Land Before Time Wristbands

All items came on wristbands.

December

Cera Water Squirter 3.00
Ducky Whistle 3.00
Chomper Action Figure 3.00
Littlefoot Pullback 3.00

Kid's Meal #85

Astronaut Version

Star Gazer Telescope 2.50
Wrist Communicator 2.50
Figurine Snap-on Space Suit Glow Kids 2.50
Space Shuttle & Robot Freewheelers 2.50

Kid's Meal #86

Musical Instruments Version

Drum Set w/Drumstick 2.50
Tambourine 2.50
Guitar 2.50
Castanets 2.50
Maracas 2.50

This puzzle set from 1997 was designed to help kids learn problem-solving skills.

Kid's Meal #87

Elmopalooza Sesame Street Version

Activity Book 3.00
Elmo Plastic Case w/Puzzle 3.00
Elmo Swinging Straw 3.00
Character Twister Cube 3.00
Elmopalooza Kids Meal Bag 3.00

Kid's Meal #88

Kidsong Version

Paddleball Set 2.50
Maze Game 2.50
Magic Board w/Brush 2.50
Round Shaped Playing Cards (full deck) 2.50

Kid's Meal #89

Barnyard Buddies Plush Version

Duck 2.50
Rooster 2.50
Pony 2.50
Pig 2.50
Cow 2.50

Kid's Meal #90

Souvenirs From Around The World Version

Leaning Tower of Pisa 2.50
Empire State Building Telescope 2.50
Vatican Coloring Roll 2.50
Eiffel Tower Bubble Blower 2.50
Egyptian Sphinx Template Set w/Mummy Crayons 2.50

Kid's Meal #91

Summer Fun Version

Splash Ball 2.50
14" Inflatable Beach Ball 2.50
9" Inflatable Flyer 2.50
Glitter Yo Yo 3.00

Kid's Meal #92

Circus Version

Lion Squirter 2.50
Harmonica 2.50
Bendable Clown 2.50
Circus Template Set w/2 crayons 2.50

Kid's Meal #93

Travel Version

Cell Phone Squirter – 2 different colors 2.50
Train & Car Bubble Necklace 2.50

A Back-To-School set got kids thinking about the classroom in 1998.

"Summer Sport"

Available Early May!

The 1997 "Summer Sports" series celebrated the end of the school year.

Are We There Yet? Book 2.50
Coast to Coast Game Book 2.50

Kid's Meal #94

Bugs! Bugs! Bugs! Version

Blooming Flower 2.50
Bumblebee Squirter 2.50
Magnifier/Tweezer Set 2.50
Beanie Bugs
Fly 3.00
Ladybug 3.00

Kid's Meal #95

Back-to-School Version

Pencil Pouch 3.00
Ruler Maze 3.00
Sand-filled 3.00
Clipboard w/Notepad & Pencil 3.00
Crayon Case w/6 Crayons 3.00

Kid's Meal #96

Dinosaur Version

Egg Catcher Skill Game – 2 different styles 3.00
Dino Giggler 3.00
Dino Roller – 2 different styles 3.00
Egg Spinner – 2 different styles 3.00

Kid's Meal #97

Jungle Pound Version

Sticker Book 2.50
Inflatable Koala Ball 2.50
Monkey Swinging Straw 2.50
Maze Game 3.00

Kid's Meal #98

DQ Treats on Wheels Version

Ice Cream Truck 2.50
Dilly Bar Truck 2.50
Peanut Buster Parfait Truck 2.50
Blizzard Truck 2.50

Kid's Meal #99

Cartoon Factory

Magic Motion Wand 2.50
Color Me Flip Book w/one Crayon 2.50
Rubdown Sketch w/one Crayon 2.50
Cartoon Viewer 2.50

A whole set of cute DQ figures made the scene in 1998.

1999

National Wildlife Federation Figurine

(Each item comes with a continent stand & collector's card, February.)

Blue Whale w/Antarctica Stand & Card 3.00
Lear's Macaw w/S. American Stand & Card.................. 3.00
Orangutan w/Asia Stand & Card.................................. 3.00
Dugong w/Australia Stand & Card 3.00
Spanish Lynx w/Europe Stand & Card........................... 3.00
White Rhino w/Africa Stand & Card............................. 3.00
Crocodile w/N. American Stand & Card........................ 3.00

Scooby-Doo

April

Scooby Dune Buggy Pullback.. 3.00
Pirate Ship Freewheeler w/Viewer................................ 3.00
Mystery Van w/Ghost Pullback 3.00
Bobbing Head Flower Pot Push Toy 3.00
Mummy Airplane Pullback 3.00
Rolling Spinner Ball... 3.00

Garfield

Garfield Skateboarding Pullback 3.00
Garfield Hockey Push Button Squirter 3.00
Garfield Beach Ball Squirter.. 3.00
Rip Cord Tricycle Odie 3.00
Tubing Garfield 3.00
Garfield Football Wind-up 3.00

Wishbone

Each item came w/collector sheet.

June

Treasure Island Pirate Squirter 3.00
Sherlock Holmes Sticker Keeper 3.00
The Three Musketeers Inflatable Ball 3.00
The Odyssey Trojan Horse Figurine & Freewheeler........ 3.00
One Thousand and One Arabian Nights Magic Carpet
    Pullback... 3.00
Robin Hood Castle Sand Mold & Wishbone Figurine 3.00

Muppet Babies

July

Giddyap Baby Gonzo.. 3.00
Barrellin' Baby Animal.. 3.00
Baby Kermit the Frog's Kruiser..................................... 3.00
Baby Fozzie Bear's Climb Time.................................... 3.00
Baby Miss Piggy's Cup of Tea 3.00

Kid's Meal #100 (Volcano Island)

Coconut Squirter – 4 different styles............................ 2.50
Volcano Template w/Crayon 2.50

Monkey in a Coconut..2.50
Turtle Taxi Pullback..2.50

Kid's Meal #101

Outerspace

Press n Go Space Vehicle – 6 versions 2.50

Glow-in-the-Dark Prismatic Spinning

Top – 4 versions 2.50
Alien Squeesh – 3 different versions 2.50
Glow-in-the-Dark Crater Bounce Ball 2.50

Kid's Meal #102

Winter Fun Games

Round Rainbow Sprinkee..2.50
Softball..2.50
Suction Ball Paddle Set 2.50
Spinning Top w/Launcher 2.50

Kid's Meal #103

Extreme Arctic

Sliding Seal Bowling Set...2.50
Ski Accident Snowball 2.50
Skater Evader Penguin..2.50
Penguin Bobsled Team..2.50

Kid's Meal #104

Mighty Knights

Sparking Dragons..2.50
Catapult 2.50
Race & Chase Blower 2.50
Mighty Knight Figurine..2.50

Kid's Meal #105

Space Exploration

Space Log 2.50
Press 'n Go Space Shuttle – 4 styles 2.50
Domino Match Game...2.50
3-D Puzzle – 3 styles..2.50

Kid's Meal #106

Amazing Amphibians

Color Change Fabric Frog 2.50
Poison Dart Frog Book w/figurine....................................2.50
Rolling Frog Water Ball 2.50
Frog Squirter – 3 styles 2.50

Kid's Meal #107

Flying Feathered Friends

Bald Eagle Glider..2.50
Hummingbird Flyer 2.50

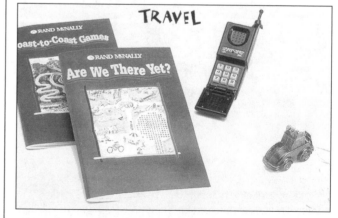

DQ tried to help out young travelers with this 1998 set.

Volcano Island was the inspiration for this 1999 collection.

Hovering Hawk..2.50
Owl Finger Puppet 2.50

Kid's Meal #108

Splish Splash
Aqua Lung...2.50
Spinning Water Whirler 2.50
Spraying Jump Rope 2.50
Spray Flyer..2.50

Muppet Babies

July 7 – Aug. 1st
Baby Kermit the Frog...2.00
Baby Fozzie Bear...2.00
Baby Gonzo 2.00
Baby Animal...2.00
Baby Miss Piggy 2.00

2000

Ready, Set, Play
Playing Cards...1.50
Tic-Tac-Toe game w/plastic mat game board 1.50
Basketball Toss Game 1.50
Memory Game 1.50

DQ Beanie figures
(Over-the-counter promo. Original retail price without purchase was $2.99.)
Berry 3.50
Curly...3.50
Chilly 3.50
Cookie...3.50
Ice Cream Sandwich 3.50
Blizzard...3.50
Dip Cone 3.50
Cone 3.50

Space Thing
2 drink Sipper (shuttle & rocket ship).................1.50
Stickers 1.50
Shuttle toy..1.50
Rocket w/parachute 1.50

Hanna-Barbera Classic Toons plush characters
(Set I, available with the purchase of a DQ Kid's meal or for 99¢ with any purchase.)
April 3
Atom Ant 2.00

Snagglepuss..2.00
Quick Draw McGraw...2.00
Wally Gator 2.00
Yogi Bear 2.00
Augie Doggie 2.00

Hanna-Barbera Classic Toons plush characters
(Set II, available with the purchase of a DQ Kid's meal or for 99¢ with any purchase.)
May 6
Peter Potamus 2.00
Top Cat 2.00
Magilla Gorilla 2.00
Secret Squirrel 2.00
Huckleberry Hound 2.00
Touché Turtle 2.00

Over-the-counter Item
Pop-Up Tents (collapsible 12" x 12" x 12" pop-up tent for characters w/full color design.)
Each tent 1.50

Curious George
June 1 – June 30
George figurine suspended from a suction cup by a
string 2.00
Fireman Pull-String Spinning Top 2.00
Rides a Bike Pullback...2.00
Rides a Ball Balancer 2.00
Yellow Hat Spinning Top.....................................2.00
Goes to the Moon Friction Sparker Rocket Ship 2.00

Back to School tools
Each item...1.50

Lost Treasures
Blow-Up Pirate Ship 1.50
Parrot squirter 1.50
Alligator Maze game...1.50
Treasure Chest w/mini puzzle 1.50

Life with Louie
Key Chain 1.50
Yo-Yo 1.50
Inflatable Ball 1.50

Christmas Books
Set of 6.
Each item..1.50

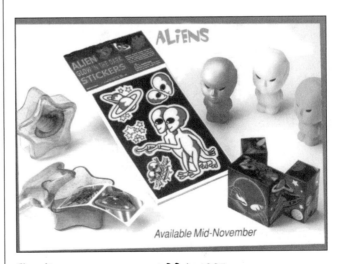

The aliens were among us at DQ in 1997.

Hardee's

Company Profile

In the fall of 1960 in North Carolina, Wilber Hardee opened a brand new restaurant. It featured a limited menu consisting only of hamburgers, french fries and soft drinks. The concept of the drive-in restaurant with a fixed menu, fast service and reduced prices was in its infancy. During his first three months of business, Hardee's averaged about $1,000 a week in net profit — not a bad sum of money in those days.

In fact, Wilber Hardee was doing so well that he attracted a pair of entrepreneurs named Leonard Rawls Jr. and Jim Gardner, who loved his concept so much they convinced him to join them as partners and Hardee's Drive-Ins, Inc. was born. They later changed the name to Hardee's Food Systems, Inc. The three men opened their first location on Friday, May 5, 1961. The original menu featured 15-cent char-broiled hamburgers, 20-cent cheeseburgers, 10-cent soft drinks, and 10-cent coffee.

Five months after the first restaurant opened, the trio sold its first franchise and others soon followed. The company grew so rapidly, it had to develop its own distribution company in 1962. In 1963, Hardee's made its first — and the fast-food industry's first — public stock offering. In 1965, Hardee's opened its first international restaurant in Heidelberg, Germany. By the end of the decade Hardee's had nearly 200 restaurants.

Hardee's acquired the 200-unit, Illinois-based Sandy's restaurant chain in 1972, bringing the number of Hardee's restaurants to 639 in 33 states. By 1975, Hardee's was opening its 1,000th restaurant.

In 1981, Hardee's began its sponsorship association with NASCAR and race-car driver Bobby Allison. In later years, Hardee's also sponsored Cale Yarborough and Ward Burton.

Continuing its expansion via acquisition, Hardee's acquired the Indianapolis-based Burger Chef chain in 1982. By 1983, Hardee's opened its 2,000th restaurant. Profits continued to rise, and by 1985 Hardee's system-wide sales had surpassed $2 billion. In 1987, Hardee's not only opened its 3,000th res-

![Hardee's logo]

taurant, but it did an unusual thing by teaming with the California Raisin Advisory Board for a promotion involving the California Raisins. Ultimately, this promotion resulted in the sale of more than 50 million raisins items and, to this day, is considered one of the most successful promotions in the fast-food industry. Hardee's system-wide sales soon went on to surpass $3 billion.

With consumer health becoming a major issue, Hardee's became the first major fast-food chain to completely switch to cholesterol-free, all-vegetable oil for all fried products in 1988. Always looking to expand, Hardee's purchased the 650-unit Roy Rogers restaurant chain in 1990 in an effort to strengthen the company's position in the Northeast. After attempting to convert those locations to Hardee's, the company was convinced by Roy Rogers consumers to restore the Roy Rogers trademark, which it eventually did.

In 1991, Hardee's introduced fresh fried chicken to its menu, making it the second largest chicken restaurant chain in the country. *Entrepreneur* Magazine ranked Hardee's among the top 10 franchises for 1995. After acquiring much of its competition, Hardee's itself was acquired in 1997 by CKE Restaurants, Inc. (NYSE:CKR).

The Business of Toys

In the 1990s, Hardee's issued what was probably one of the very first superhero-licensed fast-food toy promotions with a group of four characters

Marvel Comic's mutant outlaw heroes made a dramatic appearance at Hardee's and Roy Rogers back in 1995.

from Marvel Comics. Spider-Man, Captain America, The Hulk and Thor were melded into vehicles, with their individual logos emblazoned on them.

In 1991, Hardee's repeated this formula of characters in cars with four Archie characters (Archie, Veronica, Betty, and Jughead). In 1996, Hardee's returned to the superhero market with a more ambitious group of X-Men toys. This time, instead of combo character/vehicles that look like they hailed from the dollar mart, the chain delivered a very cool, interlocking diorama and eight-figure set of characters. A ninth figure was also available as an "under-3" toy. The diorama consisted of two PVCs (an X-man and a villain), plus a plastic base on which the characters could stand. Each of the eight characters had a hole in one foot that fit over a corresponding peg on each base, allowing them to stand. The four bases fit together to form a larger display.

These trading cards and certificates of authenticity from 1995 came with X-Men figures given away by Hardee's and Roy Rogers.

Hardee's Toy Listing

All prices are for items mint in package (MIP), unless otherwise noted.

Where applicable, the date(s) of distribution and additional information on the following premiums were provided by the individual chains.

Year Unknown

Pound Puppies Plush Toys
All Black 5.00
Brown With Black Stripes................... 5.00
Gray/Black/White 5.00
Pound Puppy #4 .... 5.00

Puppies & Purries
Black/White Dog 6.00
Gray/Black Dog 6.00
Brown Dog 6.00
Brown Kitten...................................... 6.00
Gray Kitten 6.00

Walt Disney Stuffed Animals
Minnie 8.00
Mickey 8.00
Goofy 8.00
Pluto 8.00

Walt Disney Stuffed Animals II
Bambi 7.00
Pinocchio 7.00
Dumbo 7.00
101 Dalmatians 7.00

1984

Gremlins Storybook and Record
(Clean-up period occurred July 15 – Oct. 31)
June 11 – July 14
The Gift of the Mogwai 6.00

Gizmo and the Gremlins.................... 6.00
Escape from the Gremlins 6.00
Gremlins-Trapped............................. 6.00
The Last Gremlin 6.00

1985

Halley's Comet Actionmeal Telescope
Sept. 30 – Nov .1
3X Telescope 4.00

1987

Little Little Golden Books
Mid – August promotion
Little Red Riding Hood....................... 4.00
The Pokey Little Puppy....................... 4.00
The Three Pigs.................................. 4.00

The Hulk in a bulldozer? Only at Hardee's in 1995.

The Little Red Hen 4.00
Set of 4 .... 15.00

Smurfs PVC Figurines

(Promotion occurred after depletion of Little Little Golden Books – Note: Over 100 different figurines were produced.)
Each 5.00

California Raisins I PVC Figurines

(Clean-up period occurred Nov. 1 - Nov. 14)
Oct. 4 – Oct. 31
Sunglasses 15.00
Microphone 15.00
Saxophone 15.00
Hands 15.00
Set of 4 .... 75.00

Pound Puppies Little Little Golden Books

Promotion began November 2
Problem Puppies 4.00
Pick of the Litter 4.00
Kitten Companions 4.00
The Puppy Nobody Wanted 4.00

California Raisins PVC Figures

(This set is virtually identical to a set that appeared in Post Raisin Brand. The only difference is that the Hardee's PVCs are slightly smaller in size.)
W/Shades 12.00
W/Microphone 12.00
W/Saxophone 12.00
Dancer 12.00

1988

Little Golden Book Mealbox Books

Mid – Jan.
The Little Red Caboose 4.00
The Three Bears 4.00
The Three Little Kittens 4.00
Old McDonald Had a Farm 4.00

California Raisins II

(Clean-up period occurred Aug. 14 – Aug. 20)
July 1 – Aug. 13
Waves Weaver w/surfboard 6.00
FF Strings w/guitar 6.00
Rollin' Rollo w/rollerskates 6.00
Trumpy Trunote w/trumpet 6.00
SB Stuntz w/skateboarder 6.00
Captain Toonz w/boom box 6.00

California Raisins (Plush Toys/Set 3)

W/microphone 5.00
W/hat 5.00
W/shades 5.00
In heels 5.00

California Raisins 4

Buster w/skateboard 5.00
Alotta Stille w/shopping accessories 5.00
Anita Break w/boom box 5.00
Benny w/bowling ball & bag 5.00

Smurfs (PVC Figures)

Figure #1 .... 5.00
Figure #2 .... 5.00
Figure #3 .... 5.00
Figure #4 .... 5.00

Marvel's outlaw mutant heroes, the X-Men, hid out at both Hardee's and Roy Rogers in 1995 with a very cool set of figures, cards, and comics.

1989

Beach Bunnies PVC Figurines

Promotion began April 1
Girl w/beach ball 4.00
Boy on skateboard 4.00
Girl on skates 4.00
Boy w/Frisbee 4.00
Set of 4 .... 16.00

Little Little Golden Books

The Little Red Caboose 3.00
Old McDonald's Farm 3.00
Three Little Kittens 3.00
Three Litle Bears 3.00

Ghostbusters II Ghostbuster Premium Noise Makers

(Note: Each blaster had different dual noise tones; batteries included; scarce-recalled due to hazardous detachable parts.)
June 25 – July 30
Red 9.00
Gray 9.00
Black 9.00
White 9.00

Halloween Hideaways

(Cloth Figures in Plastic Containers.)
Sept. 28 – Oct. 28
Bat in a Stump 5.00
Goblin in Blue Caldron 5.00
Cat in Pumpkin 5.00
Ghost in Trick-or-Treat Bag 5.00

Tang Mouths PVC Figurines

(Clean-up Dec. 10 – Dec. 16)
Nov. 1 – Dec. 9
Lance, The Leader 3.00
Awesome Annie, Lip Sync Kid 3.00
Flap, The Rapper 3.00
Tag, The Whistler 3.00

Ghostbusters

(Four different-colored sirens, each with a distinctive electronic sound.)
Red 6.00
White 6.00
Black 6.00
Gray 6.00

1990

Silly Sack Meal Bag

Card Games/Tang Mouths

Feb. 19 – throughout 1990 for clean-up periods. Note: This program was substituted for the finger Crayon program. Bag was used to clean up any excess premiums.

Old Maid.. 4.00
Go Fish 4.00
Crazy Eights.. 4.00
ABC.. 4.00

Food Squirters (rubber squirters)

Apr. 2 – May 22

Hamburger 3.00
Hot Dog (limited distribution).. 5.00
Strawberry Shake 3.00
French Fries... 3.00
Set of 4.. 15.00

Days of Thunder Racers cars

(There is some confusion as to whether these are Hot Wheels or Matchbox cars. (Note: there was a clean-up period between July 23 – July 29))

June – July 22

Orange Hardee's Car.. 5.00
Pink Superflo Motor Oil 5.00
Green/Yellow Mello Yellow 5.00
City Chevrolet 5.00
Set of 4.. 22.00

Tang Trio (PVC figures)

Lance the Leader 3.00
Awesome Anne 3.00
Flap the Rapper 3.00
Tag the Whistler 3.00

Surfin' Smurfs Funmeal PVC figurines

(Note: This funmeal came with one of six premiums and

That's Archie Andrews driving his jalopy into Hardee's in 1991.

optional Funmeal Deal — a coupon offering 25-cent Cool Twist Cone or Big Cookie.)

July 30 – Sept. 9

Smurfette on Green Surfboard 5.00
Smurfette on Purple Surfboard 5.00
Smurf on Yellow Board 5.00
Smurf on Orange Board 5.00
Papa Smurf on Red Board 5.00
Dog on Blue board.. 5.00
Set of 6.. 35.00

Marvel Superheroes Figurines in Vehicles

Oct. 15 – Nov. 18

Hulk in Dozer 5.00
She-Hulk in Car 5.00
Spider-Man in Supercar 5.00
Captain Marvel 5.00
Set of 4.. 22.00

Fender Bonder 500 Figurines in Vehicles

Nov. 19 – Dec. 30

Dick Dastardly/Muttley in the Dirty Truckster................... 5.00
Huck Hound/Snagglepuss in Lucky Trucky 5.00
Yogi Bear/Boo Boo in Jellystone Jammer........................ 5.00
Quick Draw McGraw/Baba Looey in Texas Twister.......... 5.00
Magilla Gorilla/Wally Gator in the Swamp Stomper.......... 5.00
Set of 5.. 22.00

Super Bowl

(Pin Premium Promotion (Note: There were a series of 25 pins depicting the Super Bowl logo for each year, football helmets of the opposing teams and the date and final score of first 24 games. size of each: 1-1/2" x 3/4".))

Dec. 26, 1990 – Jan. 27, 1991

I-XXIV, each 5.00

1991

Finger Crayons Funmeal

(Consisted of four sets of two finger Crayons and a coloring sheet.)

Feb. 1 – Mar. 7

Yellow/Red... 3.00
Blue/Magenta 3.00
Green/Orange... 3.00
Pink/Purple 3.00

California Raisins PVC figurines

(There were four figures in this series and each included a collector card depicting the character and his/her biography.)

Feb. 25 – Mar. 31

Buster 4.00
Anita Break 4.00
Alotta Stile 4.00
Benny 4.00

Kazoo Sailing Crew Sailors kazoos

(There were four different plastic collectible Kazoo Crew Kazoos, which were animals with a nautical theme.)

Apr. 22 – May 19

Deck Hand Rabbit (white).. 4.00
Lookout Monkey (orange)... 4.00
Captain Rhino (purple) 4.00
First Mate Bear (brown).. 4.00
Set of 4.. 20.00

Archies

Archie in red car 5.00

Marvel's outlaw heroes, the X-Men, graced one of the niftiest sets to date in 1995.

Jughead in green car	5.00
Veronica in purple car	5.00
Betty in blue car	5.00
Set of 4	20.00

Flintstones: First 30 Years figures w/gadgets
July 1 – Aug. 4

Dino w/Jukebox	5.00
Fred w/Television	5.00
Bamm Bamm w/pin Ball Machine	5.00
Pebbles w/Phone	5.00
Barney w/Barbecue	5.00
Set of 5	30.00

Waldo & Friends Straw Buddies
(Waldo Straw Buddies are PVC plastic figurines that fit Hardee's straws and sit on the lid of Hardee's cups.)
Aug. 4 – Sept. 28

Waldo	3.00
Wenda	3.00
Wizard Whitebeard	3.00
Woof	3.00
Set of 4	13.00

Where's Waldo Christmas Tree Ornaments
(There were three sets of three 4" plastic ornaments. Each set contained a different Waldo and two other characters or friends.)
Nov. 22 – Dec. 31

Waldo/Snowman/Waldo Watcher	4.00
Waldo/Wizard Whitebeard	4.00
Reindeer	4.00
Waldo/Wenda/Woof	4.00

Camp California
(Similar set distributed by Carl's Jr.)
June – July

Bear squirter	3.00
Lil' Bro Disc	3.00
Mini volleyball	3.00
Suction cup spinner	3.00

Jellystone Fender Bender 500
(Similar set distributed by Carl's Jr.)
Jan. – Mar.

Yogi & Boo Boo in Jellystone Jammer	4.00
Magilla Gorilla & Wally Gator in Swamp Stomper	4.00
Huckleberry Hound & Snagglepuss in Lucky Trucky	4.00
Quick Draw McGraw & Baba Looey in Texas Twister	4.00
Dick Dastardly & Muttley in Dirty Truckster	4.00

1993

Camp California
(Similar to the Camp CA set distributed by Carl's Jr.)

Mini flying disc	3.00
Squirter bear figure	3.00
Mini volley ball	3.00
Throwing star w/suction cup ends	3.00

Dinosaurs in My Pocket

Apatosaurus (yellow)	3.00
Stegosaurus (blue)	3.00
T-Rex (green)	3.00
Triceratops (pink)	3.00

Muppets Christmas Carol finger puppets

Miss Piggy (Mrs. Cratchet)	4.00
Kermit (Tiny Tim)	4.00
Fozzie (Bob Cratchet)	4.00
Gonzo (Scrooge)	4.00

Metal Cars

Chevy Camero Roadrunner (white)	3.50
Other cars in set	3.50

Trolls
(Each figure came w/different hair color (red, pink, yellow, green, purple, and green), and w/a different symbol on their belly (star, heart, diamond, and circle, these shapes also came in different colors). Toys were also distributed by Long John Silvers, Roy Rogers and Sonic Drive-Ins.)

Each troll	3.00

1994

Dinosaurs
(Colorful plastic w/accordion-like, stretchable necks.)

Apatosaurus (yellow)	3.00
Stegosaurus (green)	3.00
T-Rex	3.00
Triceratops	3.00

Eureeka's Castle Stampers

Magellan (heart stamp)	3.00
Eureeka (star stamp)	3.00
The Moat Twins (circle stamp)	3.00
Batly (square stamp)	3.00

Food Squirters
(Rubber squirters; same as 1990 version, only this set was in fluorescent colors instead of food colored.)
Apr. 2 – May 22

Hamburger (orange)	3.00
Hot Dog (limited distribution)	5.00
Strawberry Shake (pink)	3.00
French Fries (yellow)	3.00
Set of 4	15.00

Micro Super Soakers

Water Cannon	3.00
Water Gun	3.00
Bow & Arrow	3.00
Soak 'n Fly throwing disc	3.00

Nicktoons Cruisers

(Nickelodeon characters in vehicles.)
Ren Hoek in rocket ship..4.00
Stimpy in rocket ship..4.00
Spunky in dog dish...4.00
Tommy Pickles on rocking horse 4.00
Angelica Pickles on tricycle..4.00
Doug Funnie in racecar...4.00
Porkchops on skateboard 4.00
Rocko on robot dog...4.00

Nicktoons Bookmarks

(Two bookmarks came in each package).
Ren & Stimpy 4.00
Tommy & Angelica Pickles..4.00
Doug Funnie & Porkchops 4.00
Rocko & Spunky 4.00

Snowballs squirters

W/stovepipe hat (orange)..2.50
W/ski cap & goggles (white)..2.50
W/earmuffs & cap (blue) 2.50
W/Scottish tam (pink)..2.50

Speed Bunnies (rabbits on wheels)

Cruiser on rollerblades..3.00
Dusty on skateboard 3.00
Sunny on wind surfer 3.00
Stretch speedwalker 3.00

Swan Princess (PVCs from movie)

Prince Derek 3.50
Princess Odette/swan (skirt flips over head to reveal one or
    the other character)..3.50
Jean-Bob (frog) 3.50
Puffin walker 3.50
Rothbart w/full body mask (removable) 3.50

Tattoads (each came w/stickers)

Toadette (pink) 3.00
Toadinator (green)...3.00
Toad Dude (yellow) 3.00
Toadster (blue) 3.00

1995

Beakman's World

It's a Magnetic World (globe magnet) 4.00
D'Facts of Light (prism w/Ratman's head) 4.00
Beakman's Whirl 4.00
Physics Follies 4.00

Eek! the Cat PVC figures

(Distributed simultaneously w/Terrible Thunderlizards figures.)
Eek! the Cat w/arms that move.......................................3.00
Annabella 3.00
Sharky Squirter 3.00

The Terrible Thunderlizards

(Each vehicle came w/Launcher. Distributed simultaneously w/Eek! the Cat figures.)
Squatt..3.50
Kutter 3.50
Doc...3.50

X-Men Battle figures

PVC figures of X-Men squaring off against a supervillain. Each pair attached to a base and all four bases fit together to form a single diorama. Four different Marvel X-Men comic books and trading cards also came with this series, as well as a "certificate of authenticity." A fifth figure of the Beast on wheels also came with this series; this was considered the "under-3" toy. Set also distributed at Roy Rogers. Toys, cards and comics were not bagged together, and thus are listed here separately.)
Cyclops vs. Commando...5.00
Wolverine vs. The Blob...5.00
Storm vs. Phantasia 5.00
Rogue vs. Avalanche..5.00
Beast Time Traveler (on wheels)......................................5.00
Comicbook #1...5.00
Comicbook #2...5.00
Comicbook #3...5.00
Comicbook #4...5.00
Comicbook #5...5.00
Trading card #1...5.00
Trading card #2...5.00
Trading card #3...5.00
Trading card #4...5.00

1998

The Tick

Human Ton (under-3) 3.50
The Tick..3.50
Arthur..3.50
Speek the dog 3.50

The Wild Cats

(This is a fill-in promotion and considered an under-3 toy.)
Wild Cat #1...2.50
Wild Cat #2...2.50
Wild Cat #3...2.50
Wild Cat #4...2.50

Hardee's was full of bugs in 1999, thanks to an entertaining plastic blazing bugs series that came with kid meals.

Earth Worm Jim

Snott Squirter 2.50
Earthworm Jim Plasma Blaster 2.50
Princess What's Her Name Spinner 2.50
Monster Dog Peter Puppy 2.50

Munsters Cool Combo Buckets (4 buckets)

Bucket #1 .... 4.50
Bucket #2 .... 4.50
Bucket #3 .... 4.50
Bucket #4 .... 4.50

Garfield the Christmas Racers

Clearing the Way 4.00
Snowmobile 4.00
Slippin & Sliding 4.00
Downhill Racer 4.00

Where is Carmen Sandiego

Spy Camera 3.00
Vanishing Landmark Viewer 3.00
Map Airplane Magnifer 3.00
Locator Game 3.00

Bad Atti-Toads

Charga-Toad 2.50
Dunka-Toad 2.50
Goalie-Toad 2.50
Socca-Toad 2.50

1999

Blazing Bugs

Bug Jumper 2.00
Other items in series 2.00

This "cool combo for kids" bag was how Hardee's packaged its kids meals during the Blazing Bugs promotion in 1999.

NASCAR Cups

Mark Martin/Jeff Burton 3.00
Other Drivers 3.00

Jack In The Box

Company Profile

Founded in 1951 by Robert O. Peterson, already the owner of a successful chain of restaurants, Jack in the Box was the first drive-through restaurant. Peterson named this new chain Jack in the Box because he wanted to attract children. He also wished to convey the message that the food was served fast. An oversized version of a toy clown popping out of a box was soon installed as the main attraction.

In the 1950s, a Jack in the Box hamburger sold for 29 cents, and a hot apple turnover sold for 17 cents. Jack in the Box had introduced its own soft drink called Jack Cola in 1968, only to replace it with Coca-Cola in 1971.

Jack in the Box restaurants are primarily located in California, Texas, and Arizona, and used to prominently feature Jack, a smiling clown, who greeted motorists who ordered via a two-way speaker device inside Jack's head.

In a 1980 TV ad, the company blew up Jack the clown in an effort to indicate that the company was altering its market position to attract adult tastes as well as offer upscale menu choices. In 1995, Jack was reintroduced as the company's icon/spokesperson in a new "Jack's Back" advertising and marketing campaign. The ads featured Jack as a 1990s corporate executive. The campaign helped promote innovative new products and value menus as well as the company's core burger menu.

A Jack PEZ head gave PEZ collectors a treat.

Known as a trendsetter and innovator, Jack in the Box introduced the industry's first breakfast sandwich and the first pre-packaged portable salad. Today, Jack in the Box tailors its menu to adult tastes and features one of the most varied and high-quality menus in the fast-food industry.

During the company's early years, Jack in the Box business operations were conducted under various names and structures, including Foodmaker, Inc. In 1968, Foodmaker was acquired by Ralston Purina. Foodmaker's management achieved a leveraged buyout in 1985, and the company went public two years later. In 1988, management took the company private once again. In 1992 it went public once more and is publicly traded on the New York Stock Exchange (FM).

The company partners with national consumer organizations to educate the public about the best ways families can protect themselves against food poisoning.

Foodmaker, Inc. operates and franchises more than 1,300 Jack in the Box restaurants in 12 states. With over $1 billion in annual revenues, the company has more than 29,000 employees and is among the nation's largest hamburger fast-food

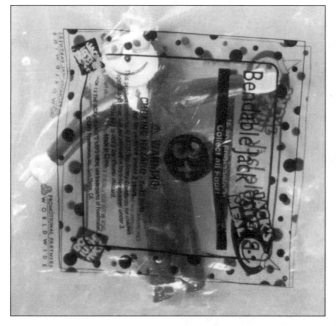

A Jack bendable (MIP) came on the scene in 1999.

Jack, the company's CEO, returned after a brief retirement.

chains. Based in San Diego, Jack in the Box operates more than two-thirds of its restaurants and franchises the rest.

Some Toy Info

In June of 1998, the chain brought back Jack vehicles. The five toys were: Jack in a golf cart, complete with golf clubs; Jack on a vintage motorcycle: in a convertible sports car; on a farm tractor; and in a helicopter. One toy was included with each Jack in the Box Kid's Meal, or sold separately for 99 cents. In August of 1999, Jack in the Box issued toys based on DC Comics characters Wonder Woman, Batman, Superman, Clark Kent, The Flash, Green Lantern, Aquaman and Darkseid.

The Story of Jack

According to Jack's official bio posted at the company's Web site (www.jackinthebox.com), Jack was a young entrepreneur who opened his first restaurant in the San Diego area way back in 1951. He named the restaurant after a favored toy, a Jack in the Box. Apparently, he looks just like the toy. Jack in the Box is among the nation's largest fast-food restaurant chains, sporting over

Another Jack bendy came out in 1999.

1,450 locations in 11 western states, plus locations in Hong Kong.

Jack's Back

After what was called a "retirement" period, the company brought Jack back into the limelight and has once again made him the keystone of its advertising and marketing campaign. A native of southern California, Jack currently resides in La Jolla and enjoys cruising in his 1968 GTO convertible and Rollerblading.

A company spokesperson indicated that while Jack in the Box is in the restaurant — not the toy — business, the toys do help extend the reach and influence of the brand. Over 4 million Jack car antenna toppers and bendable figures have been sold. The PEZ dispensers, announced in May 1999, were so appealing to the collectors market that the company was getting numerous requests prior to their release.

Jack in the Box Toy Listing

All prices are for items mint in package (MIP), unless otherwise noted.

Where applicable, the date(s) of distribution and additional information on the following premiums were provided by the individual chains.

Year Unknown

Zanny Space Buddies (sticker sets)

Set #1	10.00
Set #2	10.00
Set #3	10.00

1980

Jack Pack People (PVC figures)

Jack	20.00
Spy	20.00
Clown	20.00
German	20.00
O Ring	20.00

1991

Jack Pack Bendable Buddies

Jumbo Jack	15.00

Sly Fry 15.00
Ollie O. Ring 15.00
Edgar E. Eggroll 15.00
Betty Burger 15.00

1992

Jack Pack Bendable Buddies #2 (Same as previous year, except different colors)

Jumbo Jack 12.00
Sly Fry 12.00
Ollie O. Ring 12.00
Edgar E. Eggroll 12.00
Betty Burger 12.00

1993

Jack Pack Finger Puppets

Jumbo Jack 10.00
Sly Fry 10.00
Ollie O. Ring 10.00
Edgar E. Eggroll 10.00
Betty Burger 10.00

1998

Halloween Buckets

Wolf Man 2.00
Mummy 2.00
Count Dracula 2.00
Lady Bug rattle 2.00

Legos Animal sets

Lego Alligator 2.50
Lego Monkey 2.50
Lego Giraffe 2.50
Lego Bear 2.50

Jack Bendies

Jack with Burger 2.00
Jack with Newspaper 2.00
Jack with Notebook Computer 2.00
Jack with Golf Club 2.00

Eerie Indiana

Twins in a tub 2.00
Crow welcome to Eerie 2.00
Twins mix up 2.00
Puzzle Cube 2.00

Casper Ghost Train

(This promotion came with an exclusive offer for a Deluxe Kibosh – a green scare machine with deluxe lights and sound. Packed w/mail-in order form to Trendmasters.)

Jack bendies were out in force in '99.

Casper 2.50
Fats 2.50
Stretch 2.50
Stinky 2.50
Toy #5 .... 2.50

Jack Vehicles

Jack in Red Car 2.00
Jack on Yellow Tractor 2.00
Jack on a Motorcycle 2.00
Jack in a Helicopter 2.00
Jack in Boat 2.00
Jack in Golf Cart 2.00

1999

Kratts' Creatures Keychains

Shark 2.00
The Polar Bear 2.00
Fins the Dolphin 2.00
Fred the Snake 2.00
Theo the Monkey 2.00
Tootsie the Toucan 2.00

Glow in the Dark Fun Shapes

Each item 2.50

Hasbro Mini Game Classics

Hungry Hippo Pinball 2.50
Cootie Wind up Walker 2.50
Battleship Water Game 2.50
Finger Twister 2.50

Jack Bendies

Hawaiian Jack in a Hawaiian shirt 2.00
Disco Jack with 70s hair, clothes and glasses 2.00
College Jack holding a college '51 pendant 2.00
Business Jack holding a stock report 2.00

Sega

Sonic Push-down Racer 2.50
Dolphin Wind-up Swimmer 2.50
Knuckles Articulating Figurine 2.50
Bug Wind-up Walker 2.50

Over-the-counter items:

(A set of 4 CD-ROM games, each originally sold for $1.99.)
Each CD 3.00

Ooh It's Magic (Set of 6 toys)

June
Sword through Finger toy 2.00
Disappearing Jewel 2.00
Multiplying Coin 2.00
Guess the Card 2.00
Pierce the Coin 2.00
Magic Coin Lamp 2.00

PEZ Dispensers: featuring Jack's head.

(The set of three (w/red, blue and yellow bases), also came w/four flavors of candy. Each retailed for $1.99 with any food purchase.)
Each PEZ dispenser 4.00

Jock Jack Set of 7 toys (Bendies, some have parts with them, others roll)

June 28 – July
Fishing Jack — w/fishing pole and fish 2.00
Scuba Jack 2.00

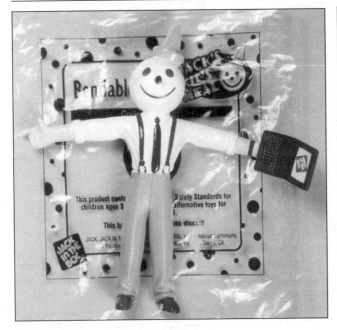

Another version of the Jack bendie.

Bob Sled Jack	2.00
Sky Diving Jack	2.00
Skateboard Jack	2.00
Race Car Driver Jack	2.00
Kayak Jack	2.00

DC Superheroes
Aug. 28 – Sept.

Batman in Batmobile	2.50
Superman in phone booth	2.50
Wonder Woman	2.50
Flash	2.50
Green Hornet	2.50
Aquaman — Wind-up water toy	2.50
Darkseid	2.50

Universal Monsters
October

Dracula	2.50
Frankenstein's Monster	2.50
Creature from the Black Lagoon	2.50
The Phantom of the Opera	2.50
The Mummy	2.50
Wolfman	2.50

Jack In the Box Antenna Balls
November

Millennium Ball	2.00
Jack Ornament	2.00
Other Ornaments	2.00

My Personal Pets
(Each pet comes with his or her own house.)
December

Each pet	2.00

2000

Pocket Toys

Tinker Toy	2.00
Mouse Trap — wind-up green mouse	2.00
Perfection	2.00
Operation	2.00
Life	2.00
Mr. Mouth	2.00
Aggravation	2.00

Spring Fever

Sun Shades	1.50
Glider	1.50
Frisbee	1.50
Koosh Ball	1.50
Mini Football	1.50
Clear Soccer Ball	1.50

Travel Games (all w/Jack in the Box logo)

Tic Tac Toe	1.50
Memory	1.50
Ball & Cup	1.50
Sketch	1.50
Ball Maze	1.50
Shake Balls	1.50

PHOTO OPS

Interested in flying? Well, you could build you own Lego helicopter courtesy of McDonald's (1999).

A pair of the original Power Rangers from McDonald's.

Spider-Man, "Spider-Sense" Peter Parker, Mary Jane Watson-Parker, and Dr. Octopus, from McDonald's.

Here comes a quartet of Barbie babes from McDonald's.

A quartet of McDonald's Muppet figurines.

A pair of cute bugs, from the 1999 Disney film A Bug's Life; issued by McDonald's.

McDonald's Aladdin figurines from the Disney animated movie.

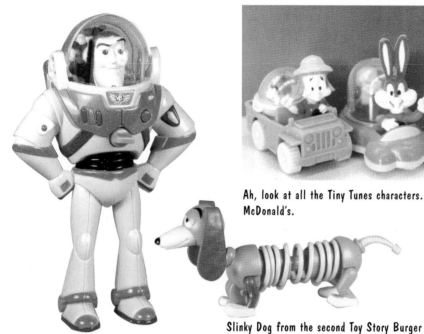

Ah, look at all the Tiny Tunes characters. These WB animated characters appeared at McDonald's.

Slinky Dog from the second Toy Story Burger King set.

Four (non-talking) plush animals from the cute animal flick Babe, courtesy of McDonald's.

This Buzz Lightyear over-the-counter candy dispenser (complete with a pack of Nerds) appeared in 1999 with the release of the fabulously animated Disney/Pixar flick, Toy Story 2.

Boo! A gaggle of "scary" McDonald's characters dressed up for All Hallows Eve.

Critters from the second McDonald's Ty Teenie Beanie Baby set.

Young Tarzan and his buddy ape, from the 1999 animated Disney film via McDonald's.

A pair of characters from the McDonald's toy series based on the 1999 Tarzan Film.

Two of eight, interlocking McDonald's Goof Troop action figurines (2000).

Nickelodeon's Action League Now! figures from Burger King's Nickel-O-Zone series (1998).

Superman, from the animated TV series. Burger King, 1997.

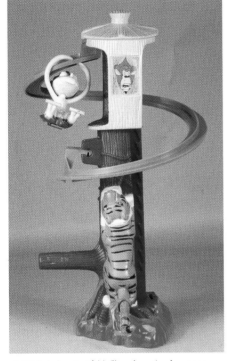

Toys from 2nd set of Burger King Pokémon collection (1999).

A Nickelodeon's Wild Thornberry's character from Burger King (2000).

Over-the-counter, gold-plated Pokémon (Poliwhirl), from Burger King (1999).

Mewtwo and clip-on "container" from the first set of Pokémon toys from Burger King (1999).

Debbie and Donnie go for a ride as part of a 2000 Burger King Wild Thornberry's promotion.

Nine-card, uncut sheet of 1999 Yankee lineup. Number one of three. Includes 1999 calendar, and BK coupon.

Nickelodeon's back-to-school set from a Burger King promotion (1997).

Burger King glow-in-the-dark figurine from the Glo Force set (1996).

Batman Beyond characters from the animated WB series and Burger King (2000).

Burger King Backstreet Project, based on characters developed by Stan Lee Media and the Backstreet Boys (2000).

Toy Story 1's Sheriff Woody from Burger King (2000).

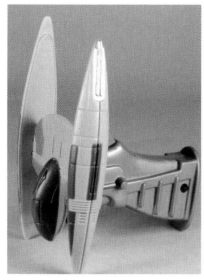

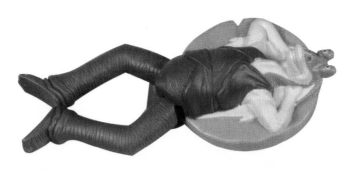

While many wished that computer-generated Jar Jar Binks would drown, this one could swim (1999).

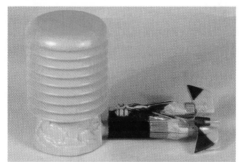

Darth Maul Sith Infiltrator toy from from Episode I: Star Wars Episode I: The Phantom Menace (1999).

The nasty Sebulba's Podracer from Star Wars Episode I: The Phantom Menace (1999).

Young Anakin's Podracer, from The Phantom Menace (1999).

Darth Vader/Yoda magic cube from the Taco Bell anniversary edition of Star Wars in 1997.

Yoda/Darth Vader magic cube from the Taco Bell anniversary edition of Star Wars in 1997.

Here's a rare find, a pair of The Empire Strikes Back Glasses from Burger King's 1980 promotion.

The sides of the boxes from the kid meal toys formed a mini poster. This set is from the Tatooine series. From Star Wars Episode I: The Phantom Menace (1999).

Yoda destiny tell you much, yes? From Star Wars Episode I: The Phantom Menace (1999).

101

You could explode your own Death Star with the Taco Bell anniversary edition of Star Wars in 1997.

Look, up in the air, Bobba Fett can fly! Well, at least this Taco Bell version from the Star Wars Special Edition can (1997).

Be your own Boss (Nass) with this cup topper from Star Wars Episode I: The Phantom Menace (1999).

Hey look, a mini R2-D2 Cup topper from Star Wars Episode I: The Phantom Menace (1999).

Captain Tarpals from Star Wars Episode I: The Phantom Menace (1999).

Lott Dodd walking throne toy from Star Wars Episode I: The Phantom Menace (1999).

Glass set from Burger King's 1977 promotion of Star Wars.

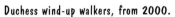
Duchess wind-up walkers, from 2000.

Aliens have invaded my Duchess kid meal, and they can swap body parts (2000).

Scary Universal Monster set from Jack in the Box, 1999.

The Big Guy and Rusty toys were based on the Dark Horse comic book and issued by Taco Bell in 2000.

Now here are some real scary monsters from KFC (2000).

Holiday wind-ups from Duchess (2000).

Universal Monster set from Jack in the Box (1999). Scary, eh?

A pair of weenie bendies from Nathen's.

To celebrate Peanuts' 50th anniversary, Wendy's issued a set of toys featuring Charlie Brown's favorite pooch, Snoopy.

Drink deep from the Millennium Loony Tune Twist 'n Go from Subway (2000)

Loony Tunes backpack clip-ons from Subway from its year-end Loony Millennium promotion (2000).

The WB's Big Cartoonie show characters appeared in this like-named promotion from Wendy's in 2000.

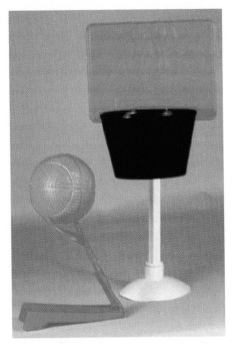

You can get nuttin' but net from this Taco Bell NCAA hoop game...if there was a net (2000).

Wendy's ended 2000 with this Grinch tie-in promotion.

KFC

Company Profile

The fast-food chain known today as KFC began back in the 1930s when Harland Sanders, born September 9, 1890, began serving chicken to the patrons of his service station in Corbin, Kentucky. He didn't have a restaurant then, but served people on his own dining table in the living quarters of his service station. Eventually the operation grew and moved across the street to a motel and restaurant. In 1935, in recognition of his contributions to the state's cuisine, Governor Ruby Laffoon made him a Kentucky Colonel.

In 1952, Pete Harman became the first Kentucky Fried Chicken franchisee, with a store in Salt Lake City. In 1956, at the ripe young age of 65, the Colonel sold the Corbin, Kentucky, location and went on the road to enlist new franchises. In 1964, he sold the chain to a group of investors, including John Y. Brown, Jr. and Jack Massey, for $2 million. The Colonel continued on as spokesman for the company, until his death in 1980. The company went public in 1969 and was sold to Heublein Inc. in 1971.

PepsiCo, Inc. acquired the chain in 1986, eventually changing its name and logo to KFC in 1991. Today, KFC has well over 9,000 locations worldwide, including restaurants in China, Russia, and Australia.

It has only been over the past few years that the company has had a kid meal program that offered

premiums. Virtually all of these have had been licensed products through Sony (Beakman's World, Ghostbusters); Marvel Comics (Spider-Man, Hulk, Fantastic Four, Wolverine); Disney (Timon & Pumbaa); Saban (Masked Rider); and others (Scholastic/ Animorphs; United Media-BBC Worldwide/Wallace & Gromit).

Unlike many of the other fast-food operations, KFC tends to keep its promotions running for longer periods of time with only four to six promotions throughout the course of the year. The advantage to this approach to meal premiums is twofold with pluses for both KFC and collectors. On KFC's side, the company incurs less traffic, marketing, and operational expenses that are associated with acquiring and scheduling promotions. For collectors, the advantage is more time to acquire preferred toys.

A New Era; A New Name

In 1991, Kentucky Fried Chicken announced that it was changing its name to "KFC" and updating its packaging and logo as well to reflect a more modern look. According to the public relations info given out at the time, the name change was an attempt to lure back customers to a restaurant now offering foods branded as "better for you."

Needless to say, there was more to the name change than just a PR face-lift. According to some sources, the real reason for the name change actually dated back to 1990 when the Commonwealth of Kentucky — which was apparently mired in debt — actually trademarked the name of the state. Needless to say, the state then required any company using the word "Kentucky" for business reasons to obtain permission from the Commonwealth, and to pay licensing fees for the use of the name. While this might have been conceived as a bold and unique scheme to alleviate the states debt, it proved spectacularly unsuccessful.

Kentucky Fried Chicken refused to pay royalties on a name it had been using since 1953, as a matter of principle. After a year of futile negotiations with Kentucky, the company simply altered its name to KFC and timed the announcement to coincide with the introduction of its new packaging and products.

Kentucky Fried Chicken was not the only company to refuse to cow-tow to the state. The Kentucky Derby officially changed its name to The Run for the Roses, while many seed and nursery companies which had previously offered Kentucky bluegrass now sell "Shenendoah bluegrass."

Jack in the Box has a toy, McDonald's has a clown, but KFC has the Colonel.

Opee See Creature from the Episode I toy 1999 toy set.

The Dawn of Darth Maul

One of the highlights of the 1999 fast-food toy season was KFC's set of *Star Wars: Episode I – The Phantom Menace* toys that were issued in conjunction with sister companies Pizza Hut and Taco Bell. The three franchises not only joined forces to issue a comprehensive set of *Star Wars Episode I* toys, they actually linked their three Web sites (via a *Star Wars* hot button), so that Web surfers could easily access the company's sister sites. Still, not wanting to do the job half way, each of the three Tricon Web sites were also linked directly to Lucas' own *Star Wars* site (www.starwars.com), so that fans could also access the very latest official *Star Wars* info direct from the grand poo-bah himself. All in all a very cool concept, no matter what might be said of the movie itself.

Further, KFC, Pizza Hut, and Taco Bell combined marketing muscle and released a very cool series of TV ads that linked up the good Colonel, the Taco Bell Chihuahua, and the new spokes-icon for Pizza Hut, a pizza delivery girl, to promote the movie, toy set, and the three restaurants.

For a more detailed look at these toys, as well as a listing of all *Star Wars* fast food toys issued over the years, check out the "May the (Fast Food), Force be with You" article and accompanying list elsewhere in this book.

KFC Toy Listing

All prices are for items mint in package (MIP), unless otherwise noted.

Where applicable, the date(s) of distribution and additional information on the following premiums were provided by the individual chains.

Year Unknown

KFC flyer (throwing disc)	10.00
KFC Truck (metal truck)	10.00

1996

Looney Tunes Cups
Feb. – Mar.
Each 3.00

Matchbox Cars
Apr. - June
Each 3.00

Koosh
July – Sept.
Each 3.00

Linkbots
Oct. – Dec.
Each 3.00

1997

Timon & Pumbaa 1
Jan. – Feb.
Out-to-Lunch Timon	2.50
Snail Snackin' Timon	2.50
Jungle River Riding Timon	2.50
Beetle Lunchin' Pumbaa	2.50
Mudbath Pumbaa	2.50
Hawaiian Luau Pumbaa	2.50

Masked Rider
Mar. – May
Magno Free Wheeler 3.00

Press and Go Super Chopper	3.00
Masked Rider with Super Blue Snap-On Helmet	3.00
Bump and Go Ferbus	3.00
Glow-in-the-Dark X-Ray Cyclopter	3.00
Ecto-Viewer Wrist Piece	3.00

Marvel Superheroes
June – Aug.
Incredible Hulk Pencil Twirler	4.00
Spider-Man Symbol Clip	4.00
Invisible Woman Escape Launcher	4.00
Wolverine Press 'n Go	4.00
Spider-Man Wall Walker	4.00

A "Battle Droid" chicken bucket top also served as a flying disc at KFC.

The Boss Nass squishy wasn't listed as an available toy when the toy list came packed in every Phantom Menace box, but it was available as an under-3 toy at KFC.

Fantastic Four Terra Craft 4.00

Carmen Sandiego
Sept. – Oct.
Jr. Sleuth Pocket Pack 4.00
Carmen's Breakaway Escape Car 4.00
Carmen's Undercover Case with Stickers 4.00
Carmen's Mystery Decoder 4.00
Carmen's World Map Puzzle 4.00
Magic Answer Globe 4.00

Extreme Ghostbusters
Nov. – Dec.
Slimer Squeezer 4.00
Ghost Top Trap 4.00
Ghostbusters Keychain Keeper 4.00
Haunted Cube 4.00
Ecto 1 Haunted Hauler 4.00
Screamin' Scrambler 4.00

Garfield
Jan. – Mar.
Each 3.00

Casper
Apr. – May
Each 4.00

Chester Cheetah
July
Each 3.00

EEK! The Cat
Aug. – Sept.
Each 3.00

Timon & Pumbaa 2
Out-to-Lunch Timon 3.00
Snail Snackin' Timon 3.00
Jungle River Riding Timon 3.00
Beetle Lunchin' Pumbaa 3.00
Mudbath Pumbaa 3.00
Hawaiian Luau Pumbaa 3.00

1998

Beakman's World
Jan. – Feb.
Dancing Liza 3.00
Beakman's Balancer 3.00
Optical Illusion Top 3.00
Diver Don 3.00
Lester Reverser 3.00
Penguin TV 3.00

Sports Illustrated for Kids
Mar. – Apr.
Hoop it up Fun Book 2.50
Basketball Flipbook 2.50
Kick it in Fun Book 2.50
Soccer Flipbook 2.50

Slimamander
June – July
Wrist Squirter 2.50
Glowing Goo 2.50
Spraying Top 2.50
Bubble Wand 2.50
Leap The Frog Launcher 2.50
Slimamander & Leap The Frog Tattoos 2.50

Wallace & Gromit
Aug. – Sept.
The Wrong Trousers 3.00
Gromit's Rollalong Slidecar 3.00
Wallace Bendable 3.00
Wallace & Gromit Character Card Set 3.00
Sheep-on-a-string 3.00
Blinking Feathers McGraw 3.00

Animorphs
Oct. – Nov.
Puzzle Cube 3.00
DNA Transferer Cards 3.00
Animorphic Box 3.00
Tobias Hawk Glider 3.00
Speak Revealer 3.00

Pokémon
(During promotion Pokémon beanbags were also available for $4.99 with purchase of meal, $5.99 if purchased separately.)

Marvel superheroes came to the rescue at KFC in the summer of 1997.

The KFC Phantom Menace toy set had it all: chicken, a collector bucket and flyer lid.

Nov. – Dec.
Pikachu Treasure Keeper (key chain/change purse) 6.00
Pokémon Tattoos (temporary)... 5.00
Ivysaur Squirter (water toy)... 5.00
Pokémon Monster Matcher (matching cube)................... 5.00
Go Pokémon Card Game 6.00
Pokémon Monster Block (character cubes) 5.00

Plush Pokémon Characters from series (over the counter toys)
Seel.. 4.00
Vulpix 4.00
Dratini.. 4.00
Zubat.. 4.00

1999

Winter WonderPals
February
Roly Poly Polar Ball (0+).. 2.00
Slick the Sled Dog Igloo Launcher.................................. 2.00
Sippy the Penguin Play Straw... 2.00
Howl E. Wolf 2.00
Wallace the Walrus Paper Puncher 2.00

The Spy Dogs as seen on Fox Kids
April
Agent Ralph's Marble Game.. 2.00
The Evil Cat Astrophe 2.00
Fidgety Scribble 2.00
Eye Popping Space Slug 2.00
Mitzy Rolling Stamper... 2.00

Star Wars: Episode I The Phantom Menace
  (This promotion was done in conjunction with sister companies Pizza Hut and Taco Bell.)

Planet Naboo toy series

Kid Meal Toys
Jar Jar Binks squirter 3.00
Queen Amidala's hidden identity 3.00
Anakin Skywalker's Naboo Fighter 3.00
Trade Federation Droid Fighter.. 3.00
Planet Naboo 3.00
Swimming Jar Jar Binks... 3.00

Opee Sea Creature Chaser..3.00
Naboo Ground Battle...3.00
Gungan Sub Squirter...3.00
Boss Nass Squirter (under-3) 3.00

Cup Toppers
Boss Nass 4.00
Captain Tarpals 4.00
Queen Amidala 4.00
R2-D2 ....4.00

Chicken Buckets w/Star Wars Scenes
Anakin Skywalker 3.00
Captain Tarpals 3.00
Battle Droid..3.00
Queen Amidala 3.00

Flying Bucket Toppers
Jar Jar Binks 3.00
Battle Droid...3.00

2000

Star Wars: Episode I The Phantom Menace
  (This set is a re-issue of the original set from 1999. Taco Bell also re-issued its version of Phantom Menace toys at the same time. It is not known if Pizza Hut also re-issued its set as well. Note: The 10th kid meal toy from KFC is not listed on the boxes.)

Planet Naboo toy series
Kid Meal Toys
Jar Jar Binks squirter 3.00
Queen Amidala's hidden identity 3.00
Anakin Skywalker's Naboo Fighter 3.00
Trade Federation Droid Fighter....................................3.00
Planet Naboo 3.00
Swimming Jar Jar Binks 3.00
Opee Sea Creature Chaser..3.00
Naboo Ground Battle...3.00
Gungan Sub Squirter...3.00

Jar Jar squirters were one of many Episode I items available at KFC.

Boss Nass Squirter (under-3)......................................3.00
Cup Toppers
    Boss Nass 4.00
    Captain Tarpals 4.00
    Queen Amidala 4.00
    R2-D2.. 4.00

Chicken Buckets w/Star Wars Scenes
Anakin Skywalker...3.00
Captain Tarpals 3.00
Battle Droid 3.00
Queen Amidala 3.00

Flying Bucket Toppers
Jar Jar Binks 3.00
Battle Droid 3.00

Final Four Basketball
NCAA Basketball 2.00
NCAA Basketball 2.00
Wrist Basketball Game 2.00
Toss Cup Game 2.00
Over-the-counter Final Four Basketball (retail $2.49)......3.50

Nova's Ark
Jumping Nova Backpack clip 2.00
Radius Mini Flyer 2.00
Surprise Stencils..2.00
Taspett Konstuctor 2.00

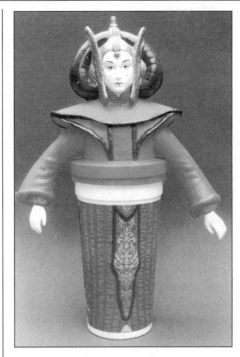

Queen Amidala got in on the act as a cup topper with the 1999 Episode I series.

Trumpet Candy Carrier 2.00
Zyte Crystal Revealer 2.00

McDonald's

Company Profile

In the late 1940s, the McDonald brothers, Dick and Mac, were searching for a way to improve their San Bernadino, California, drive-in restaurant business. Rather than monkey with the business itself, which was doing quite well, they re-invented it as an entirely new concept based on speedy service, low prices, and large volume.

They chose to do away with carhops in favor of self-service at the counter. In the process they cut their large barbecue menu in favor of a much smaller one, limiting it to just a few items, including hamburgers, cheeseburgers, three soft drink flavors, plus milk and coffee, potato chips, pie, french fries, and milkshakes. They then redesigned their kitchen for mass production and speed by instituting assembly-line procedures. They also slashed the price of their hamburger from a competitive 30 cents to 15 cents.

The new, improved McDonald's opened in December 1948. It took a while to rebuild their business, but it soon became apparent that the brothers had captured the spirit of post-war America. By the mid-1950s, their operation had annual revenues of over $350,000 — nearly double the volume of their barbecue drive-in business at the same location.

Word of their success quickly spread, and in 1952 they authorized their first franchise in Phoenix, Arizona. The Phoenix location became a prototype of future stores with a red-and-white tiled building, slanting roof, and the now familiar golden arches. The brothers actually designed the assembly-line kitchen by drawing a chalk diagram on their tennis court to the exact size of the new kitchen. They were able to design the space and place the equipment in the most efficient fashion by studying their crew during food preparation.

In those days it was possible to purchase a franchise for as little as $1,000. For this, franchises

Maple was one of four international Teenie Beanies that were sold over the counter by McDonald's in 1999.

received the right to use the McDonald's name, a basic description of the Speedy Service System, plus the services of Art Bender — the brothers' original counter man at the new restaurant — for a week or two to get them started.

Glory was another Teenie Beanie. The others were Britania and Erin.

Not just any McDonald's logo, but a Happy Meal logo.

110

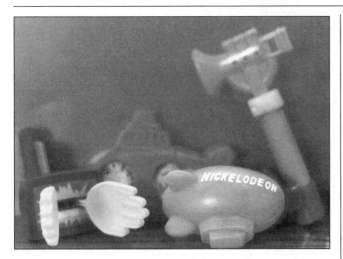

Before jumping to Burger King in '98, Nickelodeon made its home at McDonald's. This set is from 1993.

In 1954, a 52-year-old milkshake machine salesman named Ray Kroc saw the McDonald's operation for the first time. According to company history, Kroc showed up at McDonald's one morning in 1954 and, after seeing how successful the operation was, decided that he wanted in on it. He then negotiated a deal with the brothers to oversee the company's expansion, becoming their exclusive franchising agent for the entire country.

On March 2, 1955, the company officially changed its name to McDonald's System, Inc. then on April 15, 1955, Kroc's prototype McDonald's opened for business in Des Plaines, Illinois with, naturally, the help of Art Bender. Kroc continued the successful formula of a limited menu, quality food, assembly-line production system, and fast, friendly service. Still, it was in franchising where Kroc really shined.

By the end of 1956, McDonald's 14 restaurants reported sales of $1.2 million and had served over 50 million hamburgers. Four years later, there were 228 restaurants reporting $37.6 million in sales. In 1961 Kroc bought out the McDonald brothers for a million bucks apiece.

By 1963, McDonald's was selling around a million hamburgers a day. Ray Kroc actually served the billionth burger to TV personality Art Linkletter on Linkletter's national TV show. In 1965, McDonald's went public, selling for $22.50 a share and skyrocketing to $49 within a few weeks.

In 1967, the price of a McDonald's hamburger finally increased from 15 cents to 18 cents. This was the first price increase since the McDonald brothers introduced the 15-cent price two decades before. In 1970, McDonald's was reporting some $587 million in sales from 1,600 restaurants in all 50 states of the U.S. and four countries. That year, the restaurant in Waikiki, Hawaii, was the first to serve breakfast. The following year, the first McDonald's playland opened in Chula Vista, California.

In 1975, the company established its first drive-thru operation in the Sierra Vista, Arizona location. Today, drive-thru business accounts for about half of all McDonald's restaurant sales in the U.S. Today McDonald's has locations in 120 countries.

McDonald's Slogans Through the Years

A common wisdom on Madison Avenue is that a company is only as good as its marketing campaign. If this is so, then McDonald's has had perhaps one of the very best marketing campaigns ever.

Today, McDonald's serves some 38 million customers a day from 23,000 restaurants in over 100 countries (approximately 20 million of these customers and 13,000 locations are from the U.S.). This makes McDonald's one of the world's two most recognized and powerful brands – the other being Coca-Cola (which is McDonald's only soft drink supplier).

Throughout the years, McDonald's has had quite a number of catchy slogans with catchy song lyrics written by folks like Barry Manilow. Some of these catch phrases have included the following: "McDonald's Is Your Kind of Place" (1965); "You Deserve a Break Today" (1971, 1981); "We Do It All For You" (1975); "Nobody Can Do It Like McDonald's Can" (1979); "McDonald's and You" (1983); "It's a Good Time for the Great Taste of McDonald's" (1984); "Good Time, Great Taste" (1988); "Food, Folks and Fun" (1990); "McDonald's Today" (1991); "What You Want is What You Get" (1992); "Have You Had Your Break Today?" (1995); and the most recent, and perhaps the catchiest, "Did Somebody Say McDonald's?" (1997).

Having The Right Spokesman

Having a recognizable icon and/or spokesperson is also a good thing. Here again, McDonald's shoots and scores with the clown of the millennium, Ronald McDonald. In 1963, Ronald made his first appearance in Washington, D.C. He is the brain child of franchisees John Gibson and Oscar Goldstein, and was created to support their efforts to attract children to their restau-

The X-Men joined Spider-Man, Hulk and members of the Fantastic Four for an appearance at McDonald's in 1996. This is the back of the Happy Meal bag from that promotion.

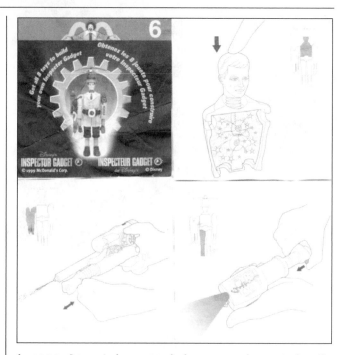

The Mystic Knights took up residence at McDonald's during the spring of 1996.

In 1999, Disney's Inspector Gadget spawned a 15-inch-tall snap-together action figure that was composed of eight separate Happy Meal toys.

rants. Ronald went on to make his first national appearance in the Macy's Thanksgiving Day parade in 1966 and was subsequently named McDonald's official spokesperson for children the following year.

Due to his appearance in TV commercials, participation in fund-raising events, and daily visits with children in hospitals, schools, and McDonald's restaurants, Ronald McDonald has become a national institution recognized by 96 percent of American children.

Backing Ronald up is an equally colorful cast of characters: the Hamburglar, Grimace, Mayor

McCheese, the Fry Kids, Officer Big Mac, Birdie the Early Bird, and the McNugget Buddies. The renowned Happy Meal was created especially for the children's market, with the first national Happy Meal "circus wagon" appearing in 1979. Children, and adults, have been enjoying and collecting special Happy Meal toys ever since.

McDonald's Toy Listing

All prices are for items mint in package (MIP), unless otherwise noted.

Where applicable, the date(s) of distribution and additional information on the following premiums were provided by the individual chains.

1971

Ronald doll, cloth, pointed collar with tab at top of
    zipper 50.00

1972

Hamburglar 17" doll, cloth, black and white-striped suit,
    detachable cape.. 35.00

1973

McDonald's Character Series
5" Glasses:
    Big Mac 14.00
    Captain Crook 14.00
    Grimace.. 14.00
    Hamburglar 14.00
    Mayor McCheese 14.00

    Ronald McDonald 14.00
Set of 6 ....85.00

Miscellaneous
Big Mac 12" hand puppet, vinyl head, blue cloth policeman
    body 25.00

1976

McDonald's Character Series
Silk Screened Glasses:
    Big Mac (has different shades of blue) 8.00

Jim Hensen's Muppet characters are always popular as McDonald's promotions. This group came from 1995.

A Disney Bambi figurine set came out in 1988.

Captain Crook (purple/lavender, black/red)................. 8.00
Grimace (dark blue, purple and lavender).................. 8.00
Hamburglar (both the top of his cape and clothing are
    lighter) 8.00
Mayor McCheese (has different shades of blue) 8.00
Ronald McDonald (has red lettering) 8.00
Set of 6, 5-1/2" 50.00

Miscellaneous
Big Mac 7" doll, blue policeman uniform (Remco) 45.00

1977

McDonaldland Series
5" Glasses:
    Big Mac On Roller Skates 5.00
    Captain Crook On Leaky Boat 5.00
    Grimace On Pogo Stick... 5.00
    Hamburglar On Flat Car.. 5.00
    Mayor McCheese Taking Pictures............................... 5.00
    Ronald Leapfrogging Into Lake 5.00
Set of 6... 30.00
6-1/4" Glasses:
    Big Mac On Roller Skates 5.00
    Captain Crook On Leaky Boat 5.00
    Grimace On Pogo Stick... 5.00
    Hamburglar On Flat Car.. 5.00
    Mayor McCheese Taking Pictures............................... 5.00
    Ronald Leapfrogging Into Lake 5.00
Set of 6... 30.00

Miscellaneous
Ronald 13" doll, cloth, red & white-striped shirt black M on
    pockets.. 35.00

1978
Ronald McDonald 22" stuffed doll 35.00

Lift-Up Mystery Games
Mayor Word Guess 7.00
Professor Dot 7.00
Ronald Maze.. 7.00
Big Mac Tic-Tac-Toe 7.00

1979

Space Theme

Space Aliens, Rubber Figures:
    Lizard Man 5.00
    Tree Trunk Monster.. 5.00
    Winged Amphibian Creature....................................... 5.00
    Vampire Creature 5.00

    Horned Cyclops 5.00
    Insectman 5.00
    Gilled-face creature 5.00
    Balloon-headed creature 5.00

Space Raiders Rubber Figures
    Pointy-eared alien..5.00
    Flying Saucer..5.00
    Round-headed alien 5.00
    Alien w/raised arms 5.00
    Rocket w/booster nozzle...5.00
    Alien w/helmet 5.00
    Narrow rocket 5.00
    Rocket w/wide wings 5.00

Star Trek
Star Trek Navigating Bracelet.......................................25.00
Starfleet Game 25.00
Captain Kirk Ring w/secret compartment 22.00
Enterprise Ring w/secret compartment 22.00
Star Trek Logo Ring w/secret compartment 22.00
Spock Ring w/secret compartment...............................22.00
Ilia Iron-On Transfer..20.00
Spock Iron-On Transfer 20.00
Kirk Iron-On Transfer...20.00
McCoy Iron-On Transfer 20.00

Boxes:
    Draw the Alien 7.00
    Planet Faces 7.00
    Federation...7.00
    Klingons 7.00
    Spacesuit..7.00
    Transporter Room..7.00

Matchbox Miniflexies
Soft, Rubber Cars:
    Turbo Fury 8.00
    Hairy Hustler...8.00
    Baja Buggy 8.00
    Cosmobile...8.00
    Fandango..8.00
    Datsun 126X 8.00
    Hi-Tailer..8.00
    Beach Hopper 8.00
    Planet Scout 8.00
    Mercedes 8.00

1980

Look Look Books 5" x 4" Books
    Animals of the Sea...7.00
    Cats In The Wild 7.00

The Busy World of Richard Scarry wasn't really scary, but it was part of a 1995 promotion.

Animals That Fly 7.00
The Biggest Animals 7.00

Safari Adventure Figurines
Alligator 5.00
Tiger 5.00
Ape 5.00
Hippo 5.00
Elephant 5.00
Monkey 5.00
Lion 5.00
Rhino 5.00

Undersea Figurines
Penguin 5.00
Pelican 5.00
Alligator 5.00
Tiger Shark 5.00
Turtle 5.00
Walrus 5.00
Whale Shark 5.00
Dolphin/Porpoise 5.00
Great White Shark 5.00
Hammerhead Shark 5.00
Seal 5.00
Snail 5.00

McDonald's Adventure Series Glasses
Big Mac Nets The Hamburglar 8.00
Captain Crook Sails The Bounding Main 8.00
Grimace Climbs a Mountain 8.00
Hamburglar Hooks The Hamburgers 8.00
Mayor McCheese Rides A Runaway Train 8.00
Ronald McDonald Saves The Falling Stars 8.00
Set of 6 .... 50.00

Miscellaneous
Ronald 5-1/2" acrobatic figure, blue plastic 35.00

1981

Adventures of Ronald McDonald 2" Rubber Figurines
Ronald 8.00
Birdie 8.00
Professor 8.00
Hamburglar 8.00
Big Mac 8.00
Grimace 8.00
Capt. Crook 8.00
Mayor McCheese 8.00

Dinosaur Days Rubber Figurines
Apatosaurus 5.00

Great jumpin' superheroes! It's the PVC figurines from the 1993 animated Batman set.

The demand for Cabbage Patch kids may have cooled, but not before McDonald's jumped on the wagon and offered a couple of sets, including this one from 1994.

Pteranodon 5.00
Stegosaurs...5.00
Dimetrodon 5.00

Old West Figurines
Sheriff 12.00
Indian w/crossed arms 12.00
Frontier Man w/knife 12.00
Indian Looking to Side 12.00
Woman w/gun 12.00
Man w/hands up 12.00

Wacky Meal Plastic Cups
Traffic Jam 6.00
Figure Skating 6.00
Jungle Gym 6.00
Country Club...6.00
Airplane Hanger...6.00
Monkey Business 6.00

Miscellaneous
Ronald 4-1/2" doll, cloth..30.00
McDonald's characters figures: plastic, blue, green, orange,
    or yellow...8.00

The Great Muppet Caper Glasses
Happiness Hotel 3.00
Kermit 3.00
Miss Piggy 3.00
The Great Gonzo 3.00
Set of 4 ....15.00

1982

Dukes of Hazzard 16 oz. Plastic Cups
Boss Hog 12.00
Bo 12.00
Luke 12.00
Daisy..12.00
Sheriff Rosco 12.00
Uncle Jesse 12.00

Meal Containers
General Lee Plastic Car...12.00
White Truck...12.00
Police Car 12.00
Boss Hog's Cadillac 12.00
White Bronco 12.00

Unidentified Space Ship Containers
Spaceship w/8 windows in blue 6.00

Mc-scary toys were part of a 1996 Halloween series.

Spaceship w/8 windows in green 6.00
Spaceship w/8 windows in red 6.00
Spaceship w/8 windows in yellow 6.00
Spaceship w/pointed nose in blue.............................. 6.00
Spaceship w/pointed nose in green 6.00
Spaceship w/pointed nose in red 6.00
Spaceship w/pointed nose in yellow 6.00
Spaceship w/4 humps in blue 6.00
Spaceship w/4 humps in green.................................. 6.00
Spaceship w/4 humps in red.................................... 6.00
Spaceship w/4 humps in yellow 6.00
Circular Spaceship in blue 6.00
Circular Spaceship in green 6.00
Circular Spaceship in red 6.00
Circular Spaceship in yellow 6.00

Little Golden Book

The Country Mouse and The City Mouse 8.00
The Monster at the End of this Book............................ 8.00
Benji, Fastest Dog in the West.................................. 8.00
Tom and Jerry's Party 8.00
The Poky Little Puppy 8.00

Playmobil

Set 1: Sheriff w/rifle, chair, hat & cape 20.00
Set 2: Indian w/shield, 2 spears, & peace pipe 20.00
Set 3: Sheriff's Brown Horse w/saddle w/water trough 20.00
Set 4: Umbrella Girl w/umbrella, suitcase, & hat 20.00
Set 5: Farmer w/hoe, rake, hat, dog 20.00
Sky-Busters Rubber Planes:
    DC-10.. 7.00
    Sky-Hawk... 7.00
    Tornado 7.00
    Mig-21 .... 7.00
    Mirage F1 .... 7.00
    Phantom.. 7.00

Miscellaneous

Goblins Bowling, six 2-1/2" plastic figures, with a 1-1/4"
    ball.. 6.00

1983

Astrosniks Figurines:

    Thirsty 8.00
    Scout... 8.00
    Astralia 8.00
    Laser 8.00
    Skater 8.00
    Snikapotamus 10.00
    Robo... 10.00
    Sport... 8.00

Circus '83

Grimace "Test Your Strength" Circus Toy 8.00
Acrobatic Ronald 10.00
Fun House Mirror of Hamburglar................................. 8.00
Fun House Mirror of Ronald.................................... 8.00
French Fry Faller 8.00

Going Places Hot Wheels Cars

Dixie Challenger 15.00
Firebird 15.00
Frontrunning Fairmont 12.00
Land Lord 10.00
Malibu Grand Prix 12.00
Mercedes 380 .... 12.00
Minitrek "Good Time Camper" 10.00
Porsche P-928 .... 10.00
Race Bait 308 .... 10.00
Sheriff Patrol 10.00
Turismo.. 9.00
Corvette Stingray 15.00
Tricar X8 .... 15.00
Jeep CJ-7 .... 15.00
Split Window '63 .... 15.00
3-Window '34 .... 12.00
'56 Hi-Tail Hauler 15.00
T-Bird 15.00
Baja Breaker 10.00
Cadillac Seville 12.00
Chevy Citation X-11 .... 12.00
Datsun 200 SX 12.00

McDonaldland Junction

Trains:
    Steam Engine w/Ronald 5.00
    Caboose w/Grimace 5.00
    Box Car w/Fry Guys.. 5.00
    Coach w/Birdie.. 5.00

Mystery '83

Assorted Items:
    Detective Kit w/tweezers, finger print kit, & decipher........ 5.00
    Magic Ball 5.00
    Magni-Finder Glass of Ronald 5.00
    Magni-Finder Glass of Fry Guy................................ 5.00
    Magni-Finder Glass of Birdie 5.00
    Unpredict-A-Ball of Ronald's Face............................ 5.00

Ship Shape '83

Meal Containers:
    River Boat 5.00
    Splash-Dasher 5.00
    Tubby-Tugger 5.00
    Rub-A-Dub Sub 5.00

The Flintstones rocked the town in 1994.

Michael Jordan, the king of the pitchmen, had his own Happy Meal sports set.

Winter Worlds

Ornaments:
    Ronald... 6.00
    Grimace.. 6.00
    Hamburglar 6.00
    Mayor McCheese............................. 6.00
    Birdie... 6.00

Peanuts Camp Snoopy

Glasses:
    Charlie Brown................................... 4.00
    Snoopy 4.00
    Lucy... 4.00
    Snoopy 4.00
    Linus.. 4.00
Set of 5.. 16.00
Charlie Brown Glass Promoting Series:
    "Good Grief! McDonald's Camp Snoopy Glasses Are Coming" 85.00

Miscellaneous

Space character, "Bully Figure" with "M" on chest,
    2" rubber 4.00

1984

Astrosniks '84 Figurines

Astrosnik Copter 8.00
Astrosnik Racing 8.00
Astrosnik Skiing 8.00
Astrosnik Commander 8.00
Astrosnik Drill.. 8.00
Astrosnik Perfido................................... 8.00

Good Sports Puffy Stickers

Sam the Olympic Eagle w/basketball............. 9.00
Birdie w/Soccer Ball 8.00
Grimace on Sled 8.00
Hamburglar Playing Hockey 8.00
Ronald Ice Skating.................................. 9.00
Mayor McCheese Skiing 8.00

Olympic Pails

Athletics Pail w/shovel 8.00
Olympic Games Pail w/shovel 8.00

Cycling Pail w/shovel...............................8.00
Swimming Pail w/shovel 8.00

Lego Building Sets '84

Set 1: 17 pieces for truck.........................5.00
Set 2: 27 pieces for ship..........................6.00
Set 3: 19 pieces for helicopter.................5.00
Set 4: 18 pieces for airplane....................5.00

Olympic Sports '84 Glowing Puzzles

"Guess Who Stole The Winning Goal" 5.00
"Who Do You Know That Can Help Them Row?"...........5.00
"Guess Who Finished Smiles Ahead"...............5.00
"Guess Which Guy Comes In Under The Wire" 5.00

School Days School Supplies

Ronald Pencil Sharpener..........................6.00
Grimace Pencil Sharpener 6.00
6" Ruler depicting Ronald and Birdie...............6.00
Captain Crook Eraser 4.00
Grimace Eraser 4.00
Hamburglar Eraser 4.00
Ronald Eraser..4.00
Birdie Eraser..4.00
Ronald/Birdie Pencil Case 4.00
Ronald Pencil 4.00
Hamburglar Pencil 4.00
Grimace Pencil 4.00

Disney Animated Classics

Glasses:
    Peter Pan..17.00
    Cinderella..17.00
    Fantasia 17.00
    Snow White and The Seven Dwarfs 17.00
Set of 4 ....75.00

Olympics '84

Mugs:
    Red 5.00
    White...5.00
    Blue...5.00
    Yellow..5.00
Set of 4 ....20.00

1985

E.T. Posters

E.T. and Elliot flying on bike...........................12.00
E.T. boy/girl w/spaceship touching fingers.......................8.00
E.T. w/radio device 10.00
E.T. w/raised finger 10.00

Barbie brought out her best threads for this 1994 collection.

McDonald's offered many Hot Wheels sets over the years. This one was from 1994.

Feeling Good Tub Floaters and Toiletries
Grimace in Wash Basin Tub Floater (under-3) 4.50
Fry Guy on Duck Tub Floater (under-3) 4.50
Hamburglar Toothbrush 4.00
Ronald Toothbrush 4.00
Grimace Soap Dish.. 4.00
Birdie Mirror 4.00
Captain Crook Comb 4.00

Halloween '85 Halloween Pails
McGoblin.. 8.00
McBoo 7.00
McPunkin 7.00
McPunky 7.00
McJack 7.00

Little Travelers Lego Sets
Set 1: 17-piece truck 4.00
Set 2: 27-piece ship 5.00
Set 3: 19-piece helicopter 4.00
Set 4: 18-piece airplane 4.00

Magic Show Happy Meal Magic Show Trinkets
Magic String Trick 5.00
Magic Tablet.. 5.00
Ronald Magic Picture 5.00
Grimace Magic Picture... 5.00

Tinosaurs Figurines (limited distribution)
Bones.. 8.00
Dinah.. 8.00
Jad 8.00
Fern... 8.00
Kobby.. 8.00
Spell 8.00
Tiny 8.00

Ship Shape '85 Meal Containers
Rub-A-Dub Sub... 12.00
River Boat 12.00
Splash-Dasher 12.00
Tubby-Tugger.. 12.00

Santa Claus, The Movie Books (limited distribution)
The Elves at the Top of the World................................. 6.00
Legend of Santa Claus 6.00
Sleigh Full of Surprises 6.00
Workshop of Activities.. 6.00

Sticker Club Stickers
Ronald and Grimace Puffy Stickers 4.00
Ronald/Professor/Hamburglar/Birdie 3-D Motion
    Stickers 4.00
Sheet of 12 McDonaldland Paper Stickers 4.00
Hamburglar, Ronald, Birdie, Fry Guy, Grimace Scratch and
    Sniff Stickers 4.00

Astrosniks III Figurines (regional)
Commander 8.00
Scout w/flag 7.00

Robo the Robot 7.00
Perfido 7.00
Astralia.. 8.00
Laser... 8.00
Snikapotamus 8.00
Bom w/cone 7.00
Puramido 8.00
First Ronik w/radio.. 8.00
Astrosnik Rocket.. 15.00
Racing 7.00
Copter 9.00
Galaxo 9.00

1986

Airport Tub Floaters and Airplanes
Fry Guy Friendly Flyer Tub Floater (under-3) 7.00
Grimace Shuttle Tub Floater (under-3)............................ 7.00
Ronald Seaplane 5.00
Fry Guy Flyer 5.00
Big Mac Helicopter 5.00
Birdie Blazer Plane 5.00
Grimace Ace 5.00

An American Tail Books
Tony and Fievel 5.00
Fievel and Tiger 5.00
Fievel's Friends 5.00
Fievel's Boat Trip 5.00

Old McDonald's Farm Figurines
Hen 5.00
Cow 5.00
Farmer's Wife 5.00
Farmer 5.00
Pig 5.00
Rooster 5.00
Sheep 5.00

Young Astronauts Spaceships
Grimace Shuttle (under-3).. 7.00
Fry Guy Flyer (under-3)... 7.00
Apollo Command Module 6.00
Cirrus Vtol 6.00
Argo Land Shuttle 6.00
White Space Shuttle 6.00

Boats 'N Floats Meal Containers
Grimace in Purple Ski Boat 5.00
McNugget Guys in Orange Life Boat............................... 4.00
Birdie on Yellow Raft... 5.00
Fry Guys on Green Raft 4.00

Colorforms Sets
Set 1: Beach Party... 5.00

Aladdin and company showed up to celebrate the 1996 animated Disney film.

There was yet another incarnation of The Jungle Book at McDonald's in 1989.

Set 2: Picnic Today 5.00
Set 3: Play Day 5.00
Set 4: Camp Out 5.00

McDonaldland Band Instruments (regional distribution)
Grimace Saxophone 4.50
Birdie Kazoo... 4.50
Fry Kid Trumpet 4.50
Ronald Train-Shaped Whistle 4.50
Red Harmonica 4.50
Fry Guy Boat-Shaped Whistle 4.50
Hamburglar Siren Whistle 4.50
Yellow Pan Pipes 4.50

Crayola Stencil Sets
Set 1: Hamburglar in Steam Engine 3.00
Set 2: Birdie in Car.. 3.00
Set 3: Grimace in Rocket 3.00
Set 4: Ronald on Tractor 3.00

Halloween '86
Halloween Pails:
   McBoo... 4.00
   McPunkin 4.00
   McGoblin 5.00

Happy Pail Beach Pails
Parade Pail 4.00
Treasure Hunt Pail 4.00
Picnic Pail 4.00
Vacation Pail 4.00

Lego Building Sets '86
Set A: 16-piece Race Car 4.00
Set B: 27-piece Tanker.................................. 5.00
Set C: 18-piece Helicopter 4.00
Set D: 19-piece Airplane 4.00

Play-Doh '86 2 oz. cans
Red 3.00
White... 3.00
Yellow... 3.00
Blue.. 3.00
Green.. 3.00
Orange.. 3.00
Purple... 3.00
Hot Pink 3.00

Stomper Mini 4 x 4s Mini Trucks
Orange/Yellow Jeep Renegade '78 .... 8.00
Maroon/White Jeep Renegade '78 .... 8.00
Blue/Yellow Toyota Tercel SR-5 .... 6.00
Gray/Maroon Toyota Tercel SR-5 .... 6.00

Yellow/Green Chevy Blazer 7.00
Red/Gray Chevy Blazer.................................7.00
Black/Silver Chevy S-10 ....7.00
Yellow/Purple Chevy S-10 ....7.00
Red/Yellow Chevy Van 6.00
Orange/Yellow Chevy Van 6.00
Orange/Blue AMC Eagle '74 ....7.00
Black/Gold AMC Eagle '74 ....7.00

McVote '86
Glasses:
   McD.L.T...5.00
   Quarter Pounder 5.00
   Big Mac 5.00
Set of 3 ....15.00

1987

Berenstain Bears Figurines
Mama Bear w/yellow shopping cart...............4.00
Papa Bear w/brown wheelbarrow...................4.00
Sister Bear w/red wagon 4.00
Brother Bear w/green/yellow scooter.............4.00

Kissyfur Figurines (regional distribution)
Kissyfur 6.00
Jolene 6.00
Gus 6.00
Lennie 6.00
Floyd..6.00
Toot..6.00
Beehonie 6.00

Bigfoot Trucks
Green Ford Bronco w/arches 7.00
Green Ford Bronco w/o arches 7.00
Dark Blue Ford Pickup w/arches 7.00
Dark Blue Ford Pickup w/o arches 7.00
Light Blue Ford Pickup w/arches 7.00
Light Blue Ford Pickup w/o arches 7.00
Pink MS Ford Pickup w/arches 7.00
Pink MS Ford Pickup w/o arches 7.00
Turquoise MS Ford Pickup w/arches 7.00
Turquoise MS Ford Pickup w/o arches...........7.00
Black/Silver Shuttle Ford w/arches 7.00
Black/Silver Shuttle Ford w/o arches..............7.00
Orange Shuttle Ford w/arches........................7.00
Orange Shuttle Ford w/o arches 7.00
Red Shuttle Ford w/arches 7.00
Red Shuttle Ford w/o arches...........................7.00

Flintstone Kids Figures in Dinosaur Cars (regional distribution)
Purple Dino (under-3) 7.25
Barney in Mastodon Car.................................7.00

These five pooches helped represent the 101 Dalmatians in 1997.

Fred in Alligator Car...7.00
Wilma in Dragon Car...7.00
Betty in Pterodactyl Car 7.00

Cosmic Crayola Sets
Set 1: 4 Crayons w/coloring page 4.00
Set 2: Marker w/coloring page 4.00
Set 3: 4 Colored Chalk w/chalk board.....................4.00
Set 4: Washable Marker and Coloring Page...............4.00
Set 5: Paint-By-Number paint set & Coloring Page 3.00

Design-O-Saurs Figurines (regional distribution)
Ronald on Tyrannosaurus Rex 6.00
Grimace on Pterodactyl 6.00
Fry Guy on Apatosaurus 6.00
Hamburglar on Triceratops 7.00

Disney Favorites Books
Dumbo Press-Out Book 5.00
Cinderella Paint with Water Coupons Book 5.00
Lady and the Tramp Sticker Book..........................5.00
The Sword in the Stone Activity Book 5.00

Duck Tales Spy Toys
Telescope..4.00
Wrist-Wallet Decoder 4.00
Duck Code Quacker 4.00
Whistle 4.00
Magnifying Glass 4.00

Muppet Babies Figurines
Kermit on Roller Skates (under-3) 5.50
Miss Piggy on Roller Skates (under-3) 5.50
Fozzie on Yellow Horse 5.00
Miss Piggy in Pink Car 5.00
Kermit on Red Skateboard...................................5.00
Gonzo on Green Tricycle 5.00

Real Ghostbusters School Supplies
The Real Ghostbusters Pencil Case........................6.00
6" Purple Real Ghostbusters Ruler.........................6.00
Real Ghostbusters Pencil w/slimer top 6.00
Sta-Puft Marshmallow Man Notepad and Ghostbuster
    Eraser..6.00
Sta-Puft Marshmallow Man Pencil Sharpener 6.50

Sailors Tub Floaters
Grimace Speedboat (under-3) 8.00
Fry Guy on Tube (under-3) 8.00
Fry Guys Ferry Boat...8.00
Grimace Submarine 8.00
Hamburglar Pirate Ship.......................................8.00
Ronald Airboat 8.00

Garfield Glasses
Poetry In Motion..5.00

Don't be scared, it's just the McBoo Buddies, circa 1995.

More Barbies than you can shake a stick at appeared at McDonald's, including this group from 1992.

Are We Having Fun Yet? 5.00
Home, James...5.00
Just Me and The Road 5.00
Set of 4 ....20.00

Garfield Mugs
I'm Easy To Get Along With When Things Go My
    Way 4.00
Use Your Friends Wisely.....................................4.00
I'm Not One Who Rises To The Occasion 4.00
It's Not A Pretty Life But Someone Has To Live It 4.00
Set of 4 ....16.00

Hawaii Glasses
Catamaran and Outrigger....................................8.00
Fisherman Bringing In The Nets 8.00
Surfing 8.00
Outrigger Racers 8.00
Set of 4 ....32.00

1988

Disney's Bambi Figurines
Bambi w/ Butterfly on Tail (under-3) 9.00
Thumper (under-3) 9.00
Bambi 5.00
Flower...5.00
Friend Owl 5.00
Thumper 5.00

Bedtime Toiletries
Set 1: Crest Toothpaste and Ronald Toothbrush..........4.00
Set 2: Ronald w/friends cup.................................4.00
Set 3: Ronald Wash Mitt 4.00
Set 4: Ronald Glow Star Figurine 4.00

New Archies Figures in Cars (limited distribution)
Archie in red car 5.00
Betty in blue car...5.00
Jughead in yellow car...5.00
Moose in pink car 5.00
Reggie in green car 5.00
Veronica in purple car..5.00

Fraggle Rock Vehicles
Gobo Holding Large Carrot (under-3)......................6.00
Red Holding Large Radish (under-3)........................6.00
Boober and Wembley in Pickle Car.........................5.00
Gobo in Carrot Car 5.00
Red in Radish Car 5.00
Mokey in Eggplant Car 5.00

Here are four of the many Dalmatians that McDonald's issued during its promotion at the close of 1987.

Mac Tonight Mac in Vehicles (regional distribution)
Mac on purple Skateboard (under-3) 5.50
Mac in green airplane 5.00
Mac in green jeep 5.00
Mac in yellow surf ski 5.00
Mac in red sports car 5.00
Mac on red motor bike 5.00
Mac in black motor scooter 5.00

McNugget Buddies Figurines
Volley 4.00
Sparky 4.00
Snorkel 4.00
Sarge 4.00
Rocker 4.00
First Class 4.00
Drummer 4.00
Cowpoke 4.00
Corny 4.00
Boomerang 4.00
Daisy 4.00
Slugger 4.00

Mickey's Birthdayland Cars
Donald on Locomotive 7.00
Minnie in Convertible 7.00
Goofy in Sports Car 7.00
Pluto in Rambler 7.00
Mickey in Roadster 7.00

Mix-Em Up Monsters Figurines (regional distribution)
Blibble 6.00
Gropple 6.00
Crokkle 6.00
Thugger 6.00

Food Changeables '88
Plastic Food Items and Robots that together form space creatures:
Cheeseburger 4.00
Fry Bot 4.00
Fry Force 4.00
Gallactica Burger 4.00
Krypto Cup 4.00
Macro Mac 4.00
Robo-Cakes 4.00
Turbo Cone 4.00

Ducktales Figurines (regional distribution)
Huey on Skates (under-3) 8.00
Huey, Louie and Dewey 7.00
Launchpad 7.00

Scrooge McDuck 7.00
Webby 7.00

Oliver and Company Finger Puppets
Oliver 5.00
Francis 5.00
Dodger 5.00
Georgette 5.00

Olympic Sports '88 Buttons
Hamburglar 4.50
Ronald 4.50
Birdie 4.50
Fry Girl 4.50
Grimace 4.50
McComs 4.50

On The Go '88 Lunch Containers
Grimace and Ronald McDonald Lunch Box w/bulletin
    board 4.00
Plastic Turquoise and Light Blue Grimace Lunch Bag 3.00
Plastic Yellow Ronald Lunch Bag 3.00
Grimace Lunch Box w/bulletin board 4.00

Storybook Muppet Babies Books
Just Kermit and Me 5.00
The Legend of the Gimme Gulch 5.00
Baby Piggy and the Living Doll 5.00

Super Summer Beach Premiums
White Beach Ball depicting Ronald 5.00
Inflatable Boat depicting Grimace 5.00
Blue Summer Fish Sand Mold 5.00
Watering Can 5.00
Sand Pail w/Shovel 5.00
Castle Mold w/Shovel 5.00

Zoo-Face Masks
Monkey 3-D Orange Face Mask (under-3) 7.00
Tiger 3-D Yellow Face Mask (under-3) 7.00
Set 1: Toucan w/Paas Make-Up Kit 3.00
Set 2: Monkey w/Paas Make-Up Kit 4.00
Set 3: Tiger w/Paas Make-Up Kit 3.00
Set 4: Alligator w/Paas Make-Up Kit 3.00

Miscellaneous
Ronald figure in 2-3/4" red rubber auto 4.00
Band Director doll, 3-1/2" rubber w/backwards hat 4.00
Hamburglar, 2-1/2" rubber 4.00

The Barbie army was out in force in 1993.

Ronald, 3" w/elbow on star, plastic 5.00
Fry Guys plastic, with attachable head dresses 2-1/2" figures,
    yellow, red or blue hair 6.00
3" figures, blue, green or purple hair.............................. 8.00
Elf character, brown plastic, "M" on chest, hole in hat, 2" 6.00

1989

Beach Toy '89 Beach Premiums
Castle-shaped sand pail 3.00
Birdie inflatable Seaside Submarine 4.00
Fry Kid inflatable Super Sailer 4.00
Ronald's inflatable Fun Flyer 4.00
Squirt Gun Rake-Propeller... 3.00
Grimace Beach Ball 3.00
Birdie w/Sand Propeller Shovel 3.00
Ronald and Grimace Sand Pail.. 3.00

Camp McDonaldland Camping Items
Collapsible Ronald Cup 4.00
Fry Guys Utensils 4.00
Birdie Mess Kit 4.00
Grimace Canteen 4.00

Chip 'N Dale Rescue Rangers Figurines in Vehicles
Chip w/Rockin' Racer (under-3)...................................... 5.50
Gadget w/Rockin' Rider (under-3) 5.50
Chip w/Whirly-Copter 5.00
Dale w/Roto-Roadster.. 5.00
Gadget w/Rescue Racer 5.00
Monterey Jack w/propel-a-phone...................................... 5.00

Fun With Food Figurines (limited distribution)
McNugget Guys 5.00
French Fry Guy 5.00
Hamburger Guy 5.00
Soft Drink Guy.. 5.00

Tom and Jerry Band Figures w/ Musical Instruments (regional distribution)
Droopy Dog (under-3).. 18.00
Tom playing keyboards 15.00
Jerry playing drums... 15.00
Spike playing bass 15.00
Droopy singing on mike 15.00

Funny Fry Friends Figurines
Li'l Chief 5.00

These Polly Pocket Pals were issued in 1995.

Ty's Teenie Beanies proved to be the biggest hit with Happy Meal customers. This group, from the second series in '97, included (from left): Bones, Zip, Inch and Mel.

Lil' Darling.. 5.00
Hoops 4.00
Sweet Cuddles 4.00
ZZZs 4.00
Tracker... 4.00
Tootall 4.00
Matey... 4.00
Gadzooks 4.00
Rollin' Rocker 4.00

Garfield Figures in Vehicles
Garfield on Roller Skates (under-3)................................. 6.00
Garfield w/Pooky on Skateboard (under-3) 6.00
Garfield w/four-wheeler 5.00
Garfield w/skateboard... 5.00
Garfield w/motorcycle (Odie in sidecar)............................. 6.00
Garfield w/scooter.. 5.00

Halloween '89 Halloween Pails
McBoo 5.00
McGhost 6.00
McWitch 5.00

Jungle Book Figurines
Mowgli in Green Pot (under-3)....................................... 5.00
Junior the Elephant (under-3)....................................... 5.00
Baloo 4.00
King Louie.. 4.00
Kaa 4.00
Shere Khan 4.00

Lego Motion '89
Set 1A: 19-piece Gyro Bird Helicopter............................... 6.00
Set 1B: 10-piece Turbo Force Car.................................... 6.00
Set 2A: 16-piece Swamp Stinger Air Boat............................. 6.00
Set 2B: 14-piece Lightning Striker Plane............................ 6.00
Set 3A: 12-piece Land Laser Car 6.00
Set 3B: 15-piece Sea Eagle Seaplane 6.00
Set 4A: 17-piece Wind Whirler Helicopter 6.00
Set 4B: 17-piece Sea Skimmer Boat 6.00

Little Gardener Gardening Premiums
Birdie Spade w/marigold seeds 4.00
Fry Guys Planter.. 4.00
Grimace Rake w/radish seeds 4.00
Ronald Watering Can 4.00

Raggedy Ann and Andy Figurines (regional distribution)
Camel (under-3) 7.25
Raggedy Ann on Swing 7.00

The Halloween McNugget Buddies probably didn't scare anybody in 1992.

Raggedy Andy on Slide	7.00
Grouchy Bear on Merry-Go-Round	7.00
Camel on Teeter Totter	7.00

Little Mermaid Figurines (movie set)
Ariel Bobbing Water Toy	7.00
Ursula Suction Cup Toy	7.00
Flounder Squirting Fish Toy	7.00
Prince Eric/Sebastian Boat Toy	7.00

Muppet Kids '89 Figures on Bicycles
Kermit on Red Bike	12.00
Ms. Piggy on Pink Bike	12.00
Gonzo on Yellow Bike	12.00
Fozzie on Green Bike	12.00

Peanuts Figures pushing carts
Snoopy carrying Potato Sack (under-3)	5.50
Charlie Brown w/Egg Basket (under-3)	5.50
Snoopy/Woodstock w/Hay Cart	5.00
Charlie Brown Pushing Tiller	5.00
Lucy pushing Apple Cart	5.00
Linus/Cat pushing Milk Cart	5.00

Disneyland Glasses
Mickey at Tomorrowland	8.00
Minnie at Fantasyland	8.00
Donald at Critter Country	8.00
Goofy at Adventureland	8.00
Set of 4	35.00

Mac Tonight Glasses
12 oz. Glass	5.00
16 oz. Glass	5.00
32 oz. Cooler	6.00

Mac Tonight Mugs
Set of 4	30.00

1990

Alvin and The Chipmunks Figurines
Alvin Leaning on Jukebox (under-3)	4.00
Alvin w/guitar	4.00
Brittney by Jukebox	4.00
Simon w/movie camera	4.00
Theodore as Disc Jockey	4.00

Berenstain Bear Books '90 Books
Eager Beavers Book	4.00
Berenstain Bears Life With Papa Book	4.00
Berenstain Bears Substitute Teacher Book	4.00
Berenstain Bears Attic Treasure Book	4.00
Eager Beavers Activity Book	4.00
Berenstain Bears Life With Papa Activity Book	4.00
Berenstain Bears Substitute Teacher Activity Book	4.00
Berenstain Bears Attic Treasure Activity Book	4.00

Dink The Dinosaur Figurines (regional distribution)
Amber	5.00
Crusty	5.00
Dink	5.00
Flapper	5.00
Scat	5.00
Shyler	5.00

Good Morning Toiletries
Ronald w/Bunny Cup	4.00
Ronald Flying Clock	4.00
5 Section McDonaldland Characters Comb	4.00
Ronald Toothbrush	4.00

Turbo Macs Cars (limited distribution)
Ronald Car (under-3)	5.00
Birdie Car	5.00
Hamburglar Car	5.00
Ronald Car	5.00
Big Mac Car	5.00

Piggsburg Pigs Figurines (regional distribution)
Portly and Pighead	4.00
Huff and Puff	4.00
Rembrandt	4.00
Piggy and Quacker	4.00

Halloween '90 Halloween Pails
Pumpkin	3.00
Witch	3.00
Ghost	3.00

From the Heart Valentines
You Warm My Heart Scratch & Sniff Valentine	2.50
You're The Frosting on My Cake Scratch & Sniff Valentine	2.50

Nature's Helper Garden Tools
Garden Rake w/ worm picture (under-3)	3.25
Blue/Yellow Water Can	3.00
Tree Shaped Bird Feeder	3.00
Double Digger w/Cucumber Seeds	3.00
Terrarium and Coleus Seeds	3.00
Garden Rake w/Marigold Seeds	3.00

Rescuers Down Under Mini-movie camera viewers
Bernard w/piece of cheese (under-3)	5.00
Wilbur	4.00
Cody	4.00
Jake	4.00
Bernard and Bianca	4.00

Super Mario 3 Nintendo Figurines
Super Mario in Blue Jeans/Red Shirt (under-3)	5.00

Disney Tailspin characters barnstormed McDonald's in 1990.

Mario on Springing Base.. 4.00
Luigi 4.00
Little Goomba... 4.00
Koopa Paratroopa... 4.00

Tale Spin Airplanes
Baloo's Rubber Seaplane (under-3) 5.00
Wildcat's Rubber Flying Machine (under-3) 5.00
Baloo in Seaplane... 4.00
Kit in Racing Plane.. 4.00
Molly in Biplane... 4.00
Wildcat in Flying Machine 4.00

Tiny Toons Adventures Flip-Over Cars
Gogo Dodo in White Bath Tub (under-3) 5.50
Plucky Duck in Red Boat (under-3)................................. 5.50
Babs Bunny/Dizzy Flipcar... 5.00
Buster Bunny/Elmyra Flipcar 5.00
Montana Max/Gogo Dodo Flipcar 5.00
Hampton Pig/Plucky Duck Flipcar 5.00

Barbie/Hot Wheels I (regional distribution)
Tea Party Barbie 5.00
Moonlight Ball Barbie 5.00
Movie Star Barbie 5.00
In Concert Barbie 5.00
Corvette 5.00
Ferrari 5.00
Hot Bird 5.00
Camaro Z-28 .... 5.00

Beach Toy II
Fry Kid Super Sailor... 5.00
Grimace Sand Pail 5.00
Grimace Bouncin' Beach Ball 5.00
Birdie with Shovel 5.00
Ronald Fun Flyer 5.00
Fry Kids Sand Castle Pail 5.00
Birdie Seaside Submarine 5.00
Ronald Squirt Gun Rake 5.00

Berenstain Bears Books
Life with Papa — Storybook.. 4.00
Life with Papa — Activity Book 4.00
Attic Treasure — Storybook... 4.00
Attic Treasure — Activity Book 4.00
Substitute Teacher — Storybook...................................... 4.00
Substitute Teacher — Activity Book................................. 4.00
Eager Beavers — Storybook 4.00
Eager Beavers — Activity Book....................................... 4.00

Among the Teenie Beanie money makers for McDonald's were (from left) Bongo, Waddle and Doby.

Even Ronald makes an appearance in a Happy Meal. This one was in 1983.

Camp McDonaldland
Fry Kid Utensils 5.00
Ronald Collapsible Cup 5.00
Fry Kid Utensils 5.00
Birdie Mess Kit...5.00
Grimace Canteen 5.00
Ronald Collapsible Cup 5.00

Dink the Little Dinosaur (regional distribution)
Flapper the Pterodactyl 4.00
Dink the Dinosaur 4.00
Scat the Alligator 4.00
Shyler the Dinosaur 4.00
Amber the Dinosaur..4.00
Crusty the Turtle 4.00

From the Heart (regional distribution)
Frosting Cake Scratch & Sniff 4.00
Hot Chocolate Scratch & Sniff 4.00

Fry Benders (regional distribution)
Roadie Grand Slam...3.00
Froggy 3.00
Free Style 3.00
Tunes..3.00

Funny Fry Friends II
Sweet Cuddles 3.00
Too Tall 3.00
ZZZs 3.00
Tracker..3.00
Gadzooks 3.00
Matey..3.00
Rollin' Rocker 3.00
Hoops 3.00
Li'l Cheif..3.00
Little Darling..3.00

Halloween '90 Pumpkin Pail
Ghost Pail...5.00
Witch Pail..5.00

Hats (regional distribution)
Birdie Derby Hat 4.00
Fry Guy Safari Hat..4.00
Grimace Construction Hat 4.00
Ronald Fireman Hat 4.00

I Like Bikes (limited regional distribution)
Horn...4.00
Mirror 4.00
Bike Basket...4.00
Spinner..4.00

Jungle Book
Shere Khan..5.00

Charlie Brown and company brought smiles to Happy Meals in 1989.

Kaa King Louie 5.00
Baloo 5.00
Mowgli the Boy 5.00
Junior the Elephant 5.00

McDonaldland Carnival (regional distribution)
Ronald 6.00
Hamburglar 6.00
Grimace 6.00
Birdie 6.00
Grimace 6.00

McDonaldland Dough (regional distribution)
Red Dough/Red Ronald Star Mold 4.00
Yellow Dough/Red Ronald Square Mold 4.00
Green Dough/Green Fry Girl Octagon Mold 4.00
Blue Dough/Green Fry Guy Hexagon Mold 4.00
Purple Dough/Purple Grimace Square Mold 4.00
Orange Dough/Purple Grimace Triangle Mold 4.00
Pink Dough/Yellow Birdie Heart Mold 4.00
White Dough/Yellow Birdie Circle Mold 4.00

McDrive Thru Crew (test market, regional distribution)
Fries in Potato Speedster 6.00
Hamburglar in Ketchup Racer 6.00
McNugget in Egg Roadster 6.00
Shake in Milk Carton 6.00

Peanuts
Linus' Milk Mover 4.00
Lucy's Apple Cart 4.00
Charlie's Seed Bag 4.00
Snoopy's Hay Hauler 4.00
Snoopy's Potato Sack 4.00
Charlie's Egg Basket 4.00

Rescuers Down Under
Wilbur Viewer 4.00
Cody Viewer 4.00
Jake Viewer 4.00
Bernard & Bianca Viewer 4.00
Bernard 4.00

Sports Ball (regional distribution)
Baseball 5.00
Basketball 5.00
Football 5.00
Soccer Ball 5.00

Super Mario 3 Nintendo
Koopa 3.00
Goomba 3.00
Luigi 3.00
Mario 3.00
Super Mario 3.00

Tale Spin
Wildcat's Flying Machine 4.00
Molly's Biplane 4.00
Kit's Racing Plane 4.00
Baloo's Seaplane 4.00
Wildcat's Flying Machine 4.00
Baloo's Seaplane 4.00

Tom & Jerry Band
Spike with Bass 7.00
Jerry with Drums 7.00
Droopy with Microphone 7.00
Tom with Keyboard 7.00
Droopy 7.00

Turbo Macs II (limited regional distribution)
Ronald 4.00
Hamburglar 4.00
Grimace 4.00
Birdie 4.00
Ronald 4.00

1991

101 Dalmatians Figures
Pongo 4.00
Lucky 4.00
Colonel & Sgt. Tibbs 4.00
Cruella DeVille 4.00

Barbie Figurines and Hot Wheels Cars
Barbie
Costume Ball Barbie Figurine (under-3) 5.00
Wedding Day Midge (under-3) 5.00
#1: All-American Barbie 4.00
#2: Costume Ball Barbie 4.00
#3: Lights and Lace Barbie 4.00
#4: Happy Birthday Barbie 4.00
#5: Hawaiian Fun Barbie 4.00
#6: Wedding Day Midge 4.00
#7: Lights and Lace Barbie 4.00
#8: My First Barbie 4.00

Hot Wheels
#1: Yellow '55 Chevy 4.00
#2: Green '63 Corvette 4.00
#3: Aqua '57 T-Bird 4.00
#4: Purple Camaro Z-28 .... 4.00
#5: White '55 Chevy 4.00
#6: Black '63 Corvette 4.00

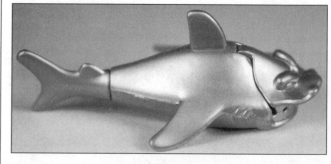

If you didn't land any of the Little Mermaid toys during the movies re-release in 1998, here's what the gold shark looked like.

#7: Red '57 T-Bird 4.00
#8: Orange Camaro Z-28 .... 4.00

Discover The Rain Forest Activity Books
Set 1: Sticker Safari 4.00
Other sets in series 4.00

McDino Changeables Toys
Set 1: 4.00
Set 2: Paint it Wild w/paint brush/pallet................ 4.00
Set 3: Ronald In The Jewel of the Amazon Kingdom 4.00
Set 4: Wonders In The Wild 4.00

Gravedale High Figurines
Cleofatra (under-3) 4.50
Cleofatra 4.00
Vinnie Stoker 4.00
Sid The Invisible Kid 4.00
Frankentyke 4.00

Halloween '91 McBoo Bags and Buckets
Blue Witch Halloween Bag 3.00
White Ghost w/bow tie halloween bag 3.00
Green Monster Halloween Bag 3.00
McBoo Pail 3.00
McGoblin Pail 3.00
Ghost Pail 3.00
Witch Pail 3.00
McPumpkin Pail 3.00

Hook Figurines
Peter Pan 3.00
Hook 3.00
Rufio 3.00
Mermaid 3.00

McDino Changeables Dinosaur Figurines
Small Fry-Ceratops (under-3) 4.50
Bronto Cheeseburger (under-3) 4.50
Week 1: Happy Meal-O-Don 4.00
Week 1: Quarter Pounder Cheese-O-Saur 4.00
Week 2: McNuggets-O-Saurus 4.00
Week 2: Hot Cakes-O-Dactyl 4.00
Week 3: Big Mac-O-Saurus Rex 4.00
Week 3: Fry-Ceratops 4.00
Week 4: Tri-Shake-Atops 4.00
Week 4: McDino Cone 4.00

Mystery of The Lost Arches
Mystery of the Lost Arches 4.00

This Happy Meal from 1989 really did look good enough to eat.

Phone/Periscope 4.00
Flashlight/Telescope (red-blue) 4.00
Variation: Flashlight/Telescope (red-yellow) 4.00
Micro-Cassette/Magnifier 4.00
Magic Lens Camera (silver 'Search Team' Decal) 4.00
Magic Lens Camera (white 'Search Team' Decal) 4.00

Super Looney Tunes Figurines
Batduck in his Batmobile (under-3) 5.00
SuperBugs 4.00
Taz Flash 4.00
Wonder Pig 4.00
Batduck 4.00

Alvin and the Chipmunks (regional distribution)
Alvin 4.00
Brittney 4.00
Simon 4.00
Theodore 4.00
Alvin 4.00

Breakfast (regional distribution)
Squeeze Bottle 4.00

McDonald's PVC figures (limited regional distribution)
Birdie 4.00
Grimace 4.00
Hamburglar 4.00
Ronald 4.00

Crazy Vehicles (limited regional distribution)
Birdie 3.00
Grimace 3.00
Hamburglar 3.00
Ronald 3.00

Friendly Skies
Ronald — White Plane 10.00
Grimace — White Plane 10.00
Ronald — Grey Plane 5.00
Grimace — Grey Plane 5.00
Ronald with Hanger 5.00

Good Morning
Toothbrush 3.00
Clock 3.00
Cup 3.00
Comb 3.00
Ronald Cup 3.00

McCharacters on Bikes (limited regional distribution)
Birdie 4.00
Grimace 4.00
Hamburglar 4.00
Ronald 4.00

McDonaldland Circus Parade (regional distribution)
Ronald 4.00
Birdie 4.00
Fry Guy 4.00
Grimace 4.00

Mighty Mini (regional distribution)
Pocket Pickup 4.00
Dune Buster 4.00
Li'l Classic T-Bird 4.00
Cargo Climber Van 4.00
Pocket Pickup 4.00

Seemingly always in the Halloween mode, McDonald's brought out this set of scary audio tapes in 1995.

Muppet Babies III (regional distribution)
Fozzie 4.00
Gonzo 4.00
Kermit 4.00
Miss Piggy.. 4.00

Nature's Helpers
Double Digger... 4.00
Bird Feeder 5.00
Water Can 6.00
Terrarium.. 6.00
Garden Rake... 3.00

Piggsburg Pigs (regional distribution)
Portly Pig... 4.00
Piggy & Quakers 4.00
Rembrant 4.00
Huff/Puff 4.00

Pizza Happy Sack (regional distribution)
Hamburglar Figure 4.00

Sports Ball (regional distribution)
Baseball 3.00
Basketball 3.00
Football 3.00
Soccer Ball... 3.00

Tiny Toon Adventures I
Hampton Pig 4.00
Montana Max 4.00
Buster Bunny.. 4.00
Babs Bunny... 4.00
(U-3) Plucky Duck 4.00
Gogo Dodo 4.00

USA/Generic (regional distribution)
Grimace Stencil... 3.00
Ronald Stencil... 3.00

1992

Barbie/Hot Wheels Mini-Streex III

Barbie
Birthday Surprise Barbie 4.50
My First Ballerina Barbie 4.50
Rappin' Rockin' Barbie... 4.50
Rollerblade Barbie.. 4.50
Rose Bride Barbie... 4.50
Snap 'n Play Barbie... 4.50

Sparkle Eyes Barbie 4.50
Sun Sensation Barbie 4.50
Sparkle Eyes Barbie 4.50

Hot Wheels
Black Arrow Hot Wheels 4.50
Blade Burner Hot Wheels 4.50
Flame-Out Hot Wheels 4.50
Hot Shock Hot Wheels 4.50
Night Shadow Hot Wheels 4.50
Quick-Flash Hot Wheels 4.50
Racer Tracer Hot Wheels 4.50
Turbo Flyer Hot Wheels 4.50
Orange Arrow Hot Wheels..4.50

Batman The Movie
Batsub 5.00
Batmobile (front detaches as a break-away jet car) 5.00
Catwoman Cat Coupe 5.00
Penguin Roto-Roadster 5.00

Behind the Scenes
Animation Wheel 3.00
Balance Builders...3.00
Rub/Draw Templates Rainbow Viewer 3.00

Cabbage Patch Kids/Tonka
All Dressed Up Cabbage Patch Kid............................3.00
Ali Marie Cabbage Patch Kid....................................3.00
Fun on Ice Cabbage Patch Kid..................................3.00
Holiday Dreamer Cabbage Patch Kid..........................3.00
Holiday Pageant Cabbage Patch Kid 3.00
Anne Louise Cabbage Patch Kid................................3.00
Loader Tonka vehicle...3.00
Cement Mixer Tonka vehicle 3.00
Dump Truck Tonka vehicle 3.00
Fire Truck Tonka vehicle 3.00
Backhoe Tonka vehicle...3.00
Dumper Truck Tonka vehicle 3.00

Crayon Squeeze Bottle (regional distribution)
Blue Squeeze Bottle 3.50
Green Squeeze Bottle 3.50
Red Squeeze Bottle...3.50
Yellow Squeeze Bottle 3.50

Fitness Fun
Baseball..3.00
Basketball 3.00
Throwing Disc 3.00
Football...3.00
Jump Rope 3.00
Soccer Ball 3.00

A set of Muppet characters from the Muppet Treasure Island, issued in 1994.

Stop Watch 3.00
Squeeze Bottle... 3.00

Halloween '92

Ghost 3.00
Pumpkin 3.00
Witch 3.00

Natures Watch

Bird Feeder 4.00
Double Shovel-Rake....................................... 3.00
Greenhouse 4.00
Sprinkler.. 4.00

Potato Head Kids II (regional distribution)

Dimples 3.00
Spike 3.00
Potato Dumpling 3.00
Slugger.. 3.00
Slick 3.00
Tulip 3.00
Potato Puff 3.00
Spud.. 3.00

Real Ghostbusters II (regional distribution)

Ecto Siren 3.50
Egon Spinner 3.50
Water Bottle 3.50
Slimer Horn 3.50
Squirting Slimer Squeezer 3.50

Tiny Toons Adventures II

Babs Bunny.. 4.00
Buster Bunny 4.00
Dizzy Devil 4.00
Elmyra 4.00
Gogo Dodo.. 4.00
Montana Max 4.00
Plucky Duck 4.00
Sweetie 4.00
Sweetie 4.00

Water Games (regional distribution)

Ronald Catching French Fries 3.00
Grimace Juggling Shakes 3.00
Hamburglar Stacking Burgers.......................... 3.00
Birdie Sorting Eggs 3.00
Grimace Squirting Camera 3.00

Wild Friends (regional distribution)

Crocodile.. 3.00
Gorilla.. 3.00
Elephant... 3.00

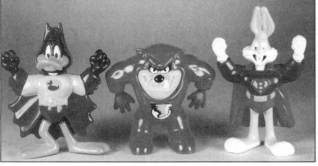

This cool 1992 set combined superheroes and Warner Bros. characters.

These happy little Potato Head Kids showed up in 1992.

Giant Panda...3.00
Giant Panda...3.00

Yo, Yogi! (regional distribution)

Yogi Bear..4.00
Cindy Bear...4.00
Huckleberry Hound..4.00
Boo Boo Bear 4.00

Young Astronauts II

Space Shuttle 3.00
Satellite Dish...3.00
Lunar Rover...3.00
Command Module 3.00
Ronald in Lunar Rover...................................3.00

1993

Barbie/Hot Wheels IV

Barbie

Romantic Bride Barbie....................................4.00
Paint and Dazzle Barbie 4.00
Hollywood Hair Barbie 4.00
Twinkle Lights Barbie.....................................4.00
Birthday Party Barbie.....................................4.00
Western Stompin' Barbie 4.00
My First Ballerina Barbie................................4.00
Secret Hearts Barbie 4.00
Rose Bride Barbie..4.00

Hot Wheels

McDonald's Funny Car Hot Wheels...........................4.00
Quaker State Racer Hot Wheels 4.00
McDonald's T-Bird Hot Wheels.........................4.00
Hot Wheels Funny Car Hot Wheels..................4.00
McDonald's Dragster Hot Wheels.....................4.00
Hot Wheels Camaro Hot Wheels......................4.00
DuraCell Racer Hot Wheels.............................4.00
Hot Wheels Dragster Hot Wheels....................4.00
Wrench and Hammer Hot Wheels....................4.00

Batman, the Animated Series (PVC figures and figure/vehicle combinations)

Batman figure w/detatchable cape 5.00
Catwoman figure w/lioness..............................5.00
Robin on motorcycle.......................................5.00
Poison Ivy in snapper vehicle 5.00
Batgirl figure 5.00
Two Face in good/evil twister car 5.00
Riddler figure 5.00
Joker in car w/battering ram head 5.00

Power Rangers came to the rescue as an over-the-counter set in 1995.

Batman (under-3 toy, same as regular figure, except cape
  was permanently attached) 5.00

Dino-Motion Dinosaurs
Baby 3.50
Grandma Ethyl 3.50
Earl.. 3.50
Charlene 3.50
Fran... 3.50
Robbie.. 3.50
Baby in Eggshell Squirter............................. 3.50

Field Trip
Explorer Bag 3.00
Kaleidoscope 3.00
Nature Viewer 3.00
Leaf Printer 3.00

Food Fundamentals
Otis the Sandwich 3.00
Milly the Milk Carton................................... 3.00
Slugger the Steak 3.00
Ruby the Apple 3.00
Duncan the Corn 3.00

Halloween '93 McNugget Buddies
Pumpkin McNugget..................................... 4.00
Monster McNugget...................................... 4.00
Mummie McNugget 4.00
McNuggula McNugget 4.00
McBoo McNugget 4.00
Witchie McNugget 4.00
McBoo (under-3 toy) 4.00

Linkables (limited regional distribution)
Birdie on Pink Tricycle 3.00
Grimace in Yellow Wagon 3.00
Hamburglar in Green Airplane 3.00
Ronald in Red Soap-Box Racer....................... 3.00

Looney Tunes Quack-Up Car Chase
Taz Tornado Tracker 4.00
Daffy Splittin' Sportster 4.00
Bugs Super Stretch Limo, orange or red 4.00
Porky Ghost Catcher................................... 4.00
Bugs Swingin' Sedan, orange or red 4.00

M-Squad
Spytracker 3.00
Spynoculars 3.00

Spycoder 3.00
Spystamper 3.00
Spytracker Watch 3.00

Nickelodeon Game Gadgets
Blimp Game...4.00
Gotcha Gusher 4.00
Loud-Mouth Mike 4.00
Applause Paws 4.00
Blimp Squirter 4.00

Out for Fun
Ronald Balloon Ball 3.00
Ronald Bubble Shoe Wand 3.00
Sunglasses 3.00
McDonaldland Pail......................................3.00

Disney's Snow White and the Seven Dwarfs
Snow White 4.00
Happy/Grumpy 4.00
Doc/Dopey/Sneezy 4.00
Prince on a Horse w/base or w/o base 4.00
Sleepy/Double Trouble Queen/Witch 4.00
Bashful..4.00
Dopey/Sneezy 4.00

Totally Toy Holiday
Magic Nursery Girl......................................3.00
Magic Nursery Boy 3.00
Attack Pack...3.00
Polly Pocket 3.00
Sally Secrets, white or black..........................3.00
Key Force Truck 3.00
Tattoo Machine 3.00
Barbie Holiday Snow Dome............................3.00
Mighty Max 3.00
Lil' Miss Candy-Stripe..................................3.00
Key Force Car 3.00
Magic Nursery Girl......................................3.00
Magic Nursery Boy 3.00
Key Force Car 3.00

1994

Animaniacs
Goodskate Goodfeathers 3.00
Upside-Down Wakko 3.00
Slappy and Skippy's Chopper 3.00
Dot's Ice Cream Machine 3.00
Pinky and the Brain Mobile............................3.00
Yakko Ridin' Ralph 3.00
Mindy and Buttons Wild Ride 3.00
Bicycle Built for Trio 3.00
Bicycle Built for Trio 3.00

Planes, boats and trucks were part of this "Attack Pack" set in 1995.

Power Rangers were all the rage in '95.

Barbie/Hot Wheels V
Barbie
Bicycling Barbie...4.00
Jewel and Glitter Shani.......................................4.00
Camp Barbie..4.00
Camp Teresa...4.00
Locket Surprise Ken, black or white.....................4.00
Locket Surprise Barbie, black or white..................4.00
Jewel and Glitter Bride.......................................4.00
Bridesmaid Skipper..4.00
Barbie Ball..4.00

Hot Wheels
Turbine 4-2 Hot Wheels......................................4.00
2-Cool Hot Wheels...4.00
Flame Rider Hot Wheels.....................................4.00
Gas Hog Hot Wheels..4.00
Bold Eagle Hot Wheels.......................................4.00
Black Cat Hot Wheels...4.00
X21J Cruiser Hot Wheels....................................4.00
Street Shocker Hot Wheels.................................4.00
Fast-Forward Hot Wheels....................................4.00

Bobby's World
Wagon/Blue Racer..3.00
Innertube/Orange Submarine...............................3.00
Tricycle/Red Spaceship.......................................3.00
Roller Skates/Green Roller Coaster.......................3.00
Bobby in Innertube...3.00

Cabbage Patch Kids/Tonka
Mimi Kristina/Angel Cabbage Patch Kid.................3.00
Kimberly Katherine/Santa's Little Helper Cabbage Patch
    Kid..3.00
Abigail Lynn/Toy Soldier Cabbage Patch Kid...........3.00
Michelle Elyse/Snow Fairy Cabbage Patch Kid.........3.00
Sarajane Cabbage Patch Kid................................3.00
Tonka Loader Tonka vehicle.................................3.00
Tonka Crane Tonka vehicle..................................3.00
Tonka Grader Tonka vehicle.................................3.00
Tonka Bulldozer Tonka vehicle.............................3.00
Plastic Dump truck Tonka vehicle.........................3.00

Earth Days
Tool Carrier/Shovel...3.00
Bird Feeder...3.00
Globe Terrarium...3.00
Earth Binoculars..3.00
Tool Carrier/Shovel...3.00

Flintstones (character in car, plus snap-together building)
Fred at Bedrock Bowl-A-Rama..............................3.50
Betty and Bamm Bamm at Roc-Donald's...............3.50
Pebbles and Dino at Toy-S-Aurus.........................3.50
Wilma at the Flinstone's House............................3.50
Barney at the Fossil Fill-Up..................................3.50
Rocking Dino...3.50

Halloween '94
Orange Pumpkin...4.00
White Ghost..4.00
Purple Witch...4.00

Magic School Bus
Collector Card Kit...3.00
Space Tracer...3.00
Undersea Adventure Game..................................3.00
Geo Fossil Finder...3.00
Undersea Adventure Game..................................3.00

Makin' Movies
Movie Camera..3.00
Sound Effects Machine..3.00
Clapboard with Chalk..3.00
Director's Megaphone..3.00
Sound Effects Machine..3.00

Mickey and Friends Epcot Center
Donald in Mexico..5.00
Daisy in Germany...5.00
Mickey in USA...5.00
Minnie in Japan...5.00
Chip in China..5.00
Pluto in France..5.00
Dale in Morocco...5.00
Goofy in Norway..5.00
Mickey in USA (under-3).....................................5.00

Ronald McDonald Celebrates Happy 15th Birthday Train
(Each vehicle was one car in a 15-car train set that hooked together.)
Ronald in Box..4.00
Barbie (recalled)..4.00
Hot Wheels...4.00
E.T...4.00
Sonic..4.00
Berenstain Bears...4.00
Tonka...4.00
Cabbage Patch Kids...4.00
101 Dalmatians..4.00
Little Mermaid...4.00
Muppet Babies-Kermit w/white or blue tie.............4.00

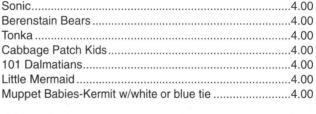

There were again bugs in the meals at McDonald's in 1996. These came as finger puppets.

Winnie the Pooh clip-ons showed up in 1999.

Snoopy	4.00
Tiny Toons	4.00
Looney Tunes	4.00
Ronald McDonald	4.00
Entire train (All 15 cars)	100.00

Sonic the Hedgehog

Miles "Tales" Prower	3.00
Dr. Ivo Robotnic	3.00
Sonic	3.00
Knucles	3.00
Sonic Soft Yellow Ball	3.00

USA/Generic Promotion

Hockey Game	4.00
Mystery of the Lost Treasure Comic Book	4.00
Mystery of the Missing Sea Horses Comic Book	4.00
License Plate	4.00
Paint Kit	4.00

Ronald and Grimace Stickers

Birdie and Hamburglar Stickers	3.00
Tattoo Fun	3.00
Time Out for Fun—Activity Book	3.00
Friends Like You—Greeting Card	3.00
You're Totally Cool—Greeting Card	3.00

1995

Runaway Robots (robot figure/vehicles)

(Also distributed by Subway, w/different markings, as "Cy* Treds.")

Beck	3.00
Coil	3.00
Bait	3.00
Skull	3.00
Jab	3.00
Flame	3.00

Amazing Wildlife (mini-plush animals)

Asiatic Lion	3.00
Chimpanzee	3.00
Koala Bear	3.00
African Elephant	3.00
Dromedary Camel	3.00
Galapagos Tortoise	3.00
Siberian Tiger	3.00
Polar Bear	3.00

Animaniacs II

Pinky and the Brain	3.50
Goodfeathers	3.50
Dot and Ralph	3.50
Wakko & Yakko	3.50
Slappy & Skippy	3.50
Mindy & Buttons	3.50
Wakko, Yakko and Dot	3.50
Hip Hippos	3.50
Goodskate Goodfeathers	3.50
Mindy & Buttons Wild Ride	3.50
Yakko Ridin' Ralph	3.50
Bicycle Built for Trio	3.50

Attack Pack/Polly Pockets

Attack Pack Truck	3.50
Attack Pack Battle Bird	3.50
Attack Pack Lunar Invader	3.50
Attack Pack Sea Creature	3.50
Attack Pack Truck	3.50
Polly Pocket Ring	3.50
Polly Pocket Locket	3.50
Polly Pocket Watch	3.50
Polly Pocket Bracelet	3.50
Polly Pocket Watch	3.50

Barbie/Hot Wheels VI

Barbie

Hot Skatin' Barbie	4.00
Dance Moves Barbie	4.00
Butterfly Princess Teresa	4.00
Cool Country Barbie	4.00
Life Guard Ken	4.00
Life Guard Barbie	4.00
Bubble Angel Barbie	4.00
Ice Skatin' Barbie	4.00

Hot Wheels

Lightning Speed Hot Wheels vehicle	4.00
Shock Force Hot Wheels vehicle	4.00
Twin Engine Hot Wheels vehicle	4.00
Radar Racer Hot Wheels vehicle	4.00
Blue Bandit Hot Wheels vehicle	4.00
Power Circuit Hot Wheels vehicle	4.00
Backburner Hot Wheels vehicle	4.00
After Blast Hot Wheels vehicle	4.00
Key Force Truck Hot Wheels vehicle	4.00

The Busy World of Richard Scarry (figure in vehicle & 2-piece building)

Lowly Worm and Post Office	3.00
Huckle Cat and School	3.00
Mr. Frumble and Fire Station	3.00

Uncle Scrooge McDuck and some of his family dropped in for lunch in 1998.

Tamagachi toy key chains were part of a disappointing set in 1998.

Bananas Gorilla and Grocery Store 3.00
Lowly Worm in Apple Car 3.00

Disneyland 40th Anniversary Viewers
Brer Bear... 4.00
Aladdin's Oasis 4.00
Simba.. 4.00
Mickey Mouse 4.00
Roger Rabbit 4.00
Winnie the Pooh, green or black cab 4.00
Peter Pan King Louie 4.00

Halloween '95
Ronald Makes It Magic Tape....................................... 3.50
Travel Tunes Tape 3.50
Silly Sing-Along Tape 3.50
Scary Sound Effects Tape.. 3.50
Hamburglar/Bat... 3.50
Grimace/Ghost.. 3.50
Ronald/Frankenstein Monster...................................... 3.50
Birdie/Pumpkin.. 3.50
Grimace in Pumpkin... 3.50

Mighty Morphin' Power Rangers
Power Com 3.50
Powermorpher Buckle... 3.50
Power Siren 3.50
Alien Detector 3.50
Power Flute.. 3.50

Mighty Morphin' Power Rangers action figure & Ninjazord vehicle (over-the-counter toys)
White Ranger w/Falcon Ninjazord 5.00
Red Ranger w/Ape Ninjazord 5.00
Blue Ranger w/Wolf Ninjazord 5.00
Pink Ranger w/Crane Ninjazord................................... 5.00
Black Ranger w/Frog Ninjazord 5.00
Yellow Ranger w/Bear Ninjazord 5.00

Muppet Workshop
Bird.. 4.00
Dog 4.00
What-Not... 4.00
Monster 4.00

Space Rescue
Astro Viewer... 4.00
Telecommunicator.. 4.00
Space Slate.. 4.00
Lunar Grabber... 4.00
Astro Viewer... 4.00

Spider-Man
Amazing Spider-Man figure 4.00
Scorpion Stringstriker vehicle 4.00
Doc Ock figure 4.00
Spider-Man Webrunner vehicle 4.00
Mary Jane Watson-Parker figure (w/2 additional snap-on outfits) 4.00
Venom Transport Vehicle.. 4.00
Spider-Sense Peter Parker figure................................... 4.00
Hobgoblin Landglider vehicle 4.00
Spider-Man figure (under-3 toy, same as regular Spidey w/slight color variation) 4.00

Totally Toy Holiday II
Holiday Barbie figurine 3.00
Hot Wheels Car with Ramp 3.00
Polly Pocket Playset 3.00
Mighty Max Playset 3.00
Cabbage Patch Playset 3.00
North Pole Explorer 3.00
Once Upon a Dream Princess figure 3.00
Key Force Car 3.00
Magic Nursery Doll—girl.. 3.00
Magic Nursery Doll—boy... 3.00

1996

Disney's 101 Dalmatians II
(Tied into the release of the live-action video, these toys came packed in opaque polystyrene packages. The entire set could have been purchased via mail-in offer for $99.)
101 different Dalmatians (each) 2.50
Entire set (mail-in promotion) 150.00
Entire set (MIP from store) 200.00
Entire set (loose) 100.00

Disney's Aladdin & The King of Thieves
Cassim... 3.00
Abu 3.00
Jasmine 3.00
Iago... 3.00
Genie 3.00
Sa-luk 3.00
Aladdin.. 3.00
Maitre d' Genie 3.00
Abu Squirter (under-3).. 3.00

Babe, Pig in the City (movie tie-in)
Babe the Pig.. 4.00

These fishy characters were from Disney's Little Mermaid promotion of 1998.

This Barbie cowgirl was riding in style in 1995.

The Cow... 4.00
Maa the Ewe 4.00
Fly the Dog... 4.00
Ferdinand the Duck................................... 4.00
Dutchess the Cat 4.00
Mouse 4.00

Barbie/Hot Wheels VII
Dutch Barbie 4.00
Kenyan Barbie 4.00
Japanese Barbie... 4.00
Mexican Barbie 4.00
USA Barbie 4.00
Barbie Puzzle (under-3)............................. 4.00
Flame Series Hot Wheels 4.00
Roarin' Road Series Hot Wheels 4.00
Dark Rider Series Hot Wheels 4.00
Hot Hubs Series Hot Wheels 4.00
Krakel Car Series Hot Wheels 4.00
Hot Wheels Squeek (under-3) 4.00

Eric Carle Finger Puppets
Very Quiet Cricket....................................... 3.00
The Grouchy Lady Bug................................ 3.00
The Very Busy Spider 3.00
The Very Hungry Caterpillar........................ 3.00
A House for Hermit Crab............................. 3.00
The Very Lonely Firefly 3.00

Halloween 1996
Dragon McNugget Buddy............................. 4.00
Spider McNugget Buddy 4.00
Fairy Princess McNugget Buddy.................. 4.00
Alien McNugget Buddy 4.00
Rock Star McNugget Buddy......................... 4.00
Ronald McNugget Buddy 4.00

The Little Pet Shop/The Transformers Beast Wars
Swan Little Pet... 3.50

Brain and his world-conquering crew landed in 1995 as part of the Warner Bros. Animaniac set.

Unicorn Little Pet 3.50
Dragon Little Pet..3.50
Tiger Little Pet..3.50
Hamster Wheel Little Pet.............................3.50
Manta Ray Transformer................................3.50
Beetle Transformer......................................3.50
Panther Transformer....................................3.50
Rhino Transformer..3.50
Lion's Head Transformer 3.50

Marvel Super Heroes (PVC figures and characters in vehicles)
Spider-Man 4.00
Storm 4.00
Wolverine..4.00
Jubilee 4.00
Color Change Invisible Woman 4.00
Thing...4.00
Hulk 4.00
Human Torch 4.00
Spider-Man Ball (under-3 toy) 4.00

Muppet Treasure Island (movie tie-in)
Miss Piggy 4.00
Kermit the Frog...4.00
Gonzo the Great 4.00
Fozzie Bear 4.00
Book for Bath..4.00

Space Jam
Lola Bunny..3.50

Cabbage Patch Baby and Gogo Dodo were the prizes for under-3 customers in 1994.

Bugs Bunny... 3.50
Taz... 3.50
Marvin the Martian 3.50
Daffy Duck 3.50
Blue Monster... 3.50
Sylvester and Tweety.. 3.50
Nerdlucks.. 3.50

Space Jam Plush
Lola Bunny 3.50
Bugs Bunny... 3.50
Taz... 3.50
Daffy Duck 3.50
Blue Monster... 3.50
Nerdlucks.. 3.50

Saban's VR Troopers (TV show tie-in)
Visor... 3.00
Wrist Spinner 3.00
Virtualizer... 3.00
Kaleidoscope 3.00
Sphere, ball with a spinner in it.................................. 3.00

Walt Disney Home Video Masterpiece Collection
(Each PVC figure came packed in a video box replica.)
Cinderella 4.00
Robin Hood 4.00
Pocahontas 4.00
Aladdin 4.00
Snow White 4.00
Sword and the Stone 4.00
Alice in Wonderland 4.00
Aristocats 4.00
Dumbo Water Squirter (under-3) 5.00

Fisher-Price Toddler Toys
(With this promotion McDonald's permanently changed its practice of including a like-themed under-3 toy with each meal promotion. From this point forward, all under-3 toys became Fisher-Price toys, regardless of the main toy promotion. The available Fisher-Price toy is rotated as supplies at each location last.)
Grimace Ball 3.00
Birdie in Car 3.00
Bear in Train 3.00
Ronald McDonald in Drive-Thru.................................. 3.00
Barn Puzzle... 3.00
Camera Bead Game 3.00
Key Ring 3.00
Pig in Barrel 3.00
Dog in House 3.00
Cow Book.. 3.00
Dog Squeak 3.00
Balls in Ball 3.00

Seamore, Pinchers, Speedy and Goldie were some of the many Teenie Beanies that just kept showing up. These four appeared in 1998.

Shortly after McDonald's cut a deal for exclusive rights to all Disney movies in 1997, these gypsy figures from the Hunchback of Notre Dame appeared.

Telephone 3.00
Horse 3.00
Puzzle Maze 3.00
Radio Rattle 3.00
Bus 3.00
Clock 3.00
Dog 3.00
Man in Car 3.00
Dog Ball 3.00
Jeep 3.00
Truck 3.00
Ball 3.00

1997
Fisher-Price Toddler Toys
Grimace Ball 3.50
Birdie in Car 3.50
Bear in Train 3.50
Ronald McDonald in Drive-Thru 3.50
Barn Puzzle 3.50
Camera Bead Game...3.50
Key Ring 3.50
Pig in Barrel 3.50
Dog in House 3.50
Cow Book...3.50
Dog Squeak 3.50
Balls in Ball 3.50
Telephone 3.50
Horse 3.50
Puzzle Maze 3.50
Radio Rattle 3.50
Bus 3.50
Clock 3.50
Dog 3.50
Man in Car 3.50
Dog Ball 3.50
Jeep 3.50
Truck 3.50
Ball..3.50

Animal Pals (mini stuffed animals)
Panda 3.00
Rhinoceros 3.00
Yak..3.00

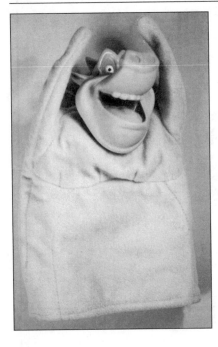

Haven't seen enough of the Hunchback characters? Here's another over-the-counter puppet from 1997.

Moose 3.00
Brown Bear 3.00
Gorilla.. 3.00

Barbie/Hot Wheels VIII
Wedding Rapunzel Barbie 3.50
Rapunzel Barbie 3.50
Angel Princess Barbie.................................. 3.50
Blossom Beauty Barbie................................. 3.50
Happy Holidays Barbie 3.50
Tow Truck Hot Wheels vehicle 3.50
Taxi Hot Wheels vehicle 3.50
Police Car Hot Wheels vehicle...................... 3.50
Ambulance Hot Wheels vehicle 3.50
Fire Truck Hot Wheels vehicle 3.50

Disney's Hercules (Movie promotion – two toys came in each pack)
Hermes and the Wind Titan 4.00
Hercules and the Hydra 4.00
Pain and Cyclops... 4.00
Megara and Pegasus.................................... 4.00
Phil and Nessus 4.00
Zeus and the Rock Titan............................... 4.00
Baby Pegasus and the Lava Titan 4.00
Panic and the Fates..................................... 4.00

Calliope and the Ice Titan.............................4.00
Hades and Cerebrus 4.00

Hercules plates (A set of four plastic kid's dinner plates were sold separately w/this promotion)
Hercules plate 6.00
Plate #2 ....6.00
Plate #3 ....6.00
Plate #4 ....6.00

Disney's Hunchback of Notre Dame
Esmerelda Amulet 4.00
Quasi Scepter..4.00
Clopin Mask 4.00
Hugo Horn 4.00
Juggling Balls 4.00
Drum...4.00
Bird Catcher..4.00
Tambourine..4.00

Disney's Jungle Book
Baloo 3.50
Junior..3.50
Bagheera 3.50
King Louie..3.50
Kaa Mowgli 3.50

Disney's The Little Mermaid II
(Movie re-release. The set also included random insertions of special gold figures of each character. The entire gold set was available for separate purchase via mail-in offer.)

Regular set
Ursula...4.00
Flounder 4.00
Scuttle...4.00
Ariel 4.00
Max...4.00
Glut...4.00
Eric...4.00
Sebastian...4.00

Gold set
(As the set came in opaque polystyrene packages, the only way to be assured of having a gold set is to have either opened the packages, or purchased it via the mail-in offer.)
Ursula...10.00
Flounder 10.00
Scuttle...10.00
Ariel 10.00
Max...10.00

Transformers were cool in 1996, and they came in Happy Meals.

To help promote its new Florida jungle park in 1998, Disney released a set of international mini-plush animals in Happy Meals.

Here's a close-up shot of the 1999 Winnie The Pooh display.

Glut	10.00
Eric	10.00
Sebastian	10.00
Entire gold set (from mail-in offer)	35.00
Entire gold set (loose)	50.00

Disney's Mighty Ducks Pucks
Wildwing	3.00
Nosedive	3.00
Mallory	3.00
Duke L'Orange	3.00

Nickelodeon's Tangle Toy
Twist-a-zoid #1	3.00
Twist-a-zoid #2	3.00
Twist-a-zoid #3	3.00
Twist-a-zoid #4	3.00
Twist-a-zoid #5	3.00
Twist-a-zoid #6	3.00
Twist-a-zoid #7	3.00
Twist-a-zoid #8	3.00

Seban's BeetleBorgs Metallix
Stinger Drill	3.00
Beetle Bonder	3.00
Hunter Claw	3.00
Platinum Purple BeetleBorg Covert Compact	3.00
Chromium Gold BeetleBorg Covert Compact	3.00
Titanium Silver BeetleBorg Covert Compact	3.00

Sky Dancers/Micro Machines
Rosemerry Sky Dancers	3.00
Swan Shimmer Sky Dancers	3.00
Princess Pegasus Sky Dancers	3.00
FlutterFly Sky Dancers	3.00
Evac Copter Micro Machine	3.00
Polar Explorer Micro Machine	3.00
Ocean Flyer Micro Machine	3.00
Deep Sea Hunter Micro Machine	3.00

Disney's Sleeping Beauty
Sleeping Beauty	4.00
Maleficent	4.00
Prince Philip	4.00
Flora	4.00
Dragon	4.00
Raven	4.00

Ty's Teenie Beanie Babies (first set of miniature Beanie Babies)
Pinky The Flamingo	20.00
Seamore the Seal	10.00
Quacks The Duck	10.00
Chocolate the Moose	10.00
Speedy the Turtle	10.00
Snort the Bull	10.00
Chops the Lamb	10.00
Patty the Platypus	10.00
Goldie the Goldfish	10.00
Liz the Lizzard	10.00
Complete set	135.00

1998

Disney's 101 Dalmatians the Series
Flip Car #1	4.00
Flip Car #2	4.00
Flip Car #3	4.00
Flip Car #4	4.00
Flip Car #5	4.00
Flip Car #6	4.00
Flip Car #7	4.00
Flip Car #8	4.00

Animal Kingdom
Gorilla and Baby	3.00
Triceratops	3.00
Crocodile	3.00
Cheetah	3.00
Rhino	3.00
Iguanadon	3.00
Ring-Tail Lemur	3.00
Lion	3.00
Tucan	3.00
Zebra	3.00
Dragon	3.00
Elephant	3.00

Disney's Hercules Sports Theme (from the animated TV show)
Pain and Panic Sound Baton	3.00
Hades Stopwatch	3.00
Pegasus Whistling Discus	3.00
Hercules Medal	3.00
Hercules Sports Bottle	3.00
Zeus Football	3.00

Mighty Morphin' Power Rangers flexed their muscles in 1995.

Power Rangers, even without their vehicles, were still pretty cool.

Eye of Fates Foot Bag 3.00
Phil Megaphone 3.00

Disney's The Legend of Mulan (PVC figures from the movie)
Mulan 3.00
Khan 3.00
Mushu 3.00
Shanyu 3.00
Shang 3.00
Chien Po, Ling, Yao 3.00
Little Brother 3.00
Cri-Kee 3.00

My Little Pony/Transformer Beast Wars
Ivy Pony 2.50
Sundance Pony 2.50
Light Heart Pony 2.50
Scorponok Transformer 2.50
Dinobot Transformer 2.50
Blackarachnia Transformer 2.50

Peter Pan series
Peter Pan 3.00
Peter Pan Glider 3.00
Tick Tock Croc Toy 3.00
Captain Hook Spyglass Toy 3.00
Tinker Bell Lantern Clip 3.00
Smee Light 3.00
Wendy & Michael Magnifier 3.00
Activity Tool 3.00

Ty's Teenie Beanie Babies II
Doby the Doberman 5.00
Bongo the Monkey 5.00
Twigs the Giraffe 5.00
Inch the Worm 5.00
Pinchers the Lobster 5.00
Happy the Hippo 5.00
Mel the Koala Bear 5.00
Scoop the Pelican 5.00
Bones the Dog 5.00
Zip the Cat 5.00
Waddle the Penguin 5.00
Peanut the Elephant 5.00

Tomagotchi
(These were plastic mock-ups of the virtual pets, some of which did one action.)
Tomagotchi #1 .... 2.50
Tomagotchi #2 .... 2.50
Tomagotchi #3 .... 2.50
Tomagotchi #4 .... 2.50
Tomagotchi #5 .... 2.50
Tomagotchi #6 .... 2.50
Tomagotchi #7 .... 2.50
Tomagotchi #8 .... 2.50

Barbie/Hot Wheels
August 14, 1998
Bead Blast Christie 3.00
Teen Skipper 3.00
Eating Fun Kelly 3.00
Barbie 3.00
Ronald NASCAR 3.00
50th Anniversary NASCAR 3.00
Hot Wheels NASCAR 3.00
Mac Tonight NASCAR 3.00

Disney Video Favorites
September 18, 1998
The Spirit of Mickey 10.00
Lady & The Tramp 10.00
Pocahontas 10.00
Mary Poppins 10.00
The Black Cauldron 10.00
Flubber 10.00

McDonaldland
(Busts of the characters wearing Halloween masks that flip up dispensing Nerds Candy. Introduces "Iam Hungry," a new character.)
October 9, 1998
Ronald w/Scarecrow Mask 3.00
Grimace w/Jack-o-lantern Mask 3.00
Birdie w/Black Cat Mask 3.00
Hamburglar w/Green Monster Mask 3.00
McNugget w/Skull Mask 3.00
Iam Hungry w/Witch Mask 3.00

Simba's Pride
October 30, 1998
(Plush toys with cords that can be used for hanging.)
Kovu 3.00
Zazu 3.00
Timon 3.00
Kiara 3.00
Pumbaa 3.00
Zira 3.00
Rafiki 3.00
Simba 3.00

A Bug's Life
Dim 3.00
Rosie 3.00
Dot 3.00
Flik 3.00
Francis 3.00
Heimlich 3.00
Hopper 3.00
Atta 3.00

Best friends Tigger and Pooh were 1999 clip-ons.

Disney's Recess (ABC Saturday cartoon)
Dec. 26 – Jan. 21

TJ	2.50
Spinelli	2.50
Vince	2.50
Gretchen	2.50
Teacher Miss Finster	2.50
Gus	2.50
Mikey	2.50

1999

Under-3 Toys Series II
(Some of the soft-plastic toys have been recalled.)

McDonald's Chicken McNuggets in the box	2.50
Grimace and Ronald at McDonald's, Yellow w/red roof	2.50
Dalmatian in fire truck	2.50
Little People Pilot & airplane	2.50
McDonald's child-size drink cup	2.50
McDonald's small-size fries	2.50
McDonald's apple pie	2.50
Little People Ronald McDonald in boat	2.50
Little People Hamburglar in hamburger car	2.50
Little People farmer on tractor	2.50
Cell Phone	2.50
Radio	2.50
Ring Toss	2.50
Green roll ball	2.50
Camera	2.50
Large & small elephant	2.50
Blue dog w/yellow heart	2.50
Red, yellow & blue stacking blocks	2.50
Gray cow w/yellow bell around neck	2.50
Yellow Taxi	2.50
Little People police officer in police car	2.50
Little People engineer in Blue train	2.50
Hamburglar teething cookie ring	2.50
McDonaldland character roll along	2.50

Mulan (each toy is a spinner or launcher)
Jan. 29 – Feb. 25

Mulan	2.50
Khan	2.50
Mushu	2.50
Shan-Yu	2.50
Chien-Po	2.50
Shang	2.50
Yao	2.50
Ling	2.50

Disney's Winnie the Pooh
Feb. 26 – Mar. 25
(Clip-ons.)

Eeyore	2.50
Owl	2.50
Winnie the Pooh	2.50
Rabbit	2.50
Roo	2.50
Piglet	2.50
Gopher	2.50
Tigger	2.50

Saban's Mystic Knights of Tir Na Nog
Apr. 23 – May 20

Rohon	2.00
Queen Moeve	2.00
Angus	2.00
Core	2.00
Deirdre	2.00
Mider	2.00
Ivan	2.00
Lugad	2.00
Bonus Toy (Buld Prism Dragon, w/parts of toys Queen Moeve, Core, Mider, and Lugad	4.50

Furby
STYLE 1 (Push tail, growls & moves eyes.)

Black w/pink tuft and belly	2.50
Black w/white tuft and belly	2.50
Blue w/pink tuft and belly	2.50
Blue w/white tuft and belly	2.50
Lt. Green w/pink tuft & belly	2.50
Lt. Green w/white tuft & belly	2.50
Purple w/white tuft and belly	2.50
Purple w/white tuft and belly	2.50
Turquoise w/pink tuft & belly	2.50
Turquoise w/white tuft & belly	2.50

STYLE 2 (Push forward, feet & ears move.)

Blue w/white tuft and belly	2.50
Blue w/yellow tuft & white belly	2.50
Gray w/white tuft & belly	2.50
Gray w/yellow tuft & belly	2.50
Green w/white tuft & belly	2.50
Green w/yellow tuft & belly	2.50

The 1995 Spider-Man collection featured the Scorpion's car.

Esmerelda and her goat friend appeared in 1997 with the Hunchback of Notre Dame series.

Orange w/white tuft & belly 2.50
Orange w/yellow tuft & belly.. 2.50
Purple w/white tuft & belly 2.50
Purple w/yellow tuft & white belly 2.50

STYLE 3 (Pull Furby backward, he rolls forward)
Lt. Blue w/green tuft 2.50
Lt. Blue w/purple tuft 2.50
Orange w/green tuft 2.50
Orange w/purple tuft.. 2.50
Pink w/green tuft 2.50
Pink w/purple tuft.. 2.50
Red w/green tuft.. 2.50
Red w/purple tuft... 2.50
Yellow w/green tuft 2.50
Yellow w/purple tuft 2.50

STYLE 4 (Press feet, beak, ears, & eyes move.)
Beige w/dots, white tuft & belly 2.50
Beige no dots, red tuft & belly 2.50
Gray w/dots, white tuft & belly....................................... 2.50
Gray no dots, red tuft & belly... 2.50
Orange w/dots, white tuft & belly................................... 2.50
Orange no dots, red tuft & belly 2.50
Purple w/dots, white tuft & belly.................................... 2.50
Purple no dots, red tuft & belly...................................... 2.50
Yellow w/dots, white tuft & belly 2.50
Yellow no dots, red tuft & belly...................................... 2.50

STYLE 5 (Furby says "Eek" when upside down.)
Blue w/white tuft 2.50
Blue w/yellow tuft 2.50
Lt. Green w/white tuft 2.50
Lt. Green w/yellow tuft... 2.50
Purple w/white tuft.. 2.50
Purple w/yellow tuft 2.50
Red w/white tuft.. 2.50
Red w/yellow tuft... 2.50
White w/white tuft... 2.50
White w/yellow tuft 2.50

STYLE 6 (Press tail, plays peekaboo w/his ears.)
Black w/black tuft 2.50
Black w/purple tuft 2.50
Blue w/black tuft 2.50
Blue w/purple tuft 2.50
Lt. Green w/black tuft 2.50
Lt. Green w/purple tuft... 2.50
Orange w/black tuft 2.50

Orange w/purple tuft 2.50
Teal w/black tuft 2.50
Teal w/purple tuft.. 2.50

STYLE 7 (Push tail, squeaks, moves eyelids & beak.)
Gray w/black tuft & belly.. 2.50
Gray w/white tuft & belly.. 2.50
Green w/black tuft & belly.. 2.50
Green w/white tuft & belly.. 2.50
Purple w/black tuft & belly... 2.50
Purple w/white tuft & belly... 2.50
Red w/black tuft & belly 2.50
Red w/white tuft & belly 2.50
Yellow w/black tuft & belly 2.50
Yellow w/white tuft & belly 2.50

STYLE 8 (Roller ball on back, moves eyes & ears.)
Black w/blue tuft & red belly.. 2.50
Black w/pink tuft & belly 2.50
Dk. Blue w/blue tuft & belly... 2.50
Dk. Blue w/pink tuft & belly 2.50
Lt. Blue w/blue tuft & red belly 2.50
Lt. Blue w/pink tuft & belly... 2.50
Gray w/blue tuft & red belly 2.50
Gray w/pink tuft & red belly 2.50
Pink w/blue tuft & red belly 2.50
Pink w/pink tuft & belly.. 2.50

Ty Beanie Babies III
May 21, 1999

Freckles 3.00
Ants 3.00
Smoochy..3.00
Spunky...3.00
Rocket 3.00
Iggy..3.00
Strut 3.00
Nuts 3.00
Claude 3.00
Stretch...3.00
Nanook 3.00
Chip 3.00

TY's International Bears (over-the-counter)

Glory 6.00
Maple...5.00
Britiania..5.00
Erin 5.00

Food Foolers

Fry box (phone) 2.50
Happy Meal box (computer) 2.50

Saban's Power Rangers as they looked at the height of their popularity in 1995.

Babe the talking pig and his farm buddies showed up in 1996 as their second movie was hitting the theaters.

McNuggets box (camera)	2.50
Drink cup (signaler)	2.50

Disney's Tarzan

Tarzan	2.50
Terk	2.50
Jane	2.50
Tantor	2.50
Sabor	2.50
Clayton	2.50
Kala	2.50
Porter	2.50

Tarzan Sound Straws

Tarzan	2.00
Tambor	2.00
Kala	2.00

Inspector Gadget

(Eight individual toys that not only performed separate functions, but also fit together to form a 15" tall Inspector Gadget toy.)

Narvik 7 sparker (head & torso)	2.50
Right arm squirter	2.50
Left arm grabber	2.50
Watch belt	2.50
Left leg tool	2.50
Right leg circuit signaler	2.50
Secret communicator (chest)	2.50
Siren hat	2.50

Barbie/Hot Wheels

Barbies

Soccer Barbie	2.50
Sleeping Beauty Barbie	2.50
Happenin' Hair Barbie	2.50
Totally Yo-Yo Barbie	2.50
Birthday Party Barbie	2.50
Giggles in Swing Barbie	2.50
Pet Lovin' Barbie	2.50
Bowling Party Barbie	2.50

Hot Wheels

Double Cross	2.50
Maximizer	2.50
Led Sled	2.50
Surf Boarder	2.50
Street Raptor	2.50
Black Track	2.50
Trail Runner	2.50
Innovator	2.50

Hercules was on one of five over-the-counter plates available in 1997.

Doug's 1st Movie

Sept. 17 – Oct. 14

Doug key chain that blushes	2.50
Doug pen pal	2.50
Pork chop squeeze-clip pooch	2.50
Patti key chain pal	2.50
Doug clip-on treasure keeper	2.50
Monster pocket protector	2.50
Skeeter key chain w/glow-in-the-dark flashlight	2.50
Quailman bouncing zipper gripper	2.50

Halloween Pails (two pails)

October 15

Each pail	2.50

Lego

(Eight limited-edition Lego sets, that, when assembled together build a Lego super model. Promotion was run in conjunction with a Lego mail catalog-only McDonald's.)

Oct. 29 – Nov. 25

Ronald—Helicopter	3.50
Sundae—Water vehicle	3.50
Birdie—Airplane	3.50
McNugett Buddy—Race Car	3.50
Grimace—Snow Plow	3.50
Yellow Fry Guy—Sea Plane	3.50
Hamburglar—Airplane	3.50

Tiny Tunes had tiny cars in 1990.

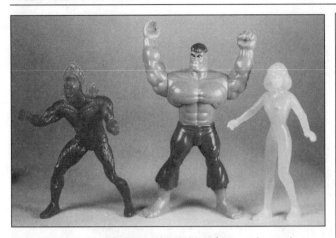

The Human Torch, Hulk and Invisible Woman, three of Marvel's best, showed up in 1996.

Blue Fry Guy—Speed Boat.. 3.50
Duplo—Parrot (under-3) 3.50

Disney PIXAR's Toy Story 2

(In addition to the 20 toys and six over-the-counter items in this promotion there are two giveaways: a large, full-color poster and a Happy Meal Visor, featuring all 20 toy designs.)

Woody.. 2.50
Mr. & Mrs. Potato Head.. 2.50
Robot 2.50
Slinky Dog... 2.50
Little Green Alien 2.50
Bo Peep 2.50
Hamm 2.50
Disney & PIXAR's Jessie 2.50
Disney & PIXAR's Rex 2.50
Lenny 2.50
Zurg... 2.50
Prospector... 2.50
Marionette Woody 2.50
Barrel of Monkeys 2.50
Buzz Lightyear 2.50
Disney & PIXAR's Bullseye... 2.50
RC Car 2.50
Etch-a-Sketch 2.50
Green Army Man.. 2.50
Tour Guide Barbie 2.50

Over-The-Counter Items

(These were larger items that dispensed various types of small candy.)

Buzz Lightyear 2.00
Hamm 2.00
Jessie... 2.00
Mr. & Mrs. Potato Head.. 2.00
Rex... 2.00
Woody & Bullseye.. 2.00

Posters

Toys kid around in Andy's room 1.50
Woody & Jessie take a wild ride 1.50
Buzz Lightyear & friends to the rescue 1.50

Ronald Scholars

December 24
Each item... 1.50

McDonald's Happy Meal Under-3 Toys

(These Fisher-Price toys are available congruently with standard toys and rotated throughout their run. There may or may not be a display of them posted. You have to ask for them.)

Grimace in a wagon...2.00
Stacking animal puzzle..2.00
Blue truck with headlight eyes.......................................2.00
Blue lantern 2.00
Large telephone...2.00
Smiling school bus...2.00
Flower rattle..2.00
Chipmunk in a tree..2.00
Ronald driving Volkswagen Beetle 2.00
Fish in fish bowl..2.00
Colored Bumble Bee 2.00
Blue/Grey Airplane 2.00
Red/Yellow Train Engine w/blue conductor 2.00
Red/Yellow Train Car w/monkey in "pop-out" window 2.00
Frog Rattle 2.00
Yellow flat Truck w/Hamburglar or Grimace in the
     window..2.00

2000

Barbie/Hot Wheels

(Half Barbies; half Hot Wheels, half of each set features "current" designs, and the other half features "future" designs. A cardboard put-together diorama was available for each series — a racing garage for the Hot Wheels, and a dollhouse for the Barbies.)

Dec. 31 – Jan..27

Barbies

Millennium Princess Barbie 2.50
#1 Barbie 2.50
Solo in the Spotlight Barbie 2.50
Hollywood Nails Barbie..2.50
Malibu Barbie 2.50
Totally Hair Barbie..2.50
Sit in Style Barbie 2.50

Goofy was honored with his own Goof Troop bucket.

Bugs was missing from this group, but the Tiny Tunes were still ready to roll.

Working Woman Barbie 2.50
Super Gymnast Barbie.. 2.50
Chic Barbie... 2.50

Hot Wheels
McDonald's current NASCAR 2.50
McDonald's future NASCAR 2.50
Hot Wheels current NASCAR 2.50
Hot Wheels future NASCAR 2.50
McLaren Grand Prix Car 2.50
Future McLaren Grand Prix Car.................................. 2.50
Del Worsham current Funny Car 2.50
Del Worsham future Funny Car 2.50
Champ Car.. 2.50
Future Champ Car 2.50

Over-The-Counter
(Cardboard item that required assembly, retailed for $2.)
Barbie's doll house... 3.50
Hot Wheel's racing garage.. 3.50

Walt Disney's Tarzan
(Video release. Each piece interlocks to form a "Rube Goldberg" machine.)
Jan. 28 – Feb. 24
Tarzan 2.50
Sabor 2.50
Tantor... 2.50
Young Tarzan 2.50
Terk 2.50
Jane 2.50
Kerchak... 2.50
Kala & Baby Tarzan 2.50

An Extremely Goofy Movie
(All toys snap together to form an Extreme Arena.)
Mar. 2 – 23
Goofy 2.50
Slouch 2.50
Sylvia 2.50
Bobby.. 2.50
Max 2.50
Tank 2.50

Like Dalmatians? Here are a few more from 1997.

This mixed bag of characters represented various sets in the '90s.

Bradley 2.50
PJ 2.50

Furby 2
(Plush clip-ons that perform some action.)
Mar. 24 – Apr. 13
Tiger (eyelids and mouth open and close).........................3.00
Tree Frog (sound chip produces a frog noise).................3.00
Elephant (ears move outward) 3.00
Monkey (tail moves) 3.00
Raccoon (light that goes on and off)...............................3.00
Lamb (body and eyes go up and down) 3.00
Giraffe (lights in belly)..3.00
Fox (magnets on back)..3.00
Dinosaur (eyes change colors when touched) 3.00
Owl (eyes glow in dark)..3.00
Cow (moos)...3.00
Diamondback Snake (mouth opens and closes) 3.00

Teletubbies Clip-ons
The new
(Teletubbies Munch & Slurp plush (pudding) includes an offer to send away for a free Teletubbies Koosh toy or Teletubbies Roto figure.)
Apr. 14 – 27
Po 3.00
Tinky 3.00
Winky 3.00
Dipsy 3.00
Laa Laa..3.00

Power Ranger Rescue
(Eleven toys; six Power Rangers in cases, which connect to form the Make-a-Zord and 5 Rescue Trains, which also hook together.)
Apr. 28 – May 18
Red Power Ranger 2.50
Yellow Rail Rescue 2.50

The Tribbles kept multiplying. This group from 1998 included (from left) Peanut, Happy, Scoop, Twigs and Bones.

Babe and his farm buddies were frequent guests at McDonald's in 1996.

Pink Power Ranger	2.50
Green Rail Rescue	2.50
Blue Power Ranger	2.50
Pink Rail Rescue	2.50
Yellow Power Ranger	2.50
Blue Rail Rescue	2.50
Green Power Ranger	2.50
Red Rail Rescue	2.50
Titanium Power Ranger	2.50

Dinosaur

(Disney Movie; Two types of toys, four plastic hand puppets, and four miniature figurines. The Lemurs spoke when their tail was depressed, snapped onto the back of the three-dinosaur toys, and said something different when affixed to the back of each.)

May 19 – June 12

Hand Puppets

Aldar	3.00
Carnotaur	3.00
Neera	3.00
Kron	3.00

Figurines

Baylane	3.00
Lemurs	3.00
Eema	3.00
Bruton	3.00

Teenie Beanie Babies IV

(These came in two series, the "regular" set, packed in w/Happy Meals, and the Superstars, over-the-counter in blister packs. Each series had subdivisions or groups of similarly themed toys released at the same time. There were also two "secret" Beanies that were part of the regular Happy Meals set.)

June 13 – July 13

Pet Pals

Lips the Fish	3.00

Here are just two of the 80 Furbys that were available from McDonald's in the early part of 1999.

During this 1999 promotion there were eight different Furbys that came in 10 different styles.

Slither the Snake	3.00
Flip the Cat	3.00
Dottie the Dalmatian	3.00

Garden Bunch

Lucky the Ladybug	3.00
Bumble the Bee	3.00
Spinner the Spider	3.00
Flitter the Butterfly	3.00

At The Zoo

Tusk the Walrus	3.00
Blizzard the Snow Tiger	3.00
Spike the Rhinoceros	3.00
Schweetheart the Orangutan	3.00

Under The Ocean

Neon the Seahorse	3.00
Coral the Fish	3.00
Sting the Stingray	3.00
Goochy the Jellyfish	3.00

Secret Surprise Beanies

Springy the Rabbit	3.00
Bushy the Lion	3.00

Over-The-Counter Superstar Teenie Beanies

Millennium Bear	5.50

Dinosaur Trio

Rex	4.00
Steg	4.00
Bronty	4.00

International Bears II

Spangles	6.00

Like we said, there were a lot of Furbys at McDonald's.

Barbie and Hot Wheels never go out of style at McDonald's.

Germania 5.00
Osito... 5.00

Legends
Peanut... 4.00
Chilly 4.00
Humphrey 4.00
The End Bear 5.00

Fingerboards
July 14 – Aug. 3
Each item 2.00

Beast Machines/Hello Kitty
Aug. 4 – 24
Hello Kitty
Crew Kid.. 2.00
Sticker Art... 2.00
Kitty Wrap (hair accessory) 2.00

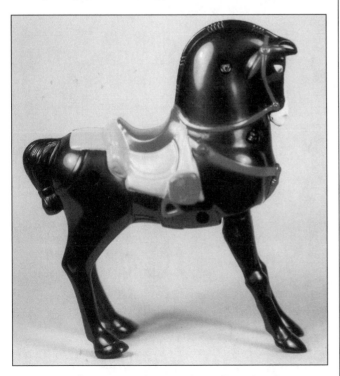

This Mulan Happy Meals horse is from the 1998 set.

Tarzan and Clayton were among the hot items in 1999.

Kimono figurine...2.00
Charm Watch 2.00
Figurine (bee costume) 2.00
Dear Daniel Stamp Mobile...........................2.00
Ballerina Scrunchy 2.00
Apple Combo Lock 2.00

Beast Machines
Cheetor 2.00
Megatron..2.00
Rattrap 2.00
Thrust...2.00
Tankor 2.00
Optimus Primal 2.00
Jetstorm 2.00
Blackarachnia 2.00
Nightscream...2.00

The Tigger Movie
(Video release. Clip-ons with removable disguises.)
Aug. 25 – Sept. 14
Tigger..2.00

Tarzan was joined in the 1999 set by gorilla friend Kala and human friend Jane.

Inspector Gadget proved to be a very popular toy, mostly due to its unique design.

Eeyore...2.00
Pooh..2.00
Roo 2.00
Piglet...2.00
Owl...2.00

Barbie/Hot Wheels
Oct. 15 – Nov. 12
Each item 2.00

Crazy Bones
Oct. 13 – Nov. 2
Each item 2.00

Disney Video
Nov. 3 – 23
Each item 2.00

102 Dalmatians
Nov. 24 – 21
Each item 2.00

These MIP toys from McDonald's were part of the recess promotion of 1998.

He is a fully assembled Inspector Gadget, all 15 inches of him.

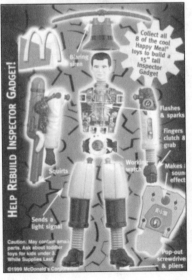

A break-away schematic showed off Inspector Gadget's parts in 1999.

Pizza Hut

Company Profile

A pair of college-age brothers in Wichita, Kansas, founded Pizza Hut in 1958 with the help of a $600 loan from their mother. The loan and the business venture paid off, as the company incorporated in 1959, with the first franchised unit opening in Topeka, Kansas. Business was doing so well that in 1965 the company was airing its first commercial with a jingle that told people to "putt-putt to Pizza Hut."

In 1967, the Fort Worth, Texas Pizza Hut baked the world's largest pizza, measuring 6 feet in diameter. By 1968, the company had not only gone international with a location in Canada, but was serving a million people a week in 310 locations. In 1969, it expanded further into the international market with locations in Mexico, Munich Germany, and Australia. During the early 1970s there were locations in Japan and England. The company went public in 1972. In 1975, the movie *The Bad News Bears* filmed scenes in the Pizza Hut in Chatsworth, California.

By 1976, the company had over 2,000 locations. In 1977, Pizza Hut merged with PepsiCo, becoming a wholly owned subsidiary. In 1982, the company's class promotion tie-in with Steven Spielberg's hit movie *E.T.* was voted as the top marketing promotion by the editorial staff of *Chain Marketing and Marketing* magazine. The 5,000th location opened in 1986, the same year that the company introduced delivery service. That was also the year that Pizza Hut delivered to the White House. First lady Barbara Bush threw a Reading Is Fundamental party for 200 Washington D.C. children at the White House, catered by Pizza Hut.

The Land Before Time debuted with the biggest opening ever for an animated feature film in 1989, and Pizza Hut sold 9.1 million Land Before Time puppets. In 1990, the company delivered some 1,340,000 pizzas on Super Bowl Sunday. During the NCAA Final Four men's basketball weekend, the chain moved 3.7 million basketballs in a co-promotion. Location number 10,000 was celebrated when soccer legend Pele kicked a soccer ball through the doors of the Sao Paulo, Brazil, restaurant.

Perhaps the company's most historic delivery was made in 1991 to Russian President Boris Yeltsin. Yeltsin and his supporters had just weathered a coup attempt and he had called the nearest Pizza Hut for a delivery as the food supplies of the Russian Parliament building were dwindling. During the 1996 Super Bowl, Pizza Hut accounted for 30 percent of the more than 12 million pizzas delivered during the game.

Some Toy Info

It wasn't until 1998 that Pizza Hut had a regular program in place that sold toys with kid's meals. Most of their previous promotions were sporadic, over-the-counter campaigns that were tied into specific events (NCAA tournament, the movie *The Land Before Time*, etc.) It wasn't until 1999 that one Pizza Hut promotion began to roll into another.

In 1994, Pizza Hut issued four comic books in conjunction with Marvel Comics. The comics dealt with pro-social issues like prejudice, substance abuse, and community service, and featured several of the company's most popular heroes, including Spider-Man, the Avengers, Daredevil, the Fantastic Four, and the X-Men.

With the Star Wars promotion, done in conjunction with sister companies KFC and Taco Bell, Pizza Hut began to aggressively seek out, attract, and competitively market its toy promotions.

One of the highlights of the 1999 toy season was Pizza Hut's set of *Star Wars: Episode I – The Phantom Menace* toys that was issued in conjunction with KFC and Taco Bell. For a more detailed look at these toys, as well as a listing of all Star Wars fast food toys issued over the years, check out the *May the (Fast-Food), Force be with You* article and accompanying list elsewhere in this book.

A Jar Jar Binks squishy was part of the Phantom Menace collection at Pizza Hut in 1999.

Pizza Hut Toy Listing

All prices are for items mint in package (MIP), unless otherwise noted.

Where applicable, the date(s) of distribution and additional information on the following premiums were provided by the individual chains.

1978

Air Garfield
Inside airball 5.00
W/parachute 5.00

1980

Aliens
(PVC figures w/Pizza Hut logo. The figures proved to be so popular that they were re-issued a number of times without logos.)
Smiley 15.00
Space Kat 15.00
Little Green Martian 15.00
Moon Man 15.00

Aliens
(PVC figures w/o Pizza Hut logo, same as above, except without logos, thus not considered as valuable.)
Smiley 10.00
Space Kat 10.00
Little Green Martian 10.00
Moon man 10.00

1988

Land Before Time Rubber Puppet Figures
Cera 6.00
Little Foot 6.00
Spike 6.00
Duckie 6.00
Petrie 6.00
Sharptooth 6.00

1990

Eureka's Castle Rubber Puppets
Batley 6.00
Eureka 6.00
Magellan 6.00
Set of 3 .... 18.00

1991

American Tail II
Beverage container 5.00
Pizza box 5.00

Rocketeer (from the Disney movie)
Glider 5.00
Pizza box 6.00
Beverage container w/ cap 6.00

Nickelodeon
Mascot beverage container 2.00

Nickelodeon Beverage Containers
Ren and Stimpy 5.00
Rug Rats 4.00
Doug 4.00

Rock Art
Each 3.00

1994

Marsupilami Houba-Douba
Glow ball 3.00
Yo-Yo 3.00
Jump Rope 3.00

Pizza Box Kit
Pizza & toppings mold w/stickers (came in a replica Pizza Hut pizza box) 3.00
Young Indiana Jones Chronicles (from TV series) telescope 4.00
Compass 4.00
Magnifying glass 4.00

Marvel's Real Heroes
(Comic books and plastic drink cups. Each comic book had the heroes dealing with an important social issue. The comics and cups were not bagged together, and thus can only be found "loose".)
Iron Man, Spider-Man, Firestar, & the Human Torch (Substance Abuse) 4.00
Captain America, Daredevil, Wasp, Falcon (Community Service) 4.00
Jubilee, Prof. X, Black Panther, Thing (Prejudice) 4.00
Comic book #4 .... 4.00
Cup #1 (Iron Man, Spider-Man, Firestar, & the Human Torch) 4.00
Cup #2 (Captain America, Daredevil, Wasp, Falcon) 4.00
Cup #3 (Jubilee, Prof. X, Black Panther, Thing) 4.00
Cup #4 .... 4.00

1999

K'Nex
May — parts from each bag make two different toys; combined parts from all four bags form a single, larger toy, Greedy Grabber.
Bag #1 butterfly or plane 3.00
Bag #2 motorcycle or red hen 3.00
Bag #3 fish or dune buggy 3.00
Bag #4 dragonfly or helicopter 3.00
Set of 4 .... 15.00

Star Wars: Episode I The Phantom Menace
(This promotion was done in conjunction with sister companies KFC and Taco Bell.)

R2-D2 greeted visitors to Pizza Hut as part of the Episode I collection.

Marvel Comics produced four comic book and cup sets for Pizza Hut in 1994. Each carried a positive social message, although that didn't stop the superheroes from pounding the stuffing out of the bad guys.

The Rocketeer was not only a very cool retro comic book from Pacific Comics (circa 1980s), but it was also a fun movie from Disney. This Pizza Hut box is from 1991.

Coruscant Toy Series
Kid Meal Toys
Jar Jar Binks Squishy (under-3)......................................3.00
Lott Dodd's Walking Throne..3.00
Yoda's Jedi Destiny..3.00
Queen Amidala's Royal Starship 3.00
R2-D2..3.00
Planet Coruscant 3.00
Sith Holoprojector 3.00
Darth Maul's Sith Infiltrator..3.00

Cup Toppers
Jar Jar Binks 4.00
Mace Windu 4.00
Nute Gunray 4.00
Yoda 4.00

Tricky Treaters
September
Web Whirler 2.00
Count Candy...2.00
Eyeball Grabber..2.00
Rattlin' Bones...2.00
Rock 'n Ghoul 2.00
Under-three toy...2.00

2000

Big Mix CD
(Mix-your-own, six-song CD available online through CDNow with the purchase of a Big New Yorker Pizza.)
Each CD..2.50

Top Secrets Mary Kate & Ashley
Spy Recorder 2.00
Wrist Decoder 2.00
Spy Scope...2.00
Spy Phone 2.00
Under-3 toy "Clue" a little Sherlock Holmes plush dog 2.00

Rocketeer made for a cool plastic cup.

The ever-cheatin' Sebulba takes a walk on the wild side as a kid meal toy in 1999.

Sonic Drive-In

Company Profile

By 1953, World War II veteran Troy Smith, who was living in Shawnee, Oklahoma, had twice attempted to enter the restaurant business. His first endeavor was a small place he named the Cottage Cafe. In fact, the place was so tiny that he was unable to support his wife and two children. Trading up to a larger place, he went on to open Troy's Panful of Chicken. This time he was successful enough to attempt to open other locations. However, being the early 1950s, no one was quite ready for franchise operations. Thus, Troy's Panful of Chicken quietly went to that great eatery in the sky.

Still, Smith wanted to run his own business, which he envisioned as a fancy steak house. When he acquired the steak house however, there was a root beer stand that came with the deal. Smith's long-range plan was to tear it down to add parking for the steak house. Needless to say, that never quite happened. As it turned out, the stand provided a steady flow of cash and was always busy. The steak house fell by the wayside.

While traveling throughout the South, Smith spotted some homemade speakers at a burger stand in Louisiana, where customers could place their food orders while remaining in their cars. The orders were broadcast directly to the kitchen. Knowing an innovation when he saw one, Smith contacted the inventor and commissioned him to make speakers for his root beer stand, the Top Hat. Smith then added a food delivery system in his operation to bring the food directly to customers' cars, thus inventing the carhop. Smith's innovation first appeared in 1953. The additions of the speakers and food delivery system expanded Smith's weekly take from around $700 to $1,750 the first week. Shortly after, he added canopies, and a new fast-food chain was well on its way.

Charles Pappe, a Safeway supermarket manager, stopped by Smith's Top Hat for dinner one night. He was so impressed with the concept, the high level of service, and operations at the drive-in that he wasted no time in introducing himself. Soon after, he became the first licensee of the future Top Hat chain. Eventually, two others were opened, but Smith and Pappe soon learned that someone else had already copyrighted the name, forcing them to come up with an alternative.

As Top Hat's slogan was "service with the speed of sound" (since the addition of the speaker system), it eventually occurred to the pair to change the name to "Sonic," which means speed of sound.

The operation continued to interest investors, partly because each location was partially owned by the on-site operator. The pair would help new franchise owners out with the layout of the new stores, site selection, and initial operations. Royalty fees were based on the number of sandwich bags sold through one of Sonic's long-time vendors, Cardinal Paper. This fee was one penny per bag. The initial franchise contract was just a page-and-a-half long and contained no advertising contribution or territorial rights clauses. If two prospects wanted to open in the same town, Smith would simply convince one to go elsewhere.

In 1967 there were 41 Sonic Drive-Ins operating. That year, Charlie Pappe died of a heart attack. Over the next six years, Smith and a pair of franchise owners who took over the supply operations at his request built 124 drive-ins in Oklahoma, Texas and Kansas.

By 1973, a group of 10 key principal franchise owners formed to restructure the company and serve as its officers and board of directors. At this time, there were 165 stores in the Sonic chain. Each store operator had the option to buy 1,250 shares of stock in the new company at $1 per share, making Sonic an over-the-counter, publicly traded company.

Sonic continued to grow and by 1978 there were over 1,000 locations. Unfortunately, the company, like the nation, was hit by inflation and recession. By the end of 1984, there were less than 1,000 Sonic Drive-Ins operating in 19 states. To help offset this, the company began to advertise as a national unit, and this helped defray expenses. Over the years, the company has led the fast-food industry in comparable store sales increases. It has since experienced 10 consecutive years of same-store sales growth. In December 1998, the 1,900th Sonic Drive-In opened.

The company now has franchise locations in 27 states and ranks as the nation's largest-running drive-in chain of restaurants. It is currently the second-largest hamburger chain in the southwest.

Sonic Drive-In Toy Listing

All prices are for items mint in package (MIP), unless otherwise noted.

Where applicable, the date(s) of distribution and additional information on the following premiums were provided by the individual chains.

Year Unknown

Sonic Village
(Each of 4 different figures came in a box that was a different village.)
Each premium... 4.00

Classic Cruisers
(Each license plate was a different color, and came with vinyl letters to make your own plate ID.)
License plate (each).. 4.00
Sticker set #1 .... 4.00
Sticker set #2 .... 4.00
Sticker set #3 .... 4.00
Sticker set #4 .... 4.00
Key Chain 4.00
Eraser 4.00

Sonic School Days
Bookmark/ruler... 4.00
Do Not Disturb doorknob sign........................... 4.00
Hush, Student Studying doorknob sign............... 4.00
Keep Out doorknob sign 4.00

Adventures of the Super Sonic Kids
(Coloring book with different color set of 3 Crayons.)
Red/blue/tan.. 4.00
Flesh/Green/tan 4.00
Pink/green/yellow... 4.00
Blue-green/purple/orange 4.00

Adventures of the Super Sonic Kids
(Four different cups w/color-changing ability.)
Each cup 5.00

Adventures of the Super Sonic Kids
(Four different sidewalk surfer w/coloring book.)
Each premium.. 4.00

Adventures of the Super Sonic Kids
(Four different PVC figures w/coloring book.)
Steve.. 4.00
Rick.. 4.00
Corkey.. 4.00
Brin.. 4.00

Sonic Drive-In Dinosaur Adventure
(Four different rubber noses & tattoo stickers.)
Each premium.. 4.00

1987

Brown Bag Juniors
(PVC figures w/storybook.)
Bookworm... 4.00
Sure Shot 4.00
Too Cool... 4.00
Marbles 4.00

1989

Adventures of the Super Sonic Kids
(Super sonic ring w/storybook.)
Steve 6.00
Rick 6.00
Corkey 6.00
Brin 6.00

Brown Bag Juniors
(PVC brown paper bag figures.)
W/bag of marbles 5.00
W/sunglasses & french fry............................... 5.00
W/basketball 5.00
W/glasses & book... 5.00

Sidewalk surfers vehicles
Ms. Sidewalk Savvy.. 6.00
Mr. Big Fun 6.00
The Sidewalk Snoot.. 6.00
The Mean Sidewalk Machine 6.00

1990

Jumpin' Juke Boxes Juke Box Banks
Red 4.00
Blue 4.00
Box #3 .... 4.00
Box #4 .... 4.00

1992

Bag-a-wag PVC figures
In car... 4.00
Skating... 4.00
Walking 4.00
Sitting on burger 4.00

Stunt-Grip Geckos
(Lizards w/suction cups on head, legs, and tail.)
Green... 4.00
Purple 4.00
Blue 4.00
Turquoise.. 4.00

1993

Trolls
(Each figure came w/different hair color and a different symbol on their belly — star, heart, diamond, and circle. Toys were also distributed by Hardee's, Long John Silvers, and Roy Rogers.)
Each troll.. 5.00

Brown Bag Sports Buddies
(PVC brown paper bag figures.)
On surfboard.. 4.00
W/inner tube 4.00
On skis... 4.00
On snow sled... 4.00

Classic Cars
'49 Mercury... 6.00
'55 Chevy.. 6.00
'57 Chevy convertible 6.00
'59 Chevy.. 6.00

Animal glass hangers
(Various colorful animals designed to hang on the edge of a drinking glass. Also distributed by Wendy's.)
Frog 3.00

Bird.. 3.00
Bear 3.00
Alligator 3.00
Beaver... 3.00
Pig 3.00
Elephant.. 3.00
Turtle 3.00
Lion 3.00

Grass Critters

(Colorful plastic critters/planters. Each came w/grass seeds to be planted in their head, which would grow "hair" for them.)
Orange 3.00
Blue 3.00
Yellow 3.00
Green 3.00

Holiday Train

(Four-car set with company logo and Dr. Pepper decals on the cars; also distributed by Dairy Queen & White Castle.)
Engine 6.00
Coal car... 6.00
Box car 6.00
Caboose... 6.00

Fast Food Squirters

French fries 3.00
Peppermint candy 3.00
Soft drink 3.00
Hamburger 3.00

Kid Squirters

Pink 3.00
Blue 3.00
Yellow 3.00

Turbo racers

Green 4.00
Orange 4.00
Yellow 4.00
Pink 4.00

1994

Brown Bag Bowlers

(Brown paper bag figures on wheels w/bowling balls.)
W/red ball.. 4.00
W/yellow ball 4.00
W/orange ball 4.00
W/blue ball 4.00

Dino pop-ups

W/burger 4.00
W/hot dog... 4.00
W/french fries 4.00
W/drink 4.00

Dino Squirters

Triceratops 4.00
Apatosaurus.. 4.00
T-Rex 4.00
Scaly-back dino.. 4.00

Flying Food Stars

(Throwing stars w/suction cups at ends.)
Taterites 4.00
Melvin the Mini-Burger 4.00
Onion Ring Squadron 4.00
Clyde the Corn Dog 4.00

Wacky Sackers

(PVC figures. Six different sacks with a total of 24 different figure/color combinations.)
Each figure 3.00

1995

Air Toads

(Six different figures w/basketballs attached to suction cups.)
Each Air Toad 3.00

Animal Squirter Balls

Bear w/honey pot...3.00
Panda bear w/ball 3.00
Rabbit 3.00
Monkey w/banana 3.00
Hound dog 3.00
Cat w/ball of yarn...3.00
Bulldog...3.00
Puppy 3.00

1996

Food Racers

Ice Cream Soda..3.00
Others in series 3.00

Food Train

Sonic Chili Float..4.00
Sonic Mustard..4.00
Sonic Engine 4.00
Sonic Caboose...4.00

1997

Hurl A Critters (4 to a set)

Each item..3.00

1998

Dinosaur Runners (4 to a set)

Each item..3.00

Sonic Wacky Chew-Chew Train

Engine w/shake on top 3.00
Fry car 3.00
Ketchup Bottle car 3.00
Hot Dog car 3.00
Nachos car 3.00
Pickle car 3.00
Hamburger car...3.00
BLT car 3.00

Super Sonic Racers Space Ships

Orange Ship racer 3.00
Red Ship racer...3.00
Blue Ship racer 3.00
Green Ship racer 3.00

Hot Rod Hot Dogs

(Each Hot Rod Dog comes w/own dog house.)
Red Hot Dog..3.00
Green Hot Dog 3.00
Red Hot Dog..3.00
Blue Hot Dog 3.00

Fast Breakin Basket Bugs

(Set of 5 bugs playing basketball.)
Each item..3.00

Sonic Wacky Lightning Lizards
Red 3.00
Green 3.00
Purple 3.00
Yellow 3.00

Sand & Sea Critters
Black Whale 3.00
Blue Orca 3.00
Orange Crab 3.00
Green Turtle 3.00

Wacky Window Clings
Neighborhood 3.00
Animals 3.00
Tic-Tac-Toe 3.00
Galatic Glowers 3.00

Wacky Splats Cool Cloth Balls (Set of 4)
Each ball 2.50

Chillin' Choo-Choo (Set of 4 cars)
Each item 2.50

Land Dolls Mini Pop-Up Books (6 to the set)
Each item 2.50

Spooky Sippers
Batty 2.50
Frank 2.50
Wolf 2.50
Mummie 2.50

TotBots
Model A-10 Standard walking robot 2.50
Model H-6227 Level 3 waddling robot 2.50
Model A10103 jumping robot 2.50
Model S-364 Class "M" pull-back zooming robot 2.50

1999

Picture Pockets
Doghouse 2.50
Car 2.50
Camera 2.50
TV 2.50

Coin Keepers
Each item 2.50

Wacky Clings
Space 2.50
Farm 2.50
School 2.50
Football 2.50

Hoops
Girl #12 .... 2.50
Boy #7 .... 2.50
Girl #10 .... 2.50
Boy #3 .... 2.50

Wrist Racers
Red Car Wrist Racer 2.50
Blue Car Wrist Racer 2.50

Yellow Car Wrist Racer 2.50
Green Car Wrist Racer 2.50

Pop-Up Books
Junior 2.50
Cherrie Makes a Big Difference 2.50
Molly Brightens Up a Rainy Day 2.50
Pete Finds a New Friend 2.50

Wacky Pack Straws
May
Red 2.50
Blue 2.50
Green 2.50
Purple 2.50

Tumblebugs (Set of 4 bugs that flip over)
July
Blue 2.00
Green 2.00
Yellow 2.00
Orange 2.00

Backpack Danglers
Girl with tater tot 2.00
Girl with drink 2.00
Boy with hot dog 2.00
Boy with hamburger 2.00

Light Up Yo-Yo
Blue w/Junior 2.00
Red w/Cherrie 2.00
Purple w/Molly 2.00
Orange w/Pete 2.00

Wacky Story Cards
Each 1.00

Glow-in-the-Dark Spooky Buckets (Set of 4)
Each 2.00

Wacky Pack Train (Set of 8)
Each car 2.00

Creativity Kits
Notepad 2.00
Pencil 2.00
Carrying Case 2.00
Eraser 2.00
Stickers 2.00
Crayons 2.00

2000

Tot Totes
Watch tote 2.00
Coin tote 2.00
Coin purse w/clip 2.00
Round plastic tote w/clip 2.00

Read Around Books (Set of 4)
Each book 1.50

Beach Balls
Each item 1.50

Subway

Company Profile

Subway was founded in 1965 by 17-year-old high school graduate Fred DeLuca, who was financed with a $1,000 loan from Dr. Peter Buck, a family friend. DeLuca opened the first shop, called Pete's Super Submarines, in Bridgeport, Connecticut, and for a year the two entrepreneurs perfected their operation. They opened a second shop a year later, but as neither shop was in a high-traveled area, neither was doing very well. Undaunted, they opened a third shop in a more visible area and shortened the name to Subway with the now-familiar yellow logo.

This third shop is still open and serving customers to the present day.

With the third location sailing along, the partners began to formulate a business plan that outlined the company's goals. It was at this time that they began to actively begin franchising operations. The first Subway franchise opened in Wallingford, Connecticut in 1974. Ten years later, Subway opened the doors of its first international shop in Bahrain. By August of 1995 Subway was celebrating 30 years of success and witnessing the opening of its 11,000th restaurant. By 1996 the operation was up to 12,000 locations.

Some Subway Toys

While Subway has tended to lean towards generic, non-licensed toys in the past, the company has issued some notable licensed premiums. Some of these have included comic book and cartoon characters such as Spider-Man, Garfield, The Flintstones and Marvin the Martian.

Cracker Jack was an original choice for a 1999 Subway promotion.

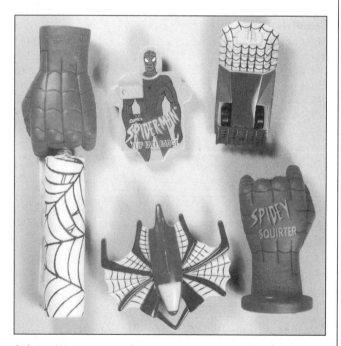

Subway loves its superheroes, as this Spider-Man collection from 1990 showed.

Plenty of superheroes were hanging around during Subway's end-of-the-year promotion in 1998.

Jetson toys rolled in in 1998.

Subway Toy Listing

All prices are for items mint in package (MIP), unless otherwise noted.

Where applicable, the date(s) of distribution and additional information on the following premiums were provided by the individual chains.

1991

Hackysack balls

(Subway logo on one side, Vegetable People image on reverse side. Also distributed by Chuck E. Cheese.)

Pappy Pepper 4.00
Petey Pickle 4.00
Lenny Lettuce 4.00
Tilly Tomato 4.00
Pearl Onion 4.00

1993

Captain Planet Rings

(Mood rings that displayed the character's symbol when warmed up.)

Quami's ring (Earth) 6.00
Linka's ring (Wind) 6.00
Wheeler's ring (Fire) 6.00
Gee's ring (Water) 6.00
Mati's ring (Heart) 6.00

Coneheads

(Pencil toppers from movie.)

Beldar 6.00
Connie 6.00
Prymaat 6.00
Marlax 6.00

Land of the Lost

(Dinosaurs from TV series.)

T-Rex 5.00
Triceratops 5.00
Dimetrodon 5.00
Stegosaurus 5.00

This MIP superhero hanger was part of the 1998 collection.

1994

Doodletop Jr.

(Plastic, spinning tops w/markers.)

Blue 5.00
Green.. 5.00
Purple 5.00
Pink... 5.00

Explore Space

(Some variations in painting and decals occur in these PVCs.)

Astronaut 5.00
Space Station 5.00
Space Shuttle 5.00
Lunar Lander 5.00

The Hurricanes

(PVC figures from a TV soccer team.)

Amanda 5.00
Gatson 5.00
Napper 5.00
Cal 5.00

Inspector Gadget

From TV cartoon.

Gadget holding magnifying glass 5.00
Gadget as ink stamper 5.00
Gadget as squirter (sitting, blue) 5.00
Gadget as squirter (standing, red) 5.00

Monkey Trouble

(Figures based on movie of same name.)

Shorty 5.00
Eva & Dodger (the monkey) 5.00
Eva 5.00
Dodger... 5.00

Disney's *The Santa Clause*

(PVC figures from the movie.)

Figure w/removable Santa outfit.. 5.00
Elf action figure.. 5.00
Santa action figure... 5.00
Comet (reindeer) 5.00
3-tier twist puzzle 5.00

Tom & Jerry

Tom on scooter 4.00
Jerry on skateboard... 4.00
Jerry in beach buggy.. 4.00
Tom in beach buggy 4.00

Wildlife Rangers (PVC animals)

Dan the lowland gorilla 4.00
Spot the Crevy's zebra 4.00
Herman the polar bear.. 4.00
Stephan the snow leopard.. 4.00

1995

Bump in the Night

(ABC TV, four action figures, plus extra credit insert about stop-motion animation.)

Aug. – Oct.

Mr. Bumpy 5.00
Squishington.. 5.00
Molly 5.00
Destructo 5.00

Bobby's World

(Fox TV, 4 Bobby figures, plus extra credit insert about Imagination.)
Oct. – Nov.
Cowboy 5.00
Knight 5.00
Astronaut 5.00
Other premiums in series 5.00

Beakman's World

(Plus extra credit insert about science & experiments.)
Nov. – Dec.
Tele Tube 4.00
Magic Movie Maker 4.00
Color Changing Penguins 4.00
Beakman Flip Top 4.00

CY*Treds

(Robot figure/vehicles. Also distributed by McDonald's, as Runaway Robots.)
Beck 4.00
Coil 4.00
Bait 4.00
Skull 4.00
Jab 4.00
Flame 4.00

Disney's Tall Tails

(PVC figures from an animated movie.)
Pecos Bill 4.00
Paul Bunyan 4.00
John Henry 4.00
Daniel Hackett 4.00
Paul Bunyan on Babe 4.00

1996

Play-Doh plus Extra Credit insert about sculpting.

(Four different color cans of Play-Doh with different model-ing tool.)
Jan. - Feb.
Subman 3.00
Tube for making stars, circles, and squares 3.00
3-D Subman in convertible car 3.00
Star shaped cutter 3.00

All Dogs Go To Heaven 2

(Plus extra credit insert about movie.)
Mar. – May
Pull-back-and-go Charlie 4.00
Itchy that scratches itself 4.00
Car Face that opens its mouth 4.00
Sasha that wags tail 4.00
David figure 4.00

Tropical Birds

(Plus extra credit insert teaching about rain forest.)
May – June
Yellow Macaw 3.00
Crimson Rosella 3.00
Blue Turaco 3.00
Flat-billed Mountain Toucan 3.00

Subway Speeders

(Four custom-made die-cast cars, and one plastic car. Each car came with different road sign, and plastic road map. Four maps combine to one large play field. Extra credit insert teaching about fuel.)

Spider-Man got top billing at Subway in 1996.

July – Aug.
Each car 4.00

Spider-Man

Marvel Comics
Sept. – Oct.
Spider-car 5.00
Spider-plane 5.00
Spidey-squirter 5.00
Spidey flip face badge 5.00
Spidey web thrower 5.00

Garfield

(Four different Garfield buckets and lid, plus extra credit insert teaching about pets and pet care.)
Oct. – Nov.
Each bucket & lid set 4.00

SNAP-ITZ

(Four interconnecting puzzles. Each kit contains 4 large pieces, and 20 small pieces, plus extra credit insert teaching about shapes and colors.)
Nov. – Dec.
Each puzzle 3.00

1997

Space Puzzles

(Plus extra credit insert teaching about space. Four NASA photos.)
January
The Columbia space shuttle lift off 4.00
American astronaut saluting flag on moon 4.00
Planets viewed from space 4.00
Atlantis docking with Mir 4.00

1998

Marvin the Martian

(Warner Bros. Four collectibles plus $3 bounce-back cou-pons for Marvin the Martian videos at Act 2 video and $5 dis-count coupons at Warner Bros. store w/$25 purchase.)
Late Aug.
Each premium 4.00

Kool-Aid

(Includes sample Kool-Aid packs and Kool-Aid man stickers.)
Sept. – Oct.
Wacky Warehouse catalog 3.00
Kool-Aid color customized straw 3.00
Mug 3.00
Activity Cup 3.00

DC Superhero Backpack Hanger Tags
(Included superhero collector cup.)
Oct. 26 – Nov. 29
Wonder Woman Plane 5.00
Batman 5.00
Flash 5.00
Superman 5.00

Flintstones/Jetsons
(Warner Bros. Four toys featuring Flintstones and the Jetsons.)
December
Each figure 4.00

Jim Henson's Bear in the Big Blue House
May
Bip and Bop Tub Fun 3.00
Cha-cha-cha Bear 3.00
Big Blue House Viewfinder 3.00
Tutter's Cheese Chase 3.00

Nick Jr.
June 7 – July 18
Flip Flop Blue 3.00
My Friend Kipper 3.00
Detective Little Bear 3.00
Dress-up Maisy 3.00
Face's Play Sack 3.00

Cracker Jacks
July 19 – Aug.
Periscope 3.00
Sailor Jack Fun Whistle 3.00
Bingo Magnifying Glass 3.00
Sailor Jack Compass 3.00

Dexter's Laboratory
Aug. 23 – Oct. 3
Each item 2.00

Batman and Superman teamed up again in 1998.

Taco Bell

Company Profile

In 1946, after the end of World War II, Glen Bell left the Marine Corps and opened his first food stand in the form of a one-man hot dog stand called Bell's Drive-In. In 1952 he sold that first stand, and opened a new place that sold hamburgers and hot dogs. It was around this time that the McDonald brothers started their first unit, also in San Bernadino.

At first Bell was worried that two stands in such close proximity would be a problem, but, as it turned out, the competition probably helped both of them. Still, he wasn't comfortable with the idea of a pair of similar stands in the same area so he began investigating alternative menu items. As an avid Mexican food take-out customer, he began to experiment with tacos. To this end he looked to open a location in a Mexican neighborhood in order to make it look like a localized store to possible competitors.

Needless to say, the idea worked and he opened up a second location and went on to build his own chain named Del Taco. Between 1954 and 1955, Bell built three Taco Tias. He also had three Bell's Drive-Ins, so he built a small commissary to serve the six places. Eventually, when Bell's partner was against expanding the Taco Tias, Bell sold out so he could grow the Taco Tias business on his own.

He moved to Los Angeles and began to do very well. He formed a partnership with four Los Angeles Rams team members, founding a chain called El Tacos. Despite the fact that business was going well, Bell found that it was tough for him to have partners and share a dream. He decided to go out on his own again and sold his share of El Tacos. In 1962, he built the first Taco Bell in Downey, California. He opened eight small

Taco Bell took off in the 1980s and '90s, as did the company's toy promotions.

A pair of Mr. Freezes and a portable Batsignal from the very cool 1997 Batman collection.

Taco Bell units that are still operating today in the Long Beach, Paramount and Los Angeles areas.

It was around this time that franchising was becoming popular, and Bell joined in the trend. Kermit Becky, a former Los Angeles policeman, bought the first Taco Bell franchise in 1964. It was his success that inspired others to tap into the growing operation. In 1966, he opened his 100th restaurant in Phoenix, Arizona. He later admitted hating it when the company took to numbering the locations.

The company went public in 1969. Bell continued to helm the operation until 1975, when he tendered his resignation as chairman of the board. By 1977, the company went international. In 1978, Bell sold Taco Bell's 868 units to PepsiCo, Inc. Under the new ownership, the franchise really took off and by 1993 the chain had increased to 9,707 locations. In 1995, Taco Bell, along with the other two PepsiCo food franchises (Pizza Hut & KFC), joined forces under the management of PepsiCo Restaurant International (PRI).

Taco Bell launched its Web site (www.taco-bell.com) in 1997, which is also the same year that PRI became Tricon Global Restaurants, Inc., a fully owned PepsiCo subsidiary.

Taco Bell Toys

Like all the other major fast-food chains, Taco Bell has taken up issuing toys with its kid's meals. However, any discussion of Taco Bell toys must include a mention of the Sylvester Stallone/Wesley Snipes 1993 film *Demolition Man*. Not only did Taco Bell issue a plastic

With the release of the special edition of George Lucas' classic film came a new wave of toys.

Matchbox cars took people for a ride in 1999.

The Mask has gone from comic book character, to TV icon, to movie star, to kid meal toy.

Chihuahuas did the talking for Taco Bell in 1998.

A puzzle cube, R2-D2, Darth Vader/Yoda magic cube, and Yoda squishy were all part of the 1997 Star Wars Taco Bell set.

Taco Bell's four PowerRings from 1998 could build a fifth toy when combined.

Yoda and Obi-Wan were part of the Star Wars special edition series in 1977. Obi-Wan was a mail-in toy.

Han Solo's Millennium Falcon Gyro took flight with a 1997 set.

157

cup as a tie-in to the movie, but during the course of the sci-fi movie, Stallone's character (who had been revived in 2032 from a 1996 cryogenic sleep) was taken out to a plush dinner at a Taco Bell and was told that Taco Bell had won the fast-food wars of the late 20th century, and now was the only restaurant.

In 1995, the company issued its first set of Tick toys that tied into the animated TV show (the Tick originally appeared in comic book form from NEC). A second Tick set appeared in 1996 and proved to be more interesting in concept, design, and execution than the original set. Another superhero/animated cartoon set featured The Mask, derived from the hit Jim Carrey movie, which, in turn, was developed off the Dark Horse comic book. A second Mask set appeared during the summer of 1997.

With the release of Star Wars Special Edition in early 1997, Taco Bell kicked kid-meal toys into the next strata with a very elaborate set of Star Wars toys that — in coming years — will be the ones to beat. This set was followed by a set of cool Batman toys. During the summer of 1998, Taco Bell released a set of Godzilla toys that was very collectible, even though the movie proved disappointing. Taco Bell's TV commercials were perhaps the best part of the "Summer of Godzilla," which probably brought people in and helped boost the collectibility of the toys.

Taco Bell wound up 1998 by capitalizing on the runaway popularity of its Chihuahua spokesdog by issuing a set of Talking Plush Chihuahua toys. Four different talking Taco Bell Chihuahuas were available during November and December 1998. Priced from $2.99 to $3.99, with no other purchase necessary, the 6-inch plush toys featured four different voice messages and accessories drawn from commercial favorites in the popular campaign. Voice chips with the actual voice of the Taco Bell Chihuahua activate when the toy's stomach is pressed.

Of course, the highlight of the 1999 toy season was Taco Bell's set of Star Wars: Episode I – The Phantom Menace toys that were issued in conjunction with sister companies KFC and Pizza Hut. For a more detailed look at these toys, as well as a listing of all Star Wars fast food toys issued over the years, check out the "May the (Fast Food), Force be with You" article and accompanying list elsewhere in this book.

Taco Bell Toy Listing

All prices are for items mint in package (MIP), unless otherwise noted.

Where applicable, the date(s) of distribution and additional information on the following premiums were provided by the individual chains.

Year Unknown

Hot Stuff Sprites (plush toys)
Spark/Yellow 3.00
Champ/Blue 3.00
Twink/White 3.00
Romeo/Red 3.00

Hugga Bunch (plush toys)
Flutter/Gold 3.00
Hug-A-Bye/Pink 3.00
Gigglet/Blue-Green 3.00
Tuggins/Blue 3.00

1992

Disney's Honey I Blew Up the Kids
(Different colors throwing rings.)
Each color 5.00

1993

The Busy World of Richard Scarry
(Finger puppets recalled.)
Heckle the Cat 3.00
Lowly Worm 3.00
Other puppets 3.00

Rocky & Bullwinkle stampers
Rocky (red) "Hokey Smoke" 4.00
Bullwinkle (yellow) "Wossamotta U." 4.00
Boris 4.00

Natasha 4.00

Matchbox cars
Each car 4.00

Demolition Man plastic cups
Each cup 4.00

1995

Congo
(Three different watches from movie of same name.)
Each 4.00

Mutant Jungle Mix-up
(Tied into Congo movie. Two colorful animals per package, each animal came in 2 different colors. Front and back of each animal could be interchanged with any other animal. Total of 12 different animals, including gorilla, elephant, rhino, lion, wart hog, alligator.)
Any package of 2 .... 4.00
Any individual animal (w/both correct halves) 4.00
Any animal with mismatching halves 4.00

Flintstones
Each item 4.00

The Tick (Fox-TV animated show)
Arthur wall climber 4.00
"Roller" Tick 4.00
Thrakkorzog squirter 4.00
Tick finger puppet 4.00
Set of 3 Tick "cling" sheets 4.00

The Mask (Fox-TV animated show)
Mask top 4.00
Ooze 'N Form with Wacky Dough 4.00
Milo with Mask finger puppet 4.00
"It's Party Time!" light switch cover 4.00

The Force could be found at Taco Bell again in 1999 with this Episode I promotion.

Street Sharks
Each item 4.00

Desert Cruisers
Each item 4.00

1996

Nacho & Dog
Each item 2.50

Earthworm Jim
Each item 2.50

Princess Tenko/Masked Rider
Each item 3.00

Kazzam (from movie)
Each item 3.00

Monster Eyes (wacky straws)
Each item 3.00

Goosebumps
Each item 3.00

The Tick II
"Balancing" Tick 4.00
Flying Arthur 4.00
Underwater Sewer Urchin 4.00
Charles the Brain Child 4.00

Life with Louie (animated TV show)
Each item 3.00

1997

Ace Ventura
Each item 3.00

Star Wars Special Edition
Millennium Falcon Gyro 4.00
3-D Puzzle Cube 4.00
Floating Cloud City 4.00
R2-D2 w/Princess Leia figurine 4.00
Flying Boba Fett 4.00
Yoda/Darth Vader 3-D cube 4.00
Yoda Squishy (under-3) 4.00

Goosebumps Activity Book
Each book 2.50

Nacho and Dog Basketball
Each item 2.50

Batman (movie set)
Mr. Freeze squirter (under-3 toy) 4.00
Break-away Batmobile 4.00
Batsignal Flashlight 4.00
Batman on Ice Freeze Pop 4.00
Poison Ivy's Hideout/Terrarium 4.00

Batman plastic cups (movie set)
Batman 3.00
Mr. Freeze 3.00
Posion Ivy 3.00
Cup #4 .... 3.00

The Mask (TV show)
Mask helicopter 4.00
Putty Thing & Fish Guy 4.00
Pretorius Wind-Up 4.00
Whistling Spinning Top Mask face 4.00
Milo the Dog (under-3) 4.00

Monster Eyes Toys
Each item 2.50

Monster Eyes Straws II
Each straw 2.00

Nintendo
Each item 2.50

1998

Goosebumps Fun Books
(Promotion contains offer to save three proof of purchases and send them in to get a free CD-Rom with 2 game samplers.)
The Abominable Snowman's Cool
Activities Book 2.50
How to Draw A Monster Book 2.50
The House in Dark Falls 3-D Puzzle 2.50
Deep Trouble II Ocean Escape Board Game 2.50

ShaQ-O Pogs
(Crayola Fun Packs could have substituted for pogs.)
Each of 4 Pog sets 3.00
Each of 4 Crayon sets 2.00

Bigger was better when it came to Star Wars reptiles.

159

Super Mario

Mario Kart 64 Joystick.................................. 2.50
Mario Maze 2.50
Star Fox 64 Shootout 2.50
Donkey Kong Tree Maze 2.50
Yoshi (under-3) 2.50

Taco Bell Matchbox Madness

'62 Corvette 3.00
Beatle Bug 3.00
Truck 3.00
Race Car.. 3.00
Nacho & Taco in Taco I Car (under-3)............ 3.00

NCAA Final Four Basketballs

Each item 2.50
Spinner Basketball (under-3) 2.50

Godzilla (from movie)

Water Tank... 3.00
Jet Shooter.. 3.00
Godzilla Action Figure................................... 3.00
Helicopter 3.00
Skyscraper 3.00
Godzilla Cup Holder 3.00

Talking Chihuahua Plush dogs

(Regional test run, Omaha: over-the-counter.)
Says "Here Lizard, Lizard" 7.00
Says "Yo Quiero Taco Bell" 7.00
Says "Viva Gorditas" 7.00

Space Goofs Fox Kids

Cosmic Cruise... 3.00
Cold Pack... 3.00
Unbeatable Bud 3.00
Bathtub Shoot Out 3.00
Face Former 3.00

Halloween Straws

(Eyeball Straws over-the-counter cleanup from 1997 promotion.)
October
Each item 2.50

Play Ball

Rawlings ball... 3.00
Pogs... 3.00
Pinball game 3.00

The Mask (from 1995) and spinner flying toy (1997) were past Taco Bell giveaways.

Looks like Unbeatable Bud to Me.................... 3.00
Nacho and Taco coloring book (under-3) 3.00

Animorphs

Yeerk On the Brain 2.00
Andalite Bean 2.00
Claw to hand Watch....................................... 2.00
Animorphing Sphere...................................... 2.00
Animorpher 2.00

Talking Chihuahua Plush Dogs Part I

(National roll-out: over-the-counter.)
"I Think I'm In Love"...................................... 7.00
"You are Getting Hungry, Very Hungry!" 7.00
"Yo Quiero Taco Bell"..................................... 7.00
"Here, Lizard, Lizard" 7.00
"Viva Gorditas" 7.00
"How Cool Is This" 7.00
"Feliz Navidad, Amigos!" 7.00

1999

Power Rings

Power Man 4.00
Reindeer... 4.00
Pirate Ship 4.00
Dune Buggy 4.00
Set of four 18.00

Matchbox Cars

Each item.. 3.00

Cow & Chicken

(Cartoon Network — apparently one in every few thousand of the walker toys goes backwards when you push the button. It was a mistake, and thus is worth more.)
Pop-A-Wheelie Tricycle 2.50
Sparking Cow 2.50
TV Animator Cow 2.50
Cereal Spinner.. 2.50
TV Animator Chicken...................................... 2.50
Huggable Cow & Chicken (under-3).................. 2.50
Backwards Walker (error toy) 5.00

Chihuahua Kids Meal

(All 5 of these toys have the Chihuahua dog as part of the toy.)
Candy Dispenser 2.50
Fire Escape Challenge 2.50
Chihuahua Figure 2.50
Message Maker 2.50
Treasure Keeper.. 2.50

Star Wars: Episode I — The Phantom Menace

(This promotion was done in conjunction with sister companies KFC and Pizza Hut.)

Tatooine toy series

Kid Meal Toys
Anakin's Podracer 3.00
Planet Tatooine 3.00
Walking Sebulba.. 3.00
Darth Maul's Sith Speeder 3.00
Hovering Watto 3.00
Joking Jar Jar Binks 3.00
Sebulba's Podracer 3.00
Levitating Queen Amidala's Royal Starship 3.00
Anakin Skywalker Transforming Bank.............. 3.00

Godzilla the movie may have stiffed back in 1998, but the Taco Bell toys were pretty cool.

Anakin Viewer 3.00
Sith Probe Droid Viewer 3.00

Cup Toppers
Anakin Skywalker 4.00
Darth Maul 4.00
Sebulba 4.00
Watto 4.00

Limited-Edition Posters
   (When combined — form an oversized picture of the planet Tatooine.)
Poster #1 .... 2.00
Poster #2 .... 2.00
Poster #3 .... 2.00
Poster #4 .... 2.00
All 4 .... 10.00

Woody Woodpecker
Mountain Bike Woody 2.50
Street Luge Woody 2.50
Air Surfin Woody 2.50
Skate Board Woody 2.50
Wave Riden Woody 2.50

Animorphs
Cassie Anteater 2.00
Tobias Hawk 2.00
Rachel Fly 2.00
Marco Shark 2.00
Jake Lizard 2.00

Woody Woodpecker Toys
Mountain Bike Woody 2.00
Street Luge Woody 2.00
Air Surfin' Woody 2.00
Skate Board Woody 2.00
Wave Ridin' Woody 2.00

Taco Bells famous Chihuahua
   (Four more versions of the little Chihuahua uttering cute catch-phrases used in commercials.)
Drop the Chalupas 7.00
Chances Are 7.00
Happy New Year, Amigos 7.00
Growlllllll 7.00

2000

Big Guy & Rusty
   (From the Dark Horse Comics series.)

This 3-D Yoda magic cube featured the profile of Darth Vader on the other side. Another bit of Jedi magic, perhaps?

Big Guy & Rusty 2.50
Stomping Big Guy 2.50
Atomic Man with Gushing Alien 2.50
Sticker Fun Kit 2.50
Flying Rusty 2.50

NCAA Basketball Toys
Watch Ball 2.50
Hoop & Ball toy 2.50
Clip-on Ball 2.50
Wall Hoop and Ball 2.50

Chihuahua Fun Notes
Chihuahua Compass 2.50
Chihuahua Fortune Teller 2.50
Chihuahua Bongo Drum 2.50
Chihuahua Photo Frame 2.50

PC in Play
   (Set of 4 computer discs.)
Taco Maker Marathon 2.00
Jumping Bean Jamboree 2.00
Tasty Temple Challenge 2.00
Moon Eater 2.00
(under-3) Coloring book 2.00

Digimon Trading Cards
   (Forty-eight embossed metal cards.)
Each ....

Look kids, a Return of the Jedi box.

Wendy's

Company Profile

Founded by Dave Thomas on November 15, 1969, Wendy's was named after Thomas' daughter. The original store is still open for business in downtown Columbus, Ohio. A second location opened a year later with a pick-up window with a second grill. The company's first franchise location followed two years later, in 1972. Revenues for the company topped $1 million in 1974. A year later it went public.

The 500th location opened in Toronto in 1976 and was also the first international location. The 1,500th location was in San Juan, Puerto Rico, in 1979. On its 10th anniversary, there were 1,767 locations in the U.S., Canada, Puerto Rico, and Europe. The company also began diversifying its menu by adding a salad bar, something that is still a big draw today. The company passed the 2,000th store mark in 1980, and the 2,500th location was opened just three years later. In 1983, Wendy's became the first national chain to introduce a baked potato to the menu. The 3,000th location opened in 1985.

Wendy's made another bold menu change in 1989 by offering nine items for 99 cents each. Then in 1990, it introduced a chicken sandwich. Dave Thomas' book, *Dave's Way*, was published, in 1991, with the proceeds donated to a national adoption awareness program. The 4,000th restaurant was opened in 1992. Thomas' second book, *Well Done*,

This Snoopy and Peanuts gang item is from 1998.

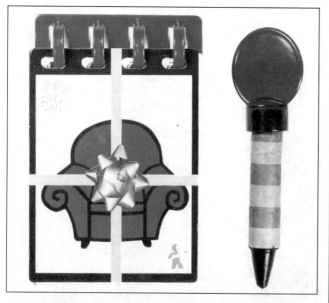

The very popular Nick Jr. series "Blues Clues" came to Wendy's in 1998.

This Felix set appeared at Wendy's in 1997.

Here are two of the many Carmen Sandiego kid meal items from Wendy's. These toys came out in 1996.

was published in 1994, with the proceeds going to the Dave Thomas Foundation for Adoption. By the company's 25th anniversary in 1994, there were over 4,400 locations.

In 1995, the company merged with Tim Hortons, a Canadian-based coffee and fresh-baked goods chain, and in 1997 Thomas opened the 5,000th location, back in Columbus, Ohio.
On the toy front:

In 1996 and 1997, Wendy's issued a pair of Felix the Cat toy sets — one each year. In 1996, the company issued a set of five 3-D comic books with 3-D glasses that were drawn by Neal Adams' studio

A Wendy's Cool Kids meal bag from 1999.

(with art by Adams himself). These comics were classic literature stories told in a comic book format. In addition, the inimitable Carmen Sandiego has made many return appearances at Wendy's.

Wendy's Toy Listing

All prices are for items mint in package (MIP), unless otherwise noted.

Where applicable, the date(s) of distribution and additional information on the following premiums were provided by the individual chains.

No Year

Spoon Tippers (PVC figures)

Frog	6.00
Alligator	6.00
Elephant	6.00
Lion	6.00
Beaver	6.00
Turtle	6.00

1983

Invisible Ink Pens (4 colors)
Each 6.00

Glo-in-the-Dark Crazy Ball
Premium 6.00

Spinning Top Game
Each 6.00

Calligraphy Stencil
Each 6.00

Pop-Up Pipe
Each 6.00

Prismatic Stickers
Each 6.00

Pumpkin Games
Each 8.00

Halloween Assorted Premiums

Witch Rocket	10.00
Ghostly Glow Stickers	10.00
Ghostly Pencil Top Eraser	10.00

Wendy's had a ball with this promotion.

Alvin and The Chipmunks
Puffy Stickers 5.00

Christmas (4 puzzle ornaments)
Each ornament.. 5.00

1984

Krazy Straws
Each item... 5.00

Fairy Tale Fun Book
Each book.. 4.00

Heart Pencil
Each item... 4.00

Moodies (PVC figurines)
Happy... 10.00
Superstar 10.00
Angry.. 10.00
Worried 10.00
Sad... 10.00
Extravagant.. 10.00
Innocent.. 10.00
Ornery... 10.00
Stickers... 10.00
Wobblers... 10.00

Bunny Trail Game
Game 8.00

Bike License Plate
License Plate 5.00

Pop-Up Paint Set
Paint Set 5.00

Press 'n Pop Toy
Premium.. 5.00

Wendy's Kaleidoscope
Kaleidoscope 5.00

Scoop 'n' Basket
Premium.. 5.00

Space Shuttle Replica
Replica 5.00

Vacation Fun Book
Book.. 5.00

Dino eggs were hatching at Wendy's in 1997. Inside each egg was a very cool skeleton of a dinosaur.

Kid-Size Flying Saucer
Saucer 5.00

Back-To-School
Ruler 4.00
Schooltime Fun Stickers 4.00

Where's The Beef (puffy stickers)
Any of the 6 sticker sets 6.00

Grabber
Premium 5.00

Ted E. Bear
Stickers..4.00
Coloring Poster 4.00

Huddles
Sticker Kit 4.00

1985

Good Stuff Gang
Fun & Games Book 4.00
Plastic Cup 4.00
Stickers..4.00

Design-A-Sticker
Sticker Kit 4.00

Brush-Tip Markers
Markers..4.00

Wide Eyes
Premium 4.00

Favorite Stickers
Stickers..4.00

Erase A Slate
Premium 4.00

Sesame Street
Storybook 5.00
"Follow That Bird" Plastic Cup 5.00

Magic Motion Nose Card
Cards...4.00

New Sticker Game
Premium 5.00

Flip-M Game
Game..5.00

Hungry Hound
Card Game 5.00

1986

Fun Stampers
Premium 4.00

Create-a-Card
Premium 4.00

Good Stuff Gang PVC Figurines
Sweet Stuff 5.00
Overstuff'd 5.00
Lite Stuff 5.00
Cool Stuff...5.00
Hot Stuff...5.00
Wendy 5.00

Gummi Bear (assorted premiums)
Drinking Cup..4.00

If you were looking for Mrs. Sandiego, you could find her hanging out at Wendy's in 1996.

Poster.. 4.00
Straws.. 4.00

Go Bots
Beaner/Sportscar 9.00
Sky-Fly/Jet 9.00
Breeze/Helicopter 9.00
Pow-Wow/Camper 9.00
Odd Ball/Monster 9.00
Fun Patches 9.00
Ruler-Stencil 9.00
Color Activity Book 9.00
Sticker Fun Book 9.00

Learn Our Land
Sticker Maps 4.00

Wendy & Good Stuff Gang
Coloring Poster w/Crayons 4.00

Good Stuff Gang
Shrinky Dinks 4.00

1987

Animal Cup Hangers
Premiums... 4.00

Pick-A-Pet
Gallery Posters 4.00

Create-a-Card
Kit/Starters 4.00

Tom Thumb Plant Starter Kits
Impatiens Seed Packet....................... 4.00
Tomatoes Seed Packet....................... 4.00
Green Peppers Seed Packet 4.00
Daisies Seed Packet........................... 4.00
Marigolds Seed Packet....................... 4.00
Zinnias Seed Packet........................... 4.00
Thyme Seed Packet............................ 4.00
Lettuce Seed Packet 4.00

Teddy Ruxpin
Plastic Drinking Cups......................... 4.00

Land of Grundo
Plastic Snack Bowls........................... 4.00

Teddy Ruxpin Poseable Figures
Teddy Ruxpin 6.00
Grubby 6.00

Newton Gimmic 6.00
Wooly What's It 6.00
Fob 6.00

Bristle Blocks
Premium 4.00

Potato Head Kids
Girl Mouse 5.00
Girl Bunny 5.00
Little Girl 5.00
Witch...5.00
Swashbuckler 5.00
Buccaneer 5.00
King 5.00
Princess...5.00
Knight 5.00
Football Player....................................5.00
Boy Moose 5.00
Girl Sheep...5.00
Pirate 5.00
Nurse 5.00
Baseball Player 5.00
Policeman..5.00
Fireman 5.00

Furskins
Storybook 4.00

Furskins on the Tear Britches Trail
Board game 4.00

Furskins 7" Dolls
Dudley 9.00
Boone 9.00
Farrell 9.00
Hattie 9.00
Fanny Fae 9.00
Jedgar..9.00
Orville 9.00
Furskins book 5.00

1988

Wendy and The Goodstuff Gang
Create-A-Scene Sticker Sets, each....................4.00
Collectible Figurines, each 6.00

Wendy and The Goodstuff Gang Plant A Spring Garden
Aster Seed Packet...............................4.00
Peppermint Seed Packet.....................4.00
Tomato Seed Packet 4.00
Green Pepper Seed Packet.................4.00
Daisy Seed Packet..............................4.00

Willow Magic Cups
Eborsisk Cup 5.00
Cherkubdrea Cup................................5.00
Madmartigan Cup................................5.00
Raziel Cup 5.00

Definitely Dinosaurs I Rubber Figures
Triceratops...6.00
Apatosaurus 6.00
Tyrannosaurus.....................................6.00
Anatosaurus 6.00

Potato Head Kids Are Back Plastic Toys

Cap'n Kid 4.00
Duke 4.00
Sparky 4.00
Krispy 4.00
Slugger 4.00
Sophie 4.00

World Wildlife Fund Meal (plush animals)

Panda 4.00
Snow Leopard 4.00
Koala 4.00
Bengal Tiger 4.00

World Wildlife Fund (books)

All About Tigers 3.00
All About Pandas 3.00
All About Snow Leopards 3.00
All About Koalas 3.00

1989

Laser Slates

Jan. 16 – Feb. 19

Seek & Find 3.00
Draw a Face 3.00
Tic-Tac-Toe 3.00
Outer Space 3.00
Animals 3.00
Costumes 3.00
Maze 3.00
Words 3.00

Mighty Mouse Clinger Characters (figurines w/ suction cups)

Scrappy 7.00
The Cow 7.00
Pearl Pureheart 7.00
Mighty Mouse 7.00
Bat Bat 7.00
Petey Pete 7.00

Wendy and The Good Stuff Gang (laser slates)

Hidden Words Slate 5.00
Draw-A-Face Slate 5.00
Tic-Tac-Toe Slate 5.00
Beings From Another Planet Slate 5.00
Animals At The Zoo Slate 5.00
Make-A-Word Slate 5.00
Let's Pretend Slate 5.00
The Maze Slate 5.00

Glo Friends (Playskool finger puppets)

Butterfly 5.00
Clutterbug 5.00
Bashfulbug 5.00
Doodlebug 5.00
Bookbug 5.00
Bopbug 5.00
Snail 5.00
Snugbug 5.00
Cricket 5.00
Grannybug 5.00
Skunkbug 5.00

Mighty Mouse Clinger Characters (figures w/ suction cups)

Scrappy 5.00

An inflatable beach toy from Wendy's made the scene in 1991.

The Cow 5.00
Pearl Pureheart 5.00
Mighty Mouse 5.00
Bat Bat 5.00
Petey Pete 5.00

Jetsons Special Edition Space Vehicles

George in round space ship 5.00
Jane in triangular space ship 5.00
Elroy in star-shaped space ship 5.00
Judy in round space ship 5.00
Mister Spacely in triangular space ship 5.00
Astro 5.00

Definitely Dinosaurs II (rubber figurines)

Parasaurolophus 5.00
Ceratosaurus 5.00
Stegosaurs 5.00
Ankylosaurus 5.00
Apatosaurus 5.00
Triceratops 5.00

All Dogs Go To Heaven (PVC figurines)

Charlie 6.00
Flo 6.00
Itchy 6.00
Anne Marie 6.00
Car Face 6.00
King Gator 6.00

Play-Doh Fingles (tub of dough and mold)

Cat Mold 5.00
Pumpkin Mold 5.00
Monster Mold 5.00
Ghost Mold 5.00
Bat Mold 5.00

Witch Mold 5.00
Complete Box 35.00

1990

Alien Mix-Ups (PVC figurines)
Blu-Zoid 5.00
Yellow-Boid 5.00
Crimson-Oid 5.00
Spotta-Soid 5.00
Purpar-Poid 5.00
Lime-Toid 5.00

Fast Food Racers (plastic food items w/wheels)
Frosty Flyer 4.00
Potato Peeler 4.00
Salad Scrambler 4.00
French Fry Raider 4.00
Single Sizzler 4.00
Kids Meal 4.00

Yogi Bear and Friends (glider figurines)
Yogi 6.00
Snagglepuss 6.00
Ranger Smith 6.00
Boo Boo 6.00
Cindy Bear 6.00
Huckleberry Hound 6.00

Jetsons (space gliders)
Astro 6.00
Elroy 6.00
Fergie 6.00
Grunchie 6.00
Judy 6.00
Premium #6 .... 6.00

Super Sky Carriers
(Vehicles that combine to make one large carrier.)
#1 Front Bottom 6.00
#2 Back Bottom................................... 6.00
#3 Front Top 6.00
#4 Back Top 6.00
#5 Starboard Wing 6.00
#6 Port Wing 6.00

Jetsons The Movie
Astro on purple scooter....................... 7.00
Elroy on blue scooter 6.00

Wendy's loved that magical cat, Felix, and invited him back again and again. At far right is a toy from the 1997 collection. The other two are from '96.

Fergie on pink scooter 6.00
Grunchie on green scooter 6.00
Judy on yellow scooter 6.00
George on red scooter 6.00

Jetsons The Movie Beverage cups
Each 5.00

ALF Tales (PVC figures)
The Three Pigs 4.00
Robin Hood...4.00
Flying Carpet 4.00
Sir Lancelot..4.00
Little Red Riding Hood............................4.00
Sleeping Beauty 4.00
Set of 6 ....22.00

Micro Machines Sky Carriers
Aug. 13 – Sept. 23
Sky Carrier 1 ....4.00
Sky Carrier 2 ....4.00
Sky Carrier 3 ....4.00
Sky Carrier 4 ....4.00
Sky Carrier 5 ....4.00
Sky Carrier 6 ....4.00

Halloween Play-Doh Fingles
Sept. 24 – Nov. 4
Pumpkin..4.00
Ghost 4.00
Cat 4.00
Monster..4.00
Bat 4.00
Witch 4.00

1991

Balls (stuffed toy balls)
Soccer Ball 4.00
Baseball...4.00
Football 4.00
Basketball...4.00

Sarus Sport Balls
Dec. 31 – Apr. 14
Footballasarus 4.00
Baseballasarus 4.00
Soccerasarus...4.00
Basketballasarus 4.00

Neon Pocket Paks
Apr. 15 – June 21
Drawstring Bag w/Keychain.....................3.00
Barrel Bag w/Keychain 3.00
Backpack w/Keychain.............................3.00
Wrist Bag 3.00

Summer Fun Sun Gear
June 3 – July 28
Bicycle Cap..3.00
Solar Wrap...3.00
Beach Bag 3.00
Inflatable Sky Saucer.............................3.00
Inflatable Pouch.....................................3.00

Speed Writers
July 29 – Sept. 15
Blue 3.00
Orange...3.00

Black/Chrome 3.00
Green 3.00
Pink 3.00
Red 3.00

Silly Sippers
Sept. 16 – Nov. 3
Dog Mask 4.00
Pig Mask 4.00
Funny Lips Mask 4.00
Lips w/Tongue Mask 4.00
Mustache Mask 4.00

Wacky Wind-Ups
Nov. 4 – Dec. 29
Hamburger Chomps & Walks 4.00
Spinning Frosty 4.00
Bouncing Hamburger in Box 4.00
Potato Rocks & Walks 4.00
Fries Wobbles & Walks 4.00

1992

Wild Games
Dec. 30 – Feb. 23
Ski Pinball Game 5.00
Target Shoot Pinball Game 5.00
Fry Box Aqua Catch 5.00
Food Fun Aqua Catch 5.00
Basketball Set 5.00

Speed Bumpers
Feb. 24 – Apr. 12
Purple 3.00
Yellow 3.00
Light Blue 3.00
Dark Blue 3.00
Dark Pink 3.00

Tricky Tints
Apr. 13 – June 7
12 oz. Water Bottle 6.00
Set of 3 Straws 6.00
Iron-on Patch 6.00
Plastic Visor 6.00
Shoe Laces 6.00

Gear Up!
June 8 – July 26
Saddle Bag 3.00
Handlebar Streamers 3.00
Reflector Wrist Band 3.00
License Plate w/Stickers 3.00
Water Bottle 3.00

RocketWriters
July 27 – Sept. 20
Purple 3.00
Yellow 3.00
Pink 3.00
Green 3.00
Blue 3.00

Too Cool! For School
Sept. 21 – Nov. 8
Hamburger Notepad 3.00
Pencil Pouch w/Ruler 3.00
French Fry Address Book 3.00

Felix began appearing in Wendy's promotions beginning in 1995.

Frosty Sharpener/Eraser 3.00
Pickle Pen 3.00

Dino Games
Nov. 9 – Jan. 3
Go Fish Dinos Card Game 5.00
Dino Catch Game 5.00
Dino Jam Basketball Pinball Game 5.00
Dino Maze Game 5.00
Dino Obstacle Course Game 5.00

1993

Animal glass hangers
(Various colorful animals designed to hang on the edge of a drinking glass. Also distributed by Sonic Drive-In.)
Frog 3.00
Bird 3.00
Bear 3.00
Alligator 3.00
Beaver 3.00
Pig 3.00
Elephant 3.00
Turtle 3.00
Lion 3.00

Fun Sips — Silly Drinking Straws
Jan. 4 – Feb. 21
Spiral Straw 3.00
Connector Straw (Style A) 3.00
Buddy Straw 3.00
Connector Straw (Style B) 3.00
Glasses Straw 3.00

Unbelievably Fun Objects
Feb. 22 – Apr. 11
Glow-in-the-Dark Moon Ball 3.00
Comet Ball 3.00
Glow-in-the-Dark Inflatable Globe 3.00
Squishy Saturn Ball 3.00
Satellite Sucker Ball 3.00

Kids' Meal Arts
Apr. 12 – June 6
Hamburger Paint Set 5.00
Finger Crayons 5.00
Hamburger Crayon Puzzle 5.00
Frosty Pen/Marker Combo 5.00
French Fry Chalk 5.00

Kids 4 Parks
June 7 – July 25
Water Bottle 3.00
Compass...3.00
Magnifying Glass 3.00
Belt Pouch...3.00
Nature's Notes Journal 3.00

WeirdWriters
July 26 – Sept. 19
Green...3.00
Pink 3.00
Blue..3.00
Orange..3.00
Yellow..3.00

Glo-Ahead
Sept. 20 – Nov. 7
Slime Glasses...3.00
Pull-Back Head Racers.......................................3.00
Sucker Figurine 3.00
Flyer Disc & Vinyl Target...................................3.00
Re-usable Stickers 3.00

Endangered Animal Games
Nov. 8 – Jan. 2
Catch Game-Eagles Nest 5.00
Tiger Pinball Game 5.00
Double Maze Game 5.00
Crazy Eights Deck of Cards...............................5.00
Mini Puzzle..5.00

1994

Drinking Tubes
Jan. 3 – Feb. 13
Cup Wrap Straw..3.00
Color Change Connector Straw A....................3.00
Color Change Connector Straw B....................3.00
Trumpet Connector Straw 3.00
Rainbow Straw 3.00

Cybercycles
Feb. 14 – Apr. 3
Eagle Style...5.00
Lightning Style 5.00
Dragon Style 5.00
Techno Style 5.00
Shark Style...5.00

A motorized cycle roared into Wendy's in 1996.

3-D Classic Comics
Apr. 4 – May 29
Treasure Island w/pink glasses 3.00
Robin Hood w/silver glasses 3.00
Call of the Wild w/purple glasses....................3.00
King Arthur w/green glasses 3.00
Swiss Family Robinson w/blue glasses............3.00

Sun Patrol
May 30 – July 24
Sailboat Drink Holder..3.00
Beach Ball 3.00
Cap 3.00
Fish Shape Water Bottle......................................3.00
Pocket Comb...3.00

Write & Sniff
July 25 – Sept. 18
Cowboy w/leather scent 3.00
Baseball Player w/grass scent...........................3.00
Fireman w/smoke scent.......................................3.00
Hiker w/pine scent 3.00
Beauty Queen w/rose scent 3.00

Carmen Sandiego
Sept. 19 – Nov. 13
Cup w/Secret Compartment 4.00
Ruler/Periscope 4.00
Magnifying Glass/Pen..4.00
Passport/Travel Kit 4.00
Book/Secret Binoculars 4.00

Good Sports
Nov. 14 – Jan. 1
Football Game 5.00
Golf Game 5.00
Basketball Game 5.00
Bowling Game 5.00
Hockey Game...5.00

1995

Make Room
Jan. 2 – Feb. 5
Photo Frame...3.00
Poster Calendar w/stickers 3.00
Door Knob Hanger w/5 paper insert signs......................3.00
Suction Cup Message Pad 3.00

Techno Tows
Feb. 6 – Mar. 19
Shovel Tow 3.00
3-Wheeler 3.00
Tow Truck 3.00
Boat Car 3.00

3-D Color Classics
Mar. 20 – May 7
(Produced by Continuity Comics & drawn, in part, by Neal Adams.)
20,000 Leagues Under the Sea.........................5.00
Gulliver's Travels 5.00
Peter Pan..5.00
The Time Machine 5.00
The Elephant's Child 5.00

Bike Trax
May 8 – June 25
Water Bottle 3.00

Two Reflectors 3.00
Helmet Stickers (3 pages)......................... 3.00
Bike Pack 3.00
Bike Sign 3.00

Ball Players
June 26 – Aug. 6
Baseball Player 3.00
Football Player 3.00
Basketball Player 3.00
Tennis Player 3.00

Animalinks
Aug. 7 – Sept. 24
Monkey 3.00
Octopus.. 3.00
Giraffe 3.00
Alligator 3.00
Doggy.. 3.00

Surprize
Sept. 25 – Nov. 12
Pullback Dino Car 3.00
Washable Tattoos 3.00
Froggie Squirt Toy 3.00
Pullback Turtle 3.00
Inflatable Pterodactyl 3.00
Dino Mechanical Puppet 3.00
Critter Rummy Cards 3.00
Clam Telescope 3.00
Felix the Cat Milk Cap Set 4.00

Mega Wheels
Nov. 13 – Dec. 31
Rock Star Car 3.00
Western Wonder 3.00
50s Flash 3.00
Rock Star Car 3.00
Wave Wagon... 3.00

1996

Laser Knights
Jan. 1 – Feb. 11
King... 3.00
Queen 3.00
Tank Warrior 3.00
Dragon 3.00

Felix the Cat
Feb. 12 – Mar. 24
Stuffed Toy 4.00
Story Board, Drawing Sheet & Stylus 4.00
Ask Felix Toy 4.00
Zoetrope (an animation wheel) 4.00
Milk Caps & Container 4.00

Screamin' (3-D Color)
Mar. 25 – May 5
Nature 2.50
Fun Facts 2.50
Extreme Sports 2.50
Wild Rides.. 2.50
Adventures 2.50

Where in the World is Carmen Sandiego
May 6 – June 16
Travel Kit 3.50
Gum Pack/Compass 3.50

Apple/Decoder..3.50
Flashlight/Telescope 3.50
Travel Viewer/Spy Mirror 3.50

Sharks
June 17 – July 28
Inflatable Shark Toy 3.00
Inflatable Shark Viewer 3.00
Shark Pump Squirt Toy 3.00
Shark Wallet 3.00
Shark Water Bottle.....................................3.00

Way 2 Go
July 29 – Sept. 8
Travel Match Game 2.50
Water Bottle 2.50
Belt Pouch 2.50
Postcard Booklet w/pencil 2.50
Travel Log w/Stickers.................................2.50

Wishbone
Sept. 9 – Oct. 20
Book Viewer 2.50
Earth Digger 2.50
Pen 2.50
Photobook w/removable stickers 2.50
Collector Cards 2.50

Cartoons
Oct. 21 – Nov. 24
Hot Rod 2.50
Bump n Go 2.50
Police Car 2.50
Split Apart 2.50

Robot Games
Nov. 25 – Dec. 29
Volcano Game 3.00
Fall in Hole Game 3.00
Top & Track Game 3.00
Pinball Game 3.00

1997

Club Cave
Dec. 30 – Feb. 9
Pick Up Bones 2.50

More Felix toys showed up later in 1996.

Sundial Toy 2.50
Dino Skeleton... 2.50
Dino Bank 2.50

Felix the Cat
Feb. 20 – Mar. 23
Felix Pattern Shoe Laces....................... 2.50
Felix Catch Game 2.50
Adjustable Felix Trophy 2.50
Stuffed Felix Toy 2.50
3-D Lenticular Puzzle............................. 2.50

Sonic Cycles
Mar. 24 – May 4
Spider Cycle 2.50
Horse Cycle 2.50
Rocket Cycle.. 2.50
Flame Cycle 2.50
Dolphin Cycle 2.50

Bruno the Kid
May 5 – June 15
Ankle/Wrist Pack................................... 2.50
Balancing Plane 2.50
Sunscreen Squirter 2.50
Pencil/Pen Decoder 2.50
Binocular Car 2.50
Turbo Craft 2.50

Cycle On
June 16 – July 27
License Plate 2.50
Stickers 2.50
Water Bottle 2.50
Wrist Reflector 2.50
Bike Bag.. 2.50

Kratts' Creatures
July 28 – Sept. 7
Jeep Freeroller 2.50
Nature Microscope 2.50
Field Utensil.. 2.50
Collector Cards...................................... 2.50
Wind-Up Flipping Ape............................. 2.50

American Youth Soccer Organization
Sept. 8 – Oct.19
Water Bottle 3.00
Kicker Game 3.00
Footbag 3.00
Collector Cards...................................... 3.00
Inflatable Soccer Ball............................. 3.00

Dexter's Laboratory
Oct. 20 – Nov. 23
Robotic Arm 3.00
Color Change Straw 3.00
Pen & Straw... 3.00
Remote Viewer Sparker 3.00
Glo Monster 3.00

Pinky & the Brain (Warner Bros.)
Nov. 24 – Jan. 4
Red Reveal TV 3.00
Note Pad w/Pencil 3.00
Brain Lab 3.00
Popper Spacecraft................................. 3.00
Mind Control Machine............................. 3.00

1998

Blues Clues
Pad & Special Marker.............................. 3.00
Other Items 3.00

The Peanuts Gang
Each Item 3.00

Soft Throwing Balls (several colors)
Yellow 3.00
Blue 3.00
Other colors 3.00

1999

Cartoon Network Character Cars
May
Jetson's Pullback Car 3.00
Alligator Sticker Car 3.00
Yogi Bear Freeroller............................... 3.00
Dexter Popper Car.................................. 3.00
Tom & Jerry Bump & Go Car 3.00
Toy Truck (under-3) 3.00

SnowBoard
Wristpack... 2.50
Snowboard Stickers................................ 2.50
Snowboarders 2.50
Ejector & Ramp 2.50

Bobby's World Rocket Car (not related to Fox-TV's Bobby's World)
Feb. 8
Basketball game 2.50
Puzzle.. 2.50
Memory Game... 2.50

Dave Thomas had his own "bag of tricks" when he offered Felix the Cat toys in 1996.

Robot 2.50
Chair 2.50
Toy (under-3).. 3.00

Tiny Toons Adventures
March 22
3-D Photo Frame (Tiny Toon Gang)................................. 2.50
Gyroscope (Dizzy Devil) 2.50
Hook-Ups (Buster & Babs).. 2.50
Red Reveal X-Ray Machine.. 2.50
U-3 Plucky's Bathtub Toy 2.50

Cartoon Network's Wacky Racing
May 3
Alligator Sticker Car 2.50
Dexter Popper Car... 2.50
Jetson's Pullback Car 2.50
Tom & Jerry's Bump & Go Car..................................... 2.50
Yogi Bear Freeroller 2.50
Toy Truck 2.50

Cartoon Network Johnny Bravo
Wrist Catch Game.. 2.50
Flipper Toy 2.50
Cool Sunglasses 2.50
Johnny Bravo Fun Kit.. 2.50
Bowling Game.. 2.50
Crazy Animal Book (under-3)..................................... 3.00

Muppets from Space (Disney movie tie-in)
Voice Changer 2.00
Gonzo Sparker 2.00
Activity Book 2.00
Kermit Keychain Clip.. 2.00
Bus Viewer 2.00
Gonzo Puzzle (under-3) 2.00

Eerie
Sept. 6
Hopping Eyeball and Skeleton Pen 2.50
Eerie Puzzle.. 2.50
Message Door Hanger 2.50
The Evidence Locker 2.50

CLUE Classic
Alias I.D. Kit 2.00
Red Reveal Game 2.00
Pocket Watch Magnifier 2.00
Modern Professor Magazine 2.00
Magnet Puzzle Game/Magnet Wand w/Sticker 2.00
Secret Safe (under-3) 2.00
Helicopter.. 2.00

2000

Snoopy 2000
Helicopter Snoopy... 2.50
Key Chain Snoopy 2.50
Time Capsule.. 2.50
Snoopy Wind-up 2.50
Light-Up Desktop Calendar....................................... 2.50
Toy Snoopy & Me Photo Album (under-3) 2.50

Wildlife
Magnetic Frog 2.00
Tropical Fish Coin Purse.. 2.00
Tiger Key Chain 2.00

This 3-D comic book was part of a 1996 Wendy's promotion.

Bean Bag Bee 2.00
U3 Cardinal Finger Puppet 2.00

Big Cartoonie Program
Feb. 7 – Mar. 19
Ask Babs 2.50
Wackko Snap-together Ladder 2.50
Yakko Wobbler... 2.50
Pinky's Brain Mini Globe.. 2.50
Phone Book w/5 pages of stickers 2.50
Purple Push-Along Train Engine w/pictures that spin
    around (under-3).. 2.50

Hasbro Classic Clip-On's
Trivial Pursuit Jr. 2.00
Hungry Hungry Hippo 2.00
Tonka dump truck 2.00
Play-Doh can 2.00
Frosty Mixer Truck (No-clip, under-3)........................... 2.00

Schwinn
Sunglasses 1.50
Card Game 1.50
Ankle Pack.. 1.50
Water Bottle 1.50
Biker (under-3)... 1.50
Stickers 1.50

Snoopy 50th Anniversary
Air Globe w/confetti 2.50
Clip-on 2.50
Jigsaw Puzzle (2-sided)... 2.50
Flying Ace Magnet 2.50
Key Ring/Clock 2.50
Wobbling Doghouse 2.50

White Castle

Company Profile

E.W. Ingram and Walt Anderson founded White Castle in 1921 in Wichita, Kansas. The company's corporate offices were moved to Columbus, Ohio in 1934. The chain was the first fast-food hamburger restaurant chain. Many individuals consider White Castle to have made fast food acceptable by using 100 percent U.S. beef in its hamburgers.

Currently, there are more than of 315 White Castle locations in operation. With franchises in Chicago, Cincinnati, Dayton, Columbus, Cleveland, Detroit, Indianapolis, Kansas City, Minneapolis/St. Paul, Louisville, Lexington, Nashville, New Jersey, New York City, St. Louis and Philadelphia.

In 1997, gross sales for the chain exceeded $384 million. The company is projecting growth of as many as 10 to 15 new stores per year in existing markets. Money for White Castle expansion comes mainly from available funds, so growth has been controlled and steady. Unlike most of the chain's competition, there are no domestic franchises issued. All of the U.S. units are owned and operated by the family-held company.

Feature Products

The signature White Castle hamburger is 100 percent USDA-inspected beef. Unique in the world of fast-food hamburgers, White Castle serves square hamburgers. The burger itself measures 2-1/2", has five evenly spaced holes, is steam-grilled on a bed of onions, and is served on a soft white-bread bun with a single slice of dill pickle. Church's Chicken products have been marketed in some White Castle restaurants since 1996 and, as of December 1998, were sold at over 70 locations.

It has been observed that White Castle customers are so loyal to the chain that on more than one occasion people who moved from a White Castle market to one served only by competitors have called the company to order dozens of the hamburgers to be delivered by air express. The company also claims to have customers who buy burgers "by the sack" to freeze and reheat later at home.

One of the earliest fast-food superheros tie-ins came from White Castle back in 1989.

White Castle Toy Listings

All prices are for items mint in package (MIP), unless otherwise noted.

Where applicable, the date(s) of distribution and additional information on the following premiums were provided by the individual chains.

1986

Color Disks & Stickers
Nov. – Aug.
Any premium from series 6.00

1987

Woolers (All-in-one rulers/bookmarks/stencils)
Aug. – Dec.
Any premium from series 5.00

Stickers & Scenes
Dec. 27 – Jan. 16
Any premium from series 5.00

1988

Castle Cups
Feb. 7 – Feb. 27
Each cup 5.00

Beach Buddy Buckets
April 3 – May 1
Each 4.00

Woozy's Magic Mania Meal Magic Tricks
June 19 – July 9
Each premium 4.00

Fabulous Funshades Sunglasses
July 3 – July 24
Yellow 4.00
Blue 4.00
Red 4.00
Green 4.00

Back To Cool
Aug. 21 – Sept. 10
Pencils 4.00
Tube Totes 4.00
Stripe-writer Crayons 4.00
Other items in set 4.00

Halloween Face Paints
Oct. 2 – Oct. 29
Each premium 4.00

Christmas Giveaways
Nov. 20 – Dec. 31
Any premium 5.00

Woofles & Willis
Woofles the Dog 6.00
Willis the Dragon 6.00
Wilfred 6.00
Other premiums in set..................... 6.00

1989

Fabulous Fun Shades
Yellow... 4.00
Red 4.00
Blue... 4.00
Green 4.00

Magic Pictures
Jan. 1 – Jan. 26
Any premium from series................ 4.00

Cups & Bowls
Feb. 3 – Mar. 2
Each premium.................................. 4.00

Dudley Easter Pals 6" Bendables
Mar. 3 – Mar. 26
Dudley... 7.00
Florence 7.00
Betty 7.00
Peter 7.00
Tommy 7.00

Color Dough
Apr. 7 – May 4
Each premium.................................. 3.50

Character Sippers
May 12 – June 8
Each premium 4.00

Marvel SuperHeroes Pails and Shovels
June 23 – July 20
Spider-Man 7.00
She-Hulk 7.00
Captain America 7.00
Silver Surfer 7.00

Vacu-Form Boats
July 21 – Aug. 31
Any premium.................................... 4.00

All-Star Stuffs By Wilson
Sept. 1 – Sept. 28
Baseball 4.00
Breakfast Bowl 4.00
Cup 1989 .... 4.00
Kids' Cup... 4.00

Bow Biters Plastic Lace Protectors
Oct. 6 – Oct. 31
Masher...4.00
Cat Zooks 4.00
Blue Meany.......................................4.00
Shades..4.00
Purple Had..4.00
Green Machine 4.00

White Castle Characters Plastic Molded Characters
Nov. 1 – Dec. 2
Any premium 6.00

Crayon Racers
Dec. 3 – Dec. 31
Any premium 4.00

911 Castle Meal Friends PVC Figurines
Dec. 31 – Feb. 3
Wendell...5.00
Sir Wencelot 5.00
Woofles...5.00
Princess Wilhelaina 5.00
Willis...5.00
Woozy Wizard 5.00
Set of 6..32.00

1990

Fat Albert & The Cosby Kids PVC Figurines
Feb. 4 – Mar. 10
Fat Albert 15.00
Russell 15.00
Dumb Donald 15.00
Weird Harold................................... 15.00
Set of 4 .... 65.00

Nestle Quik Bunny
Mar. 11 – Apr.14
Bunny Straw Holder..........................5.00
Color Change Spoon 5.00
Color Change Cup 5.00
Plush Nestle Bunny 10.00

Godzilla
Apr. 15 – May 19
Inflatable...7.00
Squirter...7.00
Mini-flyer 7.00
Suction thrower.................................7.00

Camp White Castle Plastic Camp Items
May 20 – July 7
Plate 5.00
Water bottle 5.00
Fork/spoon..5.00
Toothbrush w/case 5.00
Valuables holder 5.00

Totally U Back-To-School School Supplies
Aug. 12 – Sept. 29
Pencil Case 5.00
Wrist Wallet.......................................5.00
Lunch Box..5.00
ID Tag 5.00

PEZ Monsters & Halloween Sack
Sept. 30 – Nov. 10
Any premium from series 5.00

Holiday Huggables Stuffed Toys
Nov. 11– Dec. 29
Teddy Bells.. 4.50
Kitty Lights 4.50
Holly Hog 4.50
Candy Canine 4.50

1991

Growin' Up Fun Hats
Jan. 6 – Feb. 2
Hard Hal 3.00
Slugger.. 3.00
Fire Chief 3.00
Ballerina 3.00

Real Ghostbusters Toiletries
Feb. 4 – March 17
Toothbrush 4.00
Hair Brush 4.00
Ghost Buster Soap/Case 4.00
Slimer Toothpaste 4.00

Shape & Shout Dough
June 3 – July 6
Willis (blue) 3.00
Mold #2 .... 3.00
Mold #3 .... 3.00
Mold #4 .... 3.00
Mold #5 .... 3.00
Mold #6 .... 3.00

Sportsballs Neon Nylon Balls
July 21 – Aug. 31
Any premium.. 4.00

Totally U Back-To-School
Pencil Case 4.00
Pencils 4.00
Ruler 4.00
Name Tag... 4.00

1992

Tootsie Roll Express
Engine.. 7.00
Gondola 7.00
Hopper 7.00
Caboose... 7.00

Stunt Grip Geckos
Purple.. 5.00
Mauve 5.00
Blue... 5.00
Turquoise 5.00

Meal Family
Wobbles & Woom 10.00
Wally 10.00
King Wobbly & Queen................................ 10.00
Wilifred.. 10.00
Friar Wack... 10.00

Meal Family Bubble Makers
Princess Wilhelaina.................................... 10.00
Woozy Wizard 10.00
Wendell.. 10.00
Wilifred.. 10.00

Sir Wincelot 10.00

Wind-up Dudes
Castle Fry Dudette.....................................3.00
Castle Cheese Burger Dude........................3.00
Castle Burger Dude....................................3.00
Castle Drink Dude 3.00

1993

Mix-and-Match Dinosaurs
   (Also distributed by Carl's Jr. and White Castle)
Purple Apatosaurus....................................5.00
Blue Pterodactyl 5.00
Tyranosaurus Rex 5.00
Stegosaurus 5.00

Holiday Train
   (Four-car set with company logo and Dr. Pepper decals on the cars; also distributed by Dairy Queen & Sonic Drive-In)
Engine 3.00
Coal car 3.00
Box car 3.00
Caboose 3.00

Water Pals
Castle Fry Dudette.....................................3.00
Castle Cheese Burger Dude........................3.00
Castle Burger Dude....................................3.00
Castle Drink Dude 3.00

1994

Food Squirters
Castle Fry Dudette.....................................5.00
Castle Cheese Burger Dude........................5.00
Castle Burger Dude....................................5.00
Castle Drink Dude 5.00

Triasic Take-Aparts
Spine-Asaur...4.00
Mega-Asaur..4.00
Cool-Asaur...4.00
Sara-Asaur...4.00

Swat Kats
Razor 3.00
T-Bone 3.00
Castle 3.00

Silly Putty (3-piece set)
Set 3.00

White Castle Bendie
Woofies..5.00
Wabbles..5.00
Woozy Wizard 5.00
Wilifred..5.00

1999

Cool Air Fresheners
May
Very Vanilla...2.00
Bodacious Berry 2.00
Pleasant Pine 2.00

Crave Cups
June
Each cup...2.00

Various Franchises

Obviously, not all fast-food franchise chains are either created equal, or receive an equal share of the kid's meal premium pie. Hence, there are several other operations that offer toys with their meals, but either not much information is available about them, or they simply don't have continuous archive records of those toys. Profiles of these companies are lumped together in this section. Listings for these companies follow the profiles.

Baskin Robbins

Known for its 31 flavors of ice cream and delicious cakes, Baskin Robbins has built a reputation as the place to go for sweet treats. The individual franchise locations not only serve walk-in traffic, but many of them cater parties and will custom make cakes upon request.

Big Boy

Big Boy Restaurant and Bakery

America's Favorite Family Restaurant

The owner of a small California restaurant introduced the original "Big Boy Burger" hamburger in 1936. The burger in this new restaurant was a double-decker hamburger with fresh toppings and a special sauce. It was a few years later that the three Elias brothers from Michigan met with the restaurateur and bought into his company, becoming part of the first family-owned restaurant franchise in the U.S. The chain was renamed, Big Boy Restaurants. In 1987, the Elias clan became the worldwide franchiser of Big Boy Restaurants, Inc.

Blimpie

Launched in Hoboken, New Jersey, in 1964, the submarine sandwich food chain known as Blimpie International has quickly risen to the top of the food

chain by offering quick-service sandwiches and a family of complementary trademarks and marketing concepts. Blimpie International has grown to almost 2,000 outlets with locations in 46 states and 12 foreign countries. The company has a 60 percent interest in the international distribution of Blimpie trademarks, which began in 1995. Traditionally, Blimpie restaurants are located in shopping centers and malls, plus free-standing buildings and downtown markets. New concept locations include conve-

Collect All 4!

This toy has been safety tested for children of all ages. Toy is non-toxic. As with any toy, we suggest you provide guidance to your children regarding proper use. This bag is not a toy. Keep out of reach of children and discard properly.
©1998 BLIMPIE International, Inc. Strottman International, Inc. Made in China. Printed in Hong Kong.

nience stores, gas station food marts, colleges, office complexes, hospitals, and sports arenas. A new distribution format is the company's "Grab 'n Go" refrigeration cases, carts, kiosks, and vending machines.

A sister company to Blimpie is Pasta Central, which exists in the fast-growth "home meal replacement" category and is often co-branded with Blimpie Subs & Salads. In October 1997, Blimpie acquired the trademark and development rights to Maui Tacos, a brand of quick-service restaurants currently servicing Hawaii, and is now attempting to franchise the concept on a global level through majority-owned Maui Tacos International, Inc. Maui Tacos International is also franchising Smoothie Island, a brand serving blended fruit-based beverages. Blimpie International also owns BI Concept Systems, Inc., a professional design and equipment service company. The company is publicly traded on the American Stock Exchange. Blimpies kid meal toys are not only not licensed items, but tend to be re-used from year to year.

Boston Market

Boston Market specializes in quick, convenient meals that feature home-style entrees, fresh vegetables, sandwiches, salads, and side dishes. There were more than 850 Boston Market stores located in 33 states as of March 1999. The Boston Chicken Corp. also owns a majority interest in Einstein/Noah Bagel Corp. According to officials at Boston Chicken, the company only offered kid meal toy promotions for a very brief period of time. In 1998, only one or two sets were issued. Only one set, featuring Casper the Ghost, was ever located. As the program never really caught on with its customers, it was dropped. Boston no longer offers toys or collectible premiums.

Burger Chef

Founded by the Thomas family, Burger Chef grew out of the family's business of following county fairs around and selling milk shakes. Thomas, a mechanical engineer by trade, built a milk shake machine and traveled behind the fairs, selling his wares to the crowds.

Eventually, he and his two sons — who were also graduate engineers — thought that some food to

eat with the shake would be a good selling item, so they added a broiler to cook hamburgers. After a time, their venture became so successful that they decided to settle in one spot and sell the shakes and burgers from a stationary location.

Others soon wanted in on the action, so the Thomas family began building their broiler and franchising it. Soon they were a nationally known operation.

The first restaurant under the Burger Chef name was opened in Indianapolis in 1954. Using the restaurant as a showcase for its line of manufactured products, General Equipment contributed materials to the new endeavor. Especially popular was the gas-fired broiler with a continuously moving conveyor belt. It cooked hamburgers faster than any other known method.

In 1958, eight Burger Chef restaurants were opened in Indiana, Illinois, and Wisconsin. Franchising started, and more restaurants were opened throughout the country. A new corporation, Burger Chef Systems, Inc., was formed. In 1968, General Foods Corp. acquired Burger Chef. Around 1980, Burger Chef was one of the top fast-food chains with restaurants in 36 states.

In 1981, Hardee's acquired the Burger Chef franchise. The takeover was completed in 1982. Each franchise had the option of either becoming a Hardee's, or closing. Many of the Burger Chef owners were given extensions so that they could make the changeover to Hardee's. Many took advantage of this situation and continued to operate as a Burger Chef until 1996. Currently, there are no known Burger Chefs in operation.

Chick-Fil-A

In 1946, after the end of World War II, Truett Cathy sold his car, combined savings with his younger brother, Ben, and borrowed from the bank to acquire the $10,600 to open a tiny, 24-hour restaurant he called the Dwarf Grill (later renamed the Dwarf House) in the Atlanta suburb of Hapeville. As you would expect by its name, the restaurant was very tiny with just 10 counter stools and four tables. It was during the late 1950s that Cathy began experimenting with different seasonings and quicker ways to prepare his great-tasting chicken. By the early 1960s, he had finally developed the winning taste combination that would lead to Chick-Fil-A's success.

Utilizing the right combination of seasonings, he cooked the filleted chicken breasts in peanut oil, with both skin and bones removed, in a pressure cooker. Although it was a simple idea, there was nothing comparable to it on the market at the time.

It was in 1967 that Cathy pioneered the in-mall fast-food quick-service restaurant concept by opening the first Chick-Fil-A location in Atlanta's Greenbriar Mall. Locating his restaurants in malls also gave Cathy a niche that other quick-service restaurants did not have. The mall strategy not only proved to be a solid base, it paid off handsomely. Currently, Chick-Fil-A Chicken sandwiches can be found in over 850 restaurants in 35 states and South Africa. These locations include not just malls, but free-standing units, drive-thru outlets, and full-service restaurants. Chick-Fil-A can be found on college campuses, hospitals, airports, business and industry locations, supermarkets and school cafeterias.

The 1990s proved successful for Truett Cathy as he was named Atlanta's Most Respected CEO by *Business Atlanta* Magazine. The company reached $300 million in sales in 1990, and expansion onto college campuses started in Atlanta at Georgia Tech in 1992. Chick-Fil-A expanded throughout Southern Africa, starting in Durban, South Africa in 1996.

Today, Chick-Fil-A is one of the largest privately held restaurant chains and the third-largest quick-service chicken restaurant company in the US. With the momentum of 50 years of business success behind him, Truett Cathy continues to lead Chick-Fil-A toward its corporate goal of being a billion-dollar company.

Chuck E. Cheese's

Chuck E. Cheese (formerly known as ShowBiz Pizza Time, Inc.) is owned and operated by CEC Entertainment, Inc. This interesting and unique fast-food chain combines a restaurant with an arcade and indoor play area/gym designed especially for younger kids. Children are encouraged to play various games for tickets that can be redeemed for various prizes.

Denny's

It was 1953 when Harold Butler opened Danny's Donuts in Lakewood, California. His success with the location resulted in the opening of more locations. However, it wasn't long before Butler realized that his customers were looking for more than just donuts, so in 1954 he changed the name to Danny's Coffee shops, and expanded his menu to include sandwiches and other food.

In 1959, with about 20 locations, he renamed the chain Denny's. By the end of 1963, there were 78 Denny's operating in seven western states. The company went public in 1966 and international the following year with a location in Acapulco, Mexico. By 1968, at 192 restaurants strong, the chain merged with Sandy's Restaurant and acquired the Pioneer Restaurant chain.

In 1977, Denny's introduced what was to become its most popular meal — the grand slam breakfast. By the time 1981 rolled around, the chain had opened over 1,000 locations all across the U.S. In 1987, Denny's was purchased by TW Services, Inc. (now Advantica Restaurant Group, Inc.), one of the largest restaurant groups in the U.S. The company's headquarters moved from Irvine, California, to Spartanburg, South Carolina, in 1991. By the end of 1997, the chain had over 1,652 locations.

Domino's Pizza

Founded in 1960 by Thomas S. Monaghan, Domino's has maintained a limited menu of traditional-style, hand-tossed pizza. In 1992, the company introduced its first non-pizza product: bread sticks. In 1993, it had a national rollout of its "ultimate deep dish pizza" and its "crunchy thin crust pizza." Buffalo wings, which appeared in 1994, are the newest non-pizza addition to the menu.

In 1996, sales reached $2.8 billion, marking the fourth consecutive year of increased sales. There are currently more than 1,200 franchises operating over 6,000 stores throughout the United States and in 60 international markets.

Unfortunately, due to the company's limited experience with gift-with-purchase toys, there is no official information available in this area. According to an official spokesperson for the company, there has been considerable turnover in corporate marketing during the first part of the 1990s, and very little is known about the successes and/or failures the company may have experienced with such promotions.

Duchess

A small, local, fast-food chain located exclusively in Connecticut, Duchess began as a roadside hot dog stand in the early 1960s, and has, over the years, grown into a string of eat-in restaurants. The chain's menu features hot dogs, hamburgers, and chili, sporting items such as the big "D" burger and

the big "D" dog. The company is headquartered in Milford, Connecticut.

Dunkin' Donuts

Based in Randolph, Massachusetts, Dunkin' Donuts is the largest coffee and donut shop chain in the world. It has served up coffee, donuts, bagels, muffins and other related bakery products since 1950. The franchise currently has close to 5,000 locations in the U.S. and more than 37 other countries.

Dunkin' Donuts USA has been a wholly owned subsidiary of Allied Domecq, PLC since 1990. Allied Domecq is a food and beverage company headquartered in England. Founded by William Rosenberg in 1946, Dunkin' Donuts was originally known as Industrial Luncheon Services. At that time it delivered meals and coffee break snacks to factory workers in the outskirts of Boston. The success of Industrial Luncheon Services led Rosenberg to open his first coffee and donut shop. He called the operation The Open Kettle. It wasn't until 1950 that Rosenberg opened the first Dunkin' Donuts' in Quincy, Massachusetts. He began licensing franchises in 1955.

Dunkin' Donuts has experienced tremendous growth, with sales increasing every year. While each Dunkin' Donuts product is successful in its own right, coffee is Dunkin' Donuts top product. In New England alone, Dunkin' Donuts has doubled its coffee sales in the last five years.

IHOP

The International House of Pancakes (or IHOP) is one of America's best-known family restaurant chains. Although IHOPs are best known for their

award-winning pancakes, omelets and other breakfast specialties, IHOP restaurants are open all day and offer a broad array of lunch, dinner and snack items as well.

More than 90 percent of IHOP restaurants are franchised. There are over 800 IHOP restaurants in 36 states, Canada and Japan. While there is no official corporate toy promotion program, individual franchises do often offer toys with their standard kid meal menu items.

Some have simply purchased inexpensive plastic toys (Groucho Marx glasses have been known to have been distributed), while others simply maintain a token-operated toy machine in the front of the store, and after the meal offer children a token that can be redeemed in the machine.

Long John Silver's

 LONG JOHN SILVER'S

Founded in 1969 as Long John Silver's Fish 'n' Chips, the restaurant was conceived as a way to address the growing interest for quick-service seafood. The franchise has become one of America's largest fast-food seafood chains. Headquartered in Lexington, Kentucky, the company currently has over 1,300 units operating worldwide.

In 1998, Long John Silver went way into the past, to deliver this set of plastic dinosaurs.

Long John Silver's has locations in 35 states as well as Singapore and Thailand and serves approximately 4.6 million guests per week. Annually, the company dishes out some 45 million pounds of fish and 15 million pounds of chicken.

A proud sponsor of the Children's Miracle Network, the company also boasts that all of its packaging is "Earth friendly." The stores are designed to resemble wharf-side buildings with brass lanterns, colorful oars and signal flags.

Orange Julius

A sister fast-food franchise of the International Dairy Queen company (itself a wholly owned subsidiary of Berkshire Hathaway, Inc.), Orange Julius serves hot dogs and blended drinks made from orange juice, fruits, and other fruit flavors. There are some 410 Orange Julius locations worldwide.

Popeye's

Originally called Chicken on the Run, Popeye's has a tradition-rich history. Founded in 1972, the chain celebrated its 25th anniversary in 1997 with cross-country promotions. The first Popeye's restaurants were built with real lava rock to decorate the restaurants' exteriors. Contrary to public perception, Popeye's was not named after the spinach-eating cartoon character, but rather for the real-life police officer turned Hollywood icon, Detective "Popeye" Doyle, from the hit movie *The French Connection*.

Popeye's was founded in New Orleans by Al Copeland, a New Orleans native and entrepreneur who was raised with the tantalizing aromas and flavors of a Cajun kitchen. Popeye's is now the second-largest chicken chain in the nation in terms of sales. Popeye's raises money for Habitat for Humanity through its annual sponsorship of a golf tournament.

Red Lobster

When he was 19, Bill Darden opened his first restaurant in Waycross, Georgia. The place had a 25-by-30-foot lunch counter called The Green Frog. Its motto was "service with a hop." From there, Darden went on to found Red Lobster in Lakeland, Florida.

According to Darden, Red Lobster's success over the years goes beyond great-tasting seafood. He feels that over the past 30-plus years he and his team have satisfied the public's hunger for a restaurant offering quality, service and affordable prices. Red Lobster's success has helped create a new segment for full-service restaurants — casual dining. Today, Red Lobster is the world's leading seafood restaurant company.

7-Eleven

Not a fast-food chain, 7-Eleven is a deli/mini-mart chain with locations primarily on the eastern seaboard. 7-Eleven managed to land its spot in this guide due mostly to a legendary set of drink cups that were issued in the mid-to-late 1970s. The drinks, called Slurpees, were a fruity, frothy, frozen concoction, and proved to be very popular. In 1975, the first of two sets of plastic drink cups featuring various Marvel Comics characters was issued. Other licensed cups followed, including a second larger set of Marvel heroes and villains, as well as a Major League Baseball series featuring numerous players from both leagues.

Sbarro

In the late 1950s, an Italian immigrant, Gennaro Sbarro, along with his wife and three sons, arrived in America looking for an opportunity to succeed in business. He and his family opened up an Italian gourmet delicatessen called Salumeria in Brooklyn, New York.

That company still exists today as the renowned eatery called Sbarro. The company is still under the leadership of his three sons as well as Mama Sbarro. She still operates the Salumeria and is responsible for providing the homemade cheesecake to all stores.

The rich Sbarro tradition of serving quality food made fresh and prepared from established family recipes remains the backbone of the business. Each of the restaurants prepares all menu items on-site every day. Throughout the day, there are pots of simmering sauce, fresh-baked lasagna, baked ziti, calzones, and sausage rolls coming out of their kitchens.

They are also famous for their hand-stretched New York-style pizza. Their servings are generous, and the prices are reasonable. These elements are mixed with a passion for friendly service and absolute cleanliness. Sbarro usually delivers great value for the money.

Today, there are over 800 Sbarro Eateries all over the world. Sbarro has locations in the United States, Australia, Belgium, Canada, Chile, France, Israel, Kuwait, Lebanon, the Philippines, Puerto Rico, Qatar, Saudi Arabia, and the United Kingdom. Sbarro didn't begin serving kid's meal and toy combinations until December of 1998, but has had success with the program and plans on continuing to issue toys with their kid's meals.

Whataburger

Whataburger grew steadily from its first stand in 1950. By 1978, the company opened its 200th location. There were some 300 Whataburger locations by 1980

and a total of 500 by 1995. It was in 1995 that Whataburger was ranked No. 1 in same-store sales for top 100 chains ranked by growth of sales per unit by *Nation's Restaurant News*. The key to the franchise's success has always been its loyal customers, and the employees whose service kept them coming back.

Today's Whataburger is made much the same as the original — a grilled quarter-pound patty of 100 percent beef served on a 5-inch bun with an ample sprinkling of lettuce, three slices of tomato, four dill pickles, chopped onions, mustard, salad dressing or ketchup. As was the original, today's Whataburger is built-to-order.

Various Franchises Toy Listings

The following list groups together several operations offering toys with their meals. The listings are lumped together because there is either not enough information available relating to the individual chains or the chains simply don't have continuous archive records of toys issued.

All prices are for items mint in package (MIP), unless otherwise noted.

Where applicable, the date(s) of distribution and additional information on the following premiums were provided by the individual chains.

Baskin-Robbins
1991

Pinkie the Spoon

Bendable Pinkie the Spoon	4.00

Big Boy
1990

Big Boy PVC Characters

Skater	5.00
Pitcher	5.00
Surfer	5.00
Race driver	5.00
Set of 4	22.00

Fruit People Toys

(Small plastic or rubber toys shaped like fruit.)

Blueberry	3.00
Strawberry	3.00
Grape	3.00

Playground Toys

Sandbox	3.00
Slide	3.00
Swing	3.00
Teeter-totter	3.00

Grimm PVC Figures

Grimm playing guitar ("Dog Aid")	4.00
Grimm w/dog food dish	4.00
Grimm sitting	4.00
Grimm w/leash	4.00
Grimm w/open arms	4.00
Grimm w/sign "Fleas on Board"	4.00

1999

Various Over-the-Counter Items

Big Boy Pin	5.00
Big Boy Puzzle	7.00
Big Boy Travel Cup	7.00

Blimpie's
1996

Simpson Street Chalk

Homer (Blue)	2.50
Marge	2.50
Bart	2.50

1998

Wacky Dough (4 colors)

Green	2.50
Red	2.50
Yellow	2.50
Color #4	2.50

Spaceballs

Moon	2.50
Earth	2.50
Mars	2.50
Jupiter	2.50
Saturn	2.50
Neptune	2.50

Totem Pal Friends

Frog...2.50
Beaver...2.50
Bear...2.50
Eagle...2.50

Doodle Top, Jr.

Pink..2.50
Purple..2.50
Green...2.50
Blue..2.50

1999

Wacky Dough (4 colors)
Each...2.50

Spaceballs (6 "planets")
Each...2.50

Totem Pal Friends (4 animals)
Each...2.50

Doodle Top, Jr. (4 tops)
Each...2.50

Boston Market
1991

Helicopters (plastic)
Fire Department...4.00
Ambulance...4.00
Police..4.00

1998

Casper the Friendly Ghost
Item #1..3.00
All other items in set...3.00

Burger Chef

(Much of this list was graciously provided by Paul Browning. Visit his unofficial Burger Chef Web site: www.burgerchef.com.)

1960s

Playing Cards w/picture of pre-'70s Burger Chef on reverse
side 5.00

Pinbacks – Family Circus (buttons)
Daddy...4.00
Jeffy..4.00
Dolly..4.00
Billy...4.00
PJ..4.00
Mommy...4.00

Blimpie issued a set of five planets and Earth's moon in 1998. The other four planets and moons were left out.

Blimpie tends to create its own items, then recycle them. Here are a few examples of their critters from the mid and late 1990s.

Family Circus Comic Book (May have been part of the Pinback collection.) 4.00
Kite — Super Shef Kite (Classic diamond shape advertising the Super Shef sandwich.)...........................3.00

Coin — Wooden Nickel
(Gave patrons 5 cents off any purchase made in a Burger Chef.)
Style #1..5.00
Style #2..5.00

Hand Puppets
Character with a hamburger for a head. (Character unknown) 10.00
Character used in the logo during the '60s....................10.00

1970s

Family Classics Cards
(There were more than 90 cards in the series featuring scenes from numerous animated series.)
Arabian Nights 3.00
Swiss Family Robinson 3.00
Tom Sawyer...3.00
Snow White 3.00
Cinderella 3.00
Hiawatha..3.00
Puss-In-Boots..3.00
Johnny Appleseed 3.00
Paul Bunyan 3.00
All others..3.00

Hand Puppets
Burgerilla has Burgerilla character on it...................5.00
Burgerini has Burgerini character on it 5.00

T-Strip Racers
(Cars featured a large rear wheel that turned when you pulled a T-strip through it. Various colors.)
Model A 5.00
Model B 5.00

Wacky dough was a prize to have from Blimpie in 1998.

Record Monster Fun Records
Transylvania's Big Game 4.00
Wolfeburger's Problem 4.00
Cackleburger Casts a Spell 4.00
The Ghost of Grizzly Mountain 4.00
Fangburger's Haunted Hotel 4.00
Crankenburger, the Super Salesman 4.00

Iron-Ons Build a Burger
(Iron-ons that let you build a sandwich on your shirt.)
Bashful Buns 4.00
Chompin' Cheese Patty 4.00
Crying Onions 4.00
Mighty Mustard 4.00
Puckering Pickles 4.00
Tempting Tomatoes 4.00

Riddler
Toy that has several riddles with answers on a wheel you
turn 4.00

Window Clingers (2" x 3" window clingers)
Crankenburger 4.00
Burgerilla 4.00

Coins
(Funmoney & silver coins with pictures of several Burger
Chef characters – gave patrons 5 cents off on next purchase
of Funburger or Funmeal.)
Burger Chef & Jeff 4.00
Fangburger 4.00
Burgerilla 4.00

1971

Krazy Kreature Stickers
Pickle-Potamus 4.00
Must-Ketcher 4.00
Tomater-Gator 4.00
Chimpan-Cheese 4.00
Mynah-Burg-Er 4.00
Apple Turtle-Over 4.00

Klickety Klips
(Small bag of colored straw bits children put on the spokes
of their bikes. Also has small sticker sheet.)
Each item 3.00

1972

Flying Saucers
Burger Chef & Jeff pictured, saying "Incrediburgible" 5.00
Non-glow-in-the-dark versions 10". (Various colors; some
w/Burger Chef & Jeff. Some w/just Burger Chef on
them.) 5.00

Small Flying Saucers (Smaller non-glow-in-the-dark version
with same characters and "incrediburgible" on them. Various colors. Was alleged to have originally been a large
drink lid.) 5.00

Funburger Prize #4
Car Type 1 (Small blue car, with marble in bottom to help
roll.) 5.00
Car Type 2 (Small blue car, with marble in bottom to help
roll.) 5.00

Funmeal Prize Puzzle
(Three different puzzles featuring Burger Chef & Jeff in different situations with different characters. Puzzles were 4 x 4
pieces.)
Each puzzle 6.00

Yo-yo
(Three colored yo-yos featuring Burger Chef & Jeff.)
White & Red 10.00
White & Yellow 10.00
White & Blue 10.00

1973+

Funburger Box
(Precursor to the Funmeal. Came with puzzles on the box,
and a prize inside.)
Each Box 7.00

1975

President & Patriots Series Glasses
(Burger Chef & Jeff talk about each featured president/patriot
on back of glass.)
George Washington 4.00
Abraham Lincoln 4.00
Paul Revere 4.00
Ben Franklin 4.00
John F. Kennedy 4.00
Thomas Jefferson 4.00

Burger Chef & Jeff Glass
Characters in a standing pose 6.00

Homer's chalk wasn't meant to eat when it was available from Blimpie in '96.

This is one of the very few sets of toys issued by Boston Chicken, from 1998.

1976

Funmeal – Star Spangled
(Funmeal trays from 1976 — all were punch-outs.)
Spirit of St. Louis 6.00
Mayflower 6.00
Lincoln's Log Cabin 6.00
Independence Hall 6.00
Conestoga Wagon 6.00
Statue of Liberty 6.00
Model T 6.00
Saturn Rocket 6.00
Bald Eagle 6.00
The Riverboat 6.00
The Alamo 6.00
Tom Thumb Train 6.00

1977

Funmeal – Triple Play
(Funmeal trays – 24 in the set. Different Major League Baseball teams. Each came with 1 of 6 different baseball posters featuring the characters from Burger Chef.)
Each set 4.00

Friendly Monsters Glasses set
Burger Chef & Jeff Go Trail Riding 5.00
Burgerilla Falls in Love 5.00
Burgerini's Rabbit Hops Away 5.00
Crankenburger Scores a Touchdown 5.00
Fangburger Gets a Scare 5.00
Werewolf Goes Skateboarding. 5.00

Star Wars Posters
Chewbacca 10.00
Droids 10.00
Luke Skywalker 10.00
Darth Vader 10.00

1978+

Card Game
Go Fish (Reg. size.)
Old Maid (used items and characters from Burger Chef; small
        deck 1" x 1/2".) 5.00

Halloween Bag
(Given to children for Halloween candy collection.)
Each bag 5.00

1978

Iron-ons
Crankenburger 5.00
Burgerilla 5.00

Funmeal – Star Wars Funmeal Trays
Darth Vader's Card Game 15.00
Tie Fighter 15.00
X-Wing Fighter 15.00
Land Speeder 15.00
R2-D2 Droid Puppet 15.00
C3-PO Droid Puppet 15.00
Flight Game 15.00

1979

NFL Collectors Series Glasses – 24 Different NFL Football Teams
(Each smoky-colored glass shows a football helmet with team logo on it.)
Each team glass 5.00

1980

Star Wars Posters
(Three different Posters featuring characters from *Empire Strikes Back*.)
Each Poster 12.00

1981

Funmeal Prize
Deep Sea Treasure Search 5.00

Chick-Fil-A
1991

Animal Puzzles
Monkey 3.00
Elephant 3.00
Hippo 3.00
Lion 3.00
Water Buffalo 3.00
Ostrich 3.00
Giraffe 3.00
Zebra 3.00

An over-the-counter plush cow available from Chick-Fil-A in 1999.

1992

Pencil Topper

Purple bird... 3.00

Farm Puzzles

Goat 3.00
Cow 3.00
Horse 3.00
Sheep.. 3.00
Pig... 3.00
Farmer 3.00
Tractor... 3.00

1993

Dino Puzzles

Brontosauras.. 3.50
Stegasauras 3.50
Other premium.. 3.50

Richard Scarry Busytown Molds

Lowly Worm 3.00
Mr. Fumble 3.00
Heckle Cat 3.00
Sergeant Murphy 3.00
Hilda Hippo 3.00

1994

Drawing Doodles

(Four different shapes.)
Each premium... 3.00

Adventures From the Book of Virtues

(Six audio cassettes that contain actual stories from the *Adventures From the Book of Virtues* PBS TV show.)
Courage 3.00
Honesty... 3.00
Generosity.. 3.00
Humility 3.00
Respect... 3.00
Persistence 3.00

1999

Eyewitness Explorer Books

Rock Mining 2.00
Weather 2.00
Night Sky... 2.00
Human Body 2.00
Stuffed Cow (over-the-counter).............................. 5.00
T-shirts (various) 10.00

I Wonder Books

I Wonder If Sea Cows Give Milk 1.50
I Wonder Where Butterflies Go In Winter................ 1.50
I Wonder Which Snake Is The Longest 1.50
I Wonder Why Crocodiles Float Like Logs............... 1.50
I Wonder How Parrots Can Talk.............................. 1.50
I Wonder Why Skunks Are So Smelly...................... 1.50

Discover Letter Writing Kits

Pen Pals.. 1.00
Writing to Our Leaders and the Government 1.00
Family and Friends 1.00
Young Traveler's Journal 1.00
Special Occasions 1.00
Thank-You Letters... 1.00

A flying disc and "Space Goof" were part of a 1998 Long John Silver promotion.

2000

Adventures From the Book of Virtues Audio Cassettes

Respect 1.25
Humility... 1.25
Honesty 1.25
Courage.. 1.25
Generosity 1.25
Perseverance 1.25

Discover Sea Life with Bath Time Pals

Octopus shaped bottle... 1.50
Porpoise toothbrush holder 1.50
Anemone scrubber 1.50
Clam squirter 1.50
Blowfish hair comb 1.50
Starfish soap dish 1.50

Family Traditions

Today Is My Special Day 1.25
Table Talk.. 1.25
Crazy Questions.. 1.25

The Robinson family from "Lost in Space" got the star treatment from Long John Silver in 1998.

Family Crest.. 1.25
Family Tree 1.25
Family History 1.25

Eat Mor Chikin' Smiles toothbrush kit

(This is the first time the famous 'Eat Mor Chikin' cows were used in Chick-fil-A's kid's meals.)
Faucet friend 1.25
Toothbrush holder/carrying case....................... 1.25
Tooth brush timer 1.25
Dental floss holder 1.25

Hooked on Virtues Backpack

(Tag clip-on books.)
Honesty.. 1.25
Self-discipline... 1.25
Compassion 1.25
Work... 1.25
Courage 1.25
Responsibility.. 1.25

Adventures In Odyssey® Audio Tapes

Late Aug. – Sept.
Each... 3.00

The 7 Good Habits of Sunnyvale Kids

Early Oct. – Nov.
Each... 1.25

Chronicles of Narnia by C.S. Lewis

50th Anniversary Commemorative Set; abridged.
Late Nov. – Dec.
Each... 2.00

The Planets — An Encore

Late Dec. – Jan. 2001
Each... 1.50

DK Kid's Travel Guides

Mid-Feb. – Mid - March 2001
Each... 1.50

Chuck E. Cheese
1988

Chuck E. Cheese (various items)

Chuck E. Cheese (figure)................................. 4.00
Chuck E. Cheese (pen topper) 4.00
Pop-up Chuck E. Cheese 4.00
Car (w/picture of Chuck on side)..................... 4.00
Van (w/picture of Chuck on side) 4.00
Jeep (w/picture of Chuck on side)................... 4.00
Ball (w/picture of Chuck)................................. 4.00
Hackysack ball (w/picture of Chuck)............... 4.00

1991

Hackysack Balls

(Subway logo on one side, "Vegetable People" image on reverse side. Also distributed by Chuck E. Cheese.)
Pappy Pepper..4.00
Petey Pickle..4.00
Lenny Lettuce 4.00
Tilly Tomato...4.00
Pearl Onion...4.00

1994

Chuck E. Cheese (PVC sports figures)

Chuck E. Cheese twirling basketball 4.00
Chuck E. Cheese w/football 4.00
Chuck E. Cheese leaning on baseball bat.........4.00

Chuck E. Cheese & friends (PVC figures)

Chuck E. Cheese w/hands on hips....................3.00
Chuck E. Cheese in tux 3.00
Munch (Chuck's friend)......................................3.00
Jasper (Chuck's friend)......................................3.00
Helen (Chuck's girlfriend) 3.00

(As previously noted, Chuck E. Cheese is a combination restaurant/kid's indoor playground/arcade where kids can win tickets redeemable for prizes. The following items are not premiums that come w/meals, but rather prizes that are offered at Chuck E. Cheese locations. They are included here, as are all items imprinted with either the company's logo, Chuck E. Cheese, or both.)

1986-94

Flying Discs (various sizes and colors) 3.00
Yo-yos (various sizes and colors) 4.00
Mini telescope..3.00
Plastic stencils (various sizes, shapes, colors)................3.00
Toy watches 3.00
Picture balls (various colors) 3.00
Coloring cup (plastic cup with inner sleeve that can be colored by child; box cup comes in has Chuck E.'s image) 3.00

The snap-together "Zoobdude" came from Denny's in 1999.

This PVC figure pre-dated Domino's Noid icon by a few years.

Day-glo Chuck E. Cheese figures (pink, orange, yellow,
   green, red).. 4.00
Chuck E. Cheese w/parachute 4.00
Blue ribbon.. 3.00
Comb 3.00
Coin/token holder (various sizes, shapes, and colors) 3.00
Purse... 3.00
Pencil case... 3.00
Movie camera/viewer.. 3.00

Denny's
Year Unknown

Stencils
Jetsons (green).. 6.00
Sea Life (blue).. 6.00

1980s

Major League Baseball Cards
(Available with Grand Slam Meal.)
Each card... 5.00

1988

Flintstones
(Cloth bodies w/vinyl heads.)
Pebbles 7.00
Fred... 7.00
Barney... 7.00
Dino... 7.00
Hoppy.. 7.00
Wilma 7.00
Betty 7.00

1990

Flintstones Characters in Vehicles
Fred in car... 6.00
Barney in car... 6.00
Wilma in car 6.00
Dino in cart 6.00
Pebbles in tiny airplane... 6.00

Bamm-Bamm on tricycle 6.00
Flintstones Glacier Gliders
Bamm-Bamm...5.00
Pebbles..5.00
Barney..5.00
Fred 5.00
Dino 5.00
Hoppy 5.00
Set of 6...35.00

1988

Flintstones Stuffed Miniatures
Fred & Wilma..5.00
Barney & Betty..5.00
Dino & Hoppy 5.00
Pebbles & Bamm-Bamm 5.00

1990

Flintstones in Vehicles
Fred 5.00
Barney...5.00
Wilma..5.00
Betty 5.00
Dino 5.00
Pebbles...5.00
Bamm-Bamm...5.00
Hoppy 5.00

Flintstones Glacier Gliders
Bam Bam...5.00
Pebbles...5.00
Barney...5.00
Fred 5.00
Dino 5.00
Hoppy 5.00

1991

Flintstones Rock N' Rollers
Pink...6.00
Blue 6.00
Yellow 6.00
Green...6.00

The "Noid" became Domino's pesky corporate icon in the 1980s. This PVC bomber Noid is from 1988.

187

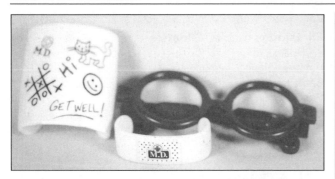

These "Dr." items — the wrist cast and ID bracelet came together — were available from Duchess in 1999.

Purple... 6.00
Orange.. 6.00
Set of 6.. 40.00

Flintstones Stone-Age Cruisers
Fred in cruiser 5.00
Dino in cruiser 5.00
Barnm-Bamm in cruiser 5.00
Wilma in cruiser 5.00
Pebbles on dinosaur 5.00
Barney in cruiser 5.00

Flintstones Rubber Character Squirters
Fred w/phone 4.00
Wilma w/camera 4.00
Bamm-Bamm w/ice cream............................. 4.00
Pebbles w/"inflatable" life ring...................... 4.00
Dino w/flower 4.00
Barney w/wristwatch 4.00
Set of 6.. 27.00

Flintstones Dino-Racers
Bamm-Bamm on dinosaur 5.00
Pebbles on dinosaur 5.00
Dino on macedon 5.00
Fred on dinosaur 5.00
Barney on dinosaur 5.00
Wilma on dinosaur 5.00

Dino-Makers
T-Rex (pink) 4.00
Triceratops (yellow)....................................... 4.00
Pterodactyl (orange) 4.00
Stegosaurus (green) 4.00
Apatosaurus (blue).. 4.00
Mastodon (purple)... 4.00

1992

Jetsons Planet Balls
(Each had picture of different character on ball.)
Earth w/Jane 5.00
Jupiter w/Judy 5.00
Moon w/Astro 5.00
Saturn w/George... 5.00
Mars w/Elroy 5.00
Neptune w/Rosie... 5.00

Jetsons Puzzles
(3-D transparent plastic puzzles w/different characters embossed on each.)
Jane 5.00
George 5.00

Astro 5.00
Elroy 5.00
Rosie 5.00
Judy 5.00

Jetson Spacecards
(These were actually POGs; each set came in a plastic case w/several POGs.)
Astronomers 5.00
Constellations 5.00
Mission Crews 5.00
Planets... 5.00
Spacecraft 5.00
Stellar Phenomenons 5.00

1993

Spinner
(Plastic throwing item w/suction cups on the end of each prong, various colors.)
Each 4.00

1994

Puzzle Ornaments
(3-D see-through, plastic puzzles.)
Diamond puzzle... 4.00
Square puzzle... 4.00
Round puzzle.. 4.00

1998

Summer Wishbone Plush Dog
Each 3.00

Fall Itchy and Scratchy Bean Bags
(Originally sold for $2.99.)
Each 3.50

1999-2000

Zoobdude
(Only one toy style was available, but each box came with plans to build various items based on how many boxes — up to four — were purchased. Denny's toys could also be combined with standard Zoobdudes available in toy stores. Each box contained a $5 off coupon for store-bought toys.)
Each toy... 4.00

A cute beach lizard was one of 16 different PVC figurines available from Duchess in 1999.

Domino's Pizza
Year Unknown

Domino PVC figure 2.00

Various Noid items

Noid bookmark 6.00
Bendable Noid 6.00
Mini throwing disc 6.00
Noid window-sticker figure 6.00

1988

Noid PVC figures

Noid in boxing gloves 6 00
Noid Night Fairy 6.00
Noid with drill 6.00
Wizard Noid 6.00
Bomber Noid 6.00
Noid w/pizza box 6.00
Noid w/arms out 6.00
Noid pulling ears 6.00

Duchess
1999

Lounging Lizards (16 PVC figures)

Each Lizard 2.00

Space Ships

Each item 2.00

Airplanes

Each item 2.00

Dr.'s Kit

Glasses 2.00
Wrist cast & medical bracelet 2.00
Other items 2.00

Elephant PVC Figurines

Elephant w/Dalmatian 2.00
Elephant drinking from bucket 2.00

Musical Instruments

Clacker 1.50

Sports Whistles

Baseball 1.50
Others 1.50

Thundra was a character that first appeared from the Fantastic Four's corner of the Marvel universe. She later popped up all over, including on 7-Eleven cups in 1995.

These under-3 items from Lost in Space made up a movie set at Long John Silver's in 1998.

Pull-back Cars

Red 1.50
Blue 1.50
Others 1.50

Christmas Vehicles

Teddy in race car 1.50
Snowman in race car 1.50
Others 1.50

Galactoids

(Two-piece colorful aliens. The tops and bottoms of which can be swapped around to create "new" species. Each alien comes in 6 different colors and with six different facial expressions.)

Tongue sticking out 2.00
Grimace 2.00
Smile 2.00
Smile w/5 buck teeth 2.00
Smile w/3 buck teeth 2.00
Two buck teeth 2.00

2000

The Cowboys of Moo Mesa

(Set of 6 figures.)
Each figure 1.50

Dunkin' Donuts
1989

Munchkins PVCs

Beach Munchkin 10.00
Munchkin on skateboard 10.00
Munchkin w/baseball & glove 10.00
Lady Munchkin 10.00

IHOP
1992

Pancake Kids PVC Figures

Cynthia Cinnamon Apple 5.00
Susie Strawberry 5.00

The Thing graced one of several dozen Marvel cups at 7-Eleven in the 1970s. This cup is from 1975.

Bonnie Blueberry	5.00
Betty Buttermilk	5.00
Rosanna Banana Nut	5.00
Peter Potato	5.00
Von Der Gus	5.00
Chocolate Chip Charlie	5.00
Harvey Harvest	5.00
Frenchy Frenchtoast	5.00

1993

Pancake Kid Cruisers (kids in vehicles)

Cynthia Cinnamon Apple	4.00
Susie Strawberry	4.00
Bonnie Blueberry	4.00
Betty Buttermilk	4.00
Von Der Gus	4.00
Chocolate Chip Charlie	4.00
Harvey Harvest	4.00
Frenchy Frenchtoast	4.00

1999

International Kid Cups

Germany	1.50
France	1.50
Others	1.50

Lee's Famous Recipe Country Chicken
1993

Cartoon Parade mini-viewers

Mighty Mouse viewer	4.00
Porky Pig viewer	4.00
Bugs Bunny viewer	4.00
Woody Woodpecker viewer	4.00
Popeye viewer	4.00

Little Caesar's
1992 – '95

Little Caesar "Action" Figures

Little Caesar squirter (blue)	4.00

Little Caesar ball (orange)	4.00
Little Caesar pop-up (yellow)	4.00
Little Caesar throwing star (suction cups on ends/ yellow)	4.00

Little Caesar Caesar Series

Roll 'em! Roll 'em! (tire)	4.00
Blimp! Blimp! (dirigible)	4.00
Scuba! Scuba!	4.00
Pepperoni Flyer	4.00
Knock Down	4.00
Pan Pipes	4.00
Secret Ring	4.00

1994

Flyer	4.00
Water Ring Catch	4.00

1995

Sports Pizza Pizza Football Game	10.00

WCW Flip-Motion Trading Cards (set of 4)

Each card	2.00

1999

Creepy Crawlers

May

Scorpion	1.50
Worm	1.50
Snake	1.50
Spider	1.50

Long John Silver's
Year Unknown

Captain Flint

Undersea Adventure	5.00

1986

Go Fish Cars

(Different fish-shaped cars of several colors — red, blue, yellow — with various colorful stickers. Came in assorted combinations.)

Each car	15.00

Sbarro's followed up its Garfield kid meal promotion with the Harvey comic book character Casper. As usual, the promotion tied into a film, this one a sequel in 1999.

These character freeze molds were available from Popeye's in 1989. Each mold came in three colors — red, orange, and blue.

1989

Playing Cards
Go Fish card game 7.00

1990

Sea Walkers Plastic Figures w/string
Sylvia (purple) 6.00
Sydney (yellow) 6.00
Flash (Turtle) 6.00
Quinn (Penguin) 6.00
Capt. Flint (Parrot) 6.00

Sea Watchers Kaleidoscope-like Items
Orange Watcher 6.00
Pink Watcher 6.00
Yellow Watcher 6.00

Water Blasters Figures
Long John Silver 4.00
Captain Flint 4.00
Ophelia Octopus 4.00

Water Blaster Balls
(Heads of various sea-faring characters that doubled as squirters.)
Long John Silver 4.00
Ophelia Octopus 4.00
Captain Flint 4.00
Billy Bones 4.00

1993

Trolls
(Each figure came with different hair color and a different symbol on their belly — star, heart, diamond, and circle. Toys were also distributed by Hardee's, Roy Rogers and Sonic Drive-Ins.)
Each troll 4.00

Once Upon a Forest straw sliders (straw holders)
Abigail 9.00
Cornelius 9.00
Edgar 9.00
Michelle 9.00
Russell (Pale and deep tan skin tones) 9.00

1994

Stone Protectors
(Troll-like PVCs w/colored gems embedded in their chest. Figures apparently based on a short-lived comic book character.)

Maxwell the Accelerator 6.00
Angus the Soldier (white stone).......................................6.00
Zink the Horrible Hatchman (pink stone) 6.00
Clifford the Rock Climber (blue stone)...............................6.00
Chester the Wrestler (red stone) 6.00
Zok the Evil Leader (purple stone) 6.00
Cornelius the Samurai (green stone)..................................6.00

1995

Free Willy II (movie set)
Little Spot..5.00
Luna 5.00
Jessy 5.00
Willy 5.00

Peanuts Christmas Boxes
Charlie Brown 5.00
Snoopy 5.00
Sally 5.00
Lucy 5.00

1996

Disney Channel
Baloo 4.00
Dale 4.00
Goofy 4.00

1997

Water Blaster
(Four different blasters.)
Each blaster...4.00

2000

Spy Dogs
Glow-in-the-dark wall toy 1.50
Colorful spinners...1.50
Keeper box 1.50
Skillful scrambler 1.50

A kid's meal bag from Popeye's featured not the chain's namesake but that "other" Popeye in 1999.

A foam fighter plane was a hot item at Orange Julius in 1999.

Nathan's
1992

Franksters (anthropomorphic hotdogs)
On roller skates... 6.00
On ice skates 6.00
On skateboard 6.00

1993

Franksters (anthropomorphic hotdogs, set II)
On surf board 6.00
W/baseball 6.00
Swimmer.. 6.00

1994

Franksters (anthropomorphic hotdogs, set III)
W/football 12.00
W/basketball 12.00
Cheerleader 12.00
W/hockey stick 12.00
Superdog 6.00

1998

Nathan Hotdog, Bendie Figures
Cowboy 2.00
Clown.. 2.00
Others in series.. 2.00

Orange Julius
1980s

Marvel Comics comic book 5.00

1999

Styrofoam airplane.. 1.00

Popeye's
1980

Popeye Plastic Figures
   (Versions of these figures were reproduced through the mid-'90s.)
Wimpy... 5.00
Brutus... 5.00
Popeye.. 5.00
Olive Oyl 5.00
Swee' Pea 5.00

Popeye Pencil Toppers
   (Versions of these figures were reproduced through the mid-'90s.)
Wimpy... 4.00
Brutus... 4.00
Popeye.. 4.00

Olive Oyl...4.00
Swee' Pea 4.00

Popeye Freezer Pop Maker
   (Each came in red, orange, and blue.)
Olive Oyl 2.00
Other characters..2.00

Roy Rogers
1988

Sand Molders
Red..4.00
Blue...4.00
Green...4.00
Yellow 4.00

Sports Kid Bike-related Premiums
Sweat band..4.00
Shoelaces..4.00
Brake lights 4.00
Shoe pocket...4.00

Rally Racers
Porsche 5.00
GT1...5.00
Car #3..5.00
Car #4..5.00
Car #5..5.00
Car #6..5.00
Car (under-3) 5.00

Neon Writers Pens
Flamingo 4.00
Palm Tree 4.00
Bird of Paradise 4.00
Sunrays 4.00

Gumby Rubber Figures
Gumby..6.00
Red Gumby w/square head.......................................6.00
Pokey...6.00
Prickle 6.00
Goo...6.00

Erasure Rings
Green Girl 4.00
Blue Robot...4.00
Yellow Robot..4.00
Red Man 4.00

Galaxy Rangers Whistles
Yellow 5.00
Blue..5.00
Green..5.00
Red...5.00

Mini-Cars
Car #1..4.00

The magic school bus rolled out at Long John Silvers in 1998.

Marvel characters pushed Slurpee cups at 7-Eleven in 1981.

Car #2 .... 4.00
Car #3 .... 4.00
Car #4 .... 4.00

Galaxy Rangers License Plates
Purple 4.00
Blue 4.00
Red 4.00
Green 4.00

Mini-Stuffs (balls)
Football 4.00
Baseball 4.00
Basketball 4.00
Soccer ball 4.00

Hide 'N Seek Dinos
Red 4.00
Blue 4.00
Purple 4.00
Green 4.00

Secret Decoder Pens (2 pens per set)
Set #1 .... 4.00
Set #2 .... 4.00
Set #3 .... 4.00
Set #4 .... 4.00

Power Pullers (male figures)
Red 5.00
Yellow 5.00
Blue 5.00
Green 5.00

Snorks
(There were four different snorks, based on characters from a comic book published in Belgium; however, some 30 variant PVC figures were produced and distributed.)
Alistar 6.00
Girlfriend 6.00
Dimmy 6.00
Tooter 6.00
Casey 6.00

Galaxy Rangers Space Ship Vehicles
Interceptor 5.00
Iron Falcon 5.00
Beta 5.00

Hyperdrive 5.00

Swamp Pets Bracelets
Aqua 4.00
Purple 4.00
Grey 4.00
Chartreuse 4.00

Rad Riders Bike-O-Mania
Funny Bone Covers - orange 4.00
Funny Bone Covers - yellow 4.00
Funny Bone Covers - green 4.00
Funny Bone Covers - purple 4.00
Spoke Clicker #1 .... 4.00
Spoke Clicker #2 .... 4.00
Spoke Clicker #3 .... 4.00
Spoke Clicker #4 .... 4.00
Refrigerator Magnet - red 4.00
Refrigerator Magnet - blue 4.00

Skateboard Gang (4 PVC Figures on Skateboards)
Figure #1 .... 4.00
Figure #2 .... 4.00
Figure #3 .... 4.00
Figure #4 .... 4.00

1989

Be-a-Sport Refrigerator Magnets
Touchdown 7.00
Slam Dunk 7.00
Score 7.00
Go For It 7.00
Set of 4 .... 30.00

Gator Tales PVC Alligators
Investi-Gator (in sneakers) 8.00
A.V. Gator (on skis) 8.00
Sneaky Gator (on snowshoes) 8.00
Skater Gator (on skates) 8.00
Set of 4 .... 35.00

Major League Baseball Mini-Batting Helmets (26 teams)
Each helmet 2.00

1990

Critters Plastic Monsters
Blue eyes/purple body 6.00
Blue eyes/red body 6.00
Blue eyes/yellow body 6.00
Blue eyes/orange body 6.00
Yellow eyes/purple body 6.00
Yellow eyes/red body 6.00
Yellow eyes/orange body 6.00
Yellow eyes/yellow body 6.00
Red eyes/purple body 6.00
Red eyes/red body 6.00
Red eyes/orange body 6.00
Red eyes/yellow body 6.00
White eyes/purple body 6.00
White eyes/red body 6.00
White eyes/orange body 6.00
White eyes/yellow body 6.00

Star Searchers Plastic Space Toys
(Four different toys; each came in various color combinations of front (f) or top (t)/middle (m)/back (ba) or bottom (bo) of three colors.)

Robot #1 orange (f)/purple (m)/green (ba)........................5.00
Robot #2 orange (f)/green (m)/purple (ba)........................5.00
Robot #3 purple (f)/orange (m)/green (ba)........................5.00
Robot #4 purple (f)/green (m)/orange (ba)........................5.00
Robot #5 green (f)/orange (m)/purple (ba)........................5.00
Robot #6 green (f)/purple (m)/orange (ba)........................5.00
Rover #1 orange (t)/purple (m)/green (bo)........................5.00
Rover #2 orange (t)/green (m)/purple (bo)........................5.00
Rover #3 purple (t)/orange (m)/green (bo)........................5.00
Rover #4 purple (t)/green (m)/orange (bo)........................5.00
Rover #5 green (t)/orange (m)/purple (bo)........................5.00
Rover #6 green (t)/purple (m)/orange (bo)........................5.00
Saucer #1 orange (t)/purple (m)/green (bo)....................5.00
Saucer #2 orange (t)/green (m)/purple (bo)....................5.00
Saucer #3 purple (t)/orange (m)/green (bo)....................5.00
Saucer #4 purple (t)/green (m)/orange (bo)....................5.00
Saucer #5 green (t)/orange (m)/purple (bo)....................5.00
Saucer #6 green (t)/purple (m)/orange (bo)....................5.00
Shuttle #1 orange (t)/purple (m)/green (bo)...................5.00
Shuttle #2 orange (t)/green (m)/purple (bo)...................5.00
Shuttle #3 purple (t)/orange (m)/green (bo)...................5.00
Shuttle #4 purple (t)/green (m)/orange (bo)...................5.00
Shuttle #5 green (t)/orange (m)/purple (bo)...................5.00
Shuttle #6 green (t)/purple (m)/orange (bo)...................5.00

Skateboard Gang PVC Figures

Standing on skateboard 6.00
Kneeling on skateboard 6.00
Handstand on skateboard... 6.00
One Foot on skateboard 6.00

Fun Flyers Airport Plastic Planes

Blue jet... 5.00
Green jet 5.00
Yellow jet 5.00
Red jet.. 5.00
Blue helicopter 5.00
Green helicopter 5.00
Yellow helicopter 5.00
Red helicopter 5.00
Blue round-nosed transport 5.00
Green round-nosed transport...................................... 5.00
Yellow round-nosed transport..................................... 5.00
Red round-nosed transport.. 5.00
Blue pointy-nosed transport 5.00
Green pointy-nosed transport..................................... 5.00
Yellow pointy-nosed transport.................................... 5.00
Red pointy-nosed transport....................................... 5.00

Ickky Stickky Buggs Rubber Bugs

Yellow Centipede 5.00
Pink Centipede... 5.00
Green Centipede... 5.00
Blue Centipede... 5.00
Yellow Grasshopper 5.00
Pink Grasshopper 5.00
Green Grasshopper 5.00
Blue Grasshopper 5.00
Yellow Spider 5.00
Pink Spider... 5.00
Green Spider... 5.00
Blue Spider 5.00
Yellow Worm 5.00
Pink Worm 5.00
Green Worm 5.00
Blue Worm 5.00

1992

Major League Baseball Helmets

(All 28 existing teams represented.)
Each Helmet 3.00

1993

Trolls

(Each figure came w/different hair and a different symbol on their belly — star, heart, diamond. Toys were also distributed by Hardee's, Long John Silver's, and Sonic Drive-Ins.)
Each troll..4.00

1995

X-Men Battle Figures

(PVC figures of X-Men squaring off against a super villain. Each pair attached to a base and all four bases fit together to form a single diorama. Four different Marvel X-Men comic books and trading cards also came with this series, as well a certificate of authenticity. A fifth figure of the Beast on Wheels also came with this series. This was considered the under-3 toy. Set also distributed at Hardee's. Toys, cards and comics were not bagged together, and thus are listed separately.)
Cyclops vs. Commando...5.00
Wolverine vs. The Blob...5.00
Storm vs. Phantasia 5.00
Rogue vs. Avalanche..5.00
Beast Time Traveler (on wheels)................................5.00
Comic book #1...5.00
Comic book #2...5.00
Comic book #3...5.00
Comic book #4...5.00
Comic book #5...5.00
Trading card #1..5.00
Trading card #2..5.00
Trading card #3..5.00
Trading card #4..5.00

1999

Lunch box 2.00

7-Eleven

(See glasses listing for extensive plastic and glass Slurpee cups issued by 7-Eleven.)

A Kid's Meal at Roy Rogers included a lunch box in 1999.

Garfield was the feature cat on the first kid meal production at Sbarro's in 1998.

This PVC hot dog character was available from the Texas hot dog chain Wienerschnitzel.

Mr. Bigbite
Year Unknown

(PVC anthropomorphic hotdog)
Holding a Slurpee cup.................................. 4.00

1990

Oscar Mayer Hot Dog Whistles
Whistle #1 w/paper band 4.00
Whistle #2 w/molded band.............................. 4.00

1992

Various Premiums
Mini flying disc... 4.00
Triprong Flyer... 4.00

Sbarro
1998

Garfield
Dec. 98 – Feb. 99
Garfield 4.00
Arlene... 4.00
Nermal 4.00
Odie 4.00

1999

Casper and the Ghostly Trio Watches
(Toy watches from the second Casper movie.)
Mar. – May
Casper watch 3.00
Fatso watch... 3.00
Stinky watch.. 3.00
Stretch watch 3.00

Sesame Street (summer)
Each premium 3.00

Muppets from Space (fall, from the movie)
Each premium 3.00

2000

Garfield Mazes
March
Odie 2.50
Garfield 2.50
Nermal 2.50
Other toys in series.......................................2.50

Wienerschnitzel
1999

Hotdog 'Tenna Topper (antenna topper).........................2.00

Whataburger
1999

Splash Bugs
June
Each premium 2.00

2000

Action Figures
Whataburger Man..1.50
AddABoy..1.50
Dr. Stale..1.50
Just Alien 1.50

Drinking Glasses & Cup Listings

Since not everything that comes out of a fast-food franchise is a toy, or even food, we've decided to add this special section, which covers many of the various glassware promotions that have been issued over the years. Items in this section are listed alphabetically by franchise, and then by year.

As glasses and cups tend to not be packaged individually, the following prices are for items mint in package (MIP), unless otherwise noted.

Where applicable, the date(s) of distribution and additional information on the following premiums were provided by the individual chains and other sources.

A&W
1993
The Great Root Bear's Nursery Rhyme Kid's Cup
Each.. 5.00

1994
The Great Root Bear's 75th Anniversary Kid's Cup
Each.. 5.00

A&W Mini Mugs
Each.. 8.00

The Great Root Bear's Magic Color Change Kid's Cup
Each.. 5.00

1995
A&W Mini Mugs
Each.. 8.00

The Great Root Bear's Monster Cups
Each.. 6.00

1996
The Great Root Bear's Cruisin' Kid's Cup
Each.. 5.00

A&W Mini Mugs
Each 5.00

The Great Root Bear's Monster Kid's Cup
Each.. 6.00

1997
The Great Root Bear's Rockin' A&W Kid's Cup
Each.. 6.00

Plastic mini mugs, circa 1999, were available in various colors at A&W in 1999.

A&W offered a dandy ceramic coffee mug in 1999.

A&W Mini Mugs
Each 5.00

The Great Root Bear's Rockin' Monster Kid's Cup
Each 5.00

1998
The Great Root Bear's Star Cruiser Kid's Cup
Each 5.00

A 60s-style logo identified this A&W baby glass mug.

A&W Mini Mugs
Each... 7.00

1999

A&W All American Food Mini Mugs
Each... 7.00

A&W Mini Mugs
Each... 7.00

Arby's
1976

Bicentennial Series
Bullwinkle To The Defense............................. 10.00
Bullwinkle Crosses The Delaware 10.00
Casper And Nightmare's Midnight Ride........................ 10.00
Dudley Takes Tea At Sea................................ 10.00
George By Woody.. 10.00
Hot Stuff Makes It Hot For The Red Coats 10.00
Never Fear, Underdog Is Here........................ 10.00
Woody Has Spirit 10.00
Rocky In The Dawn's Early Light................... 10.00
Underdog Saves The Bell 10.00
Set of 10.. 120.00

Zodiac
Aries... 7.50
Aquarius.. 7.50
Cancer 7.50
Capricorn 7.50
Gemini.. 7.50
Leo... 7.50
Libra... 7.50
Pisces... 7.50
Sagittarius... 7.50
Scorpio.. 7.50
Taurus... 7.50
Virgo... 7.50
Set of 12.. 100.00

Samuel L. Jackson found little to smile about with his Phantom Menace cup topper from Pizza Hut in 1999.

A pair of Burger Chef presidential glasses was issued in 1975.

1978

Currrier & Ives Series
(Set re-issued in 1981.)
The Road In Winter 3.50
Winter Pastime 3.50
American Farm In Winter...3.50
Frozen Up...3.50
Set of 4 ....15.00

1979

Actors Series
Charlie Chaplin 4.00
Abbott & Costello 4.00
Laurel and Hardy 4.00
Mae West 4.00
Little Rascals 4.00
W.C. Fields 4.00
Set of 6 ....35.00

Norman Rockwell Winter Scenes
A Boy Meets His Dog 5.00
Downhill Darling..5.00
Chilling Chore 5.00
Snow Sculpturing..5.00
Set of 4 ....30.00

1981

Currrier & Ives Series (re-issue)
Set of 4 ....10.00

BC Ice Age Series
Set of 6 ....20.00

Warner Brothers Looney Tunes Collector Series
(All characters have head in a star.)
Bugs Bunny 7.00
Daffy Duck 7.00
Porky Pig 7.00
Road Runner 7.00
Sylvester 7.00
Tweety 7.00
Yosemite Sam..7.00
Set of 7 ....40.00

Norman Rockwell Saturday Evening Post Covers
Knuckles Down...4.00
No Swimming 4.00
Catching The Big One 4.00
The Champ...4.00
The Spooners 4.00
Leapfrog 4.00
Set of 6 ....35.00

A younger, more active Yoda made an appearance in Phantom Menace and on this cup topper at Pizza Hut in 1999.

1983

Wizard of Id
Bung	9.00
King	9.00
Wizard	9.00
Spook	9.00
Larsen E. Pettifogger	9.00
Sir Rodney	9.00
Set of 6	65.00

Monopoly Collector Series
Just Visiting	11.50
Free Parking	11.50
Go To Jail	11.50
Collect $200	11.50
Set of 4	55.00

Norman Rockwell Summer Scenes
Sunset	4.00
Gramps	4.00
Gone Fishing	4.00
No Swimming	4.00
Set of 4	26.00

1988

Warner Brothers Looney Tunes
Bugs Bunny "Diving For Carrots"	15.00
Daffy Duck "Jungle Jitters'	15.00
Porky Pig "Lunar Lunch"	15.00
Sylvester "Anchors Away"	15.00
Set of 4	70.00

Burger Chef
1975
Burger Chef and Jeff "Now We're Glassified"	35.00

1976

Bicentennial Series Presidents & Patriots
Abraham Lincoln	8.00
Benjamin Franklin	8.00
George Washington	8.00
John Kennedy	8.00
Paul Revere	8.00
Thomas Jefferson	8.00
Set of 6	60.00

Burger Chef Characters
Burgerinis Rabbit Hops Away	10.00
Burger Chef And Jeff Go Trail Riding	10.00
Burgerilla Falling Head Over Heels	10.00
Fangburger Gets a Scare	10.00
Frankenburger Scares	10.00
Werewolf Goes Skateboarding	10.00
Set of 6	75.00

1978

Endangered Species Series
Bald Eagle	8.00
Giant Panda	8.00
Orangutan	8.00
Tiger	8.00
Set of 4	45.00

Burger King
1976

Bicentennial Series "Have It Your Way"
Liberty Bell	6.00
Fife and Drum	6.00
Eagle	6.00
Crossed Flags	6.00
Set of 4	35.00

1977

Star Wars
Darth Vader	15.00
Luke Skywalker	15.00
Chewbacca	15.00
R2-D2 and C-3PO	15.00
Set of 4	65.00

Captain America leapt into 7-Eleven in 1977, along with several other Marvel comic book heroes.

Burger King's cup holder series from 1984 didn't leave out Superman.

Darkseid was a menacing figure in this 1984 cupholder set from Burger King.

1978

The Marvelous Magical Burger King
"See These Burgers".. 13.50
"I'll Turn Onions" 13.50
"I've Got The Magic"... 13.50
"It Isn't Luck" 13.50
Set of 4, all feature The King 70.00

1979

Burger King Characters
Burger Thing 6.00
Duke of Doubt.. 6.00
Marvelous Magical Burger King.................................... 6.00
Sir Shake A Lot.. 6.00
Wizard of Fries.. 6.00
Set of 5... 40.00

1980

Star Wars: The Empire Strikes Back
Lando Calrissian 12.00
Luke Skywalker 12.00

Chick-Fil-A featured an over-the-counter thermal mug in 1999.

Darth Vader 12.00
R2-D2 And C-3PO...12.00
Set of 4...60.00

1983

Star Wars: Return of The Jedi
Jabba The Hutt..8.00
Ewok Village 8.00
Luke Skywalker and Darth Vader
   In The Emperor's Throne Room 8.00
Han Solo In The Tatooine Desert 8.00
Set of 4...50.00

1985

Mark Twain Country Series
Mark Twain 12.50
Tom Sawyer..12.50
Huck Finn 12.50
Octagonal Study 12.50
Set of 4, in box..70.00

1987

Haunted Mansion
Glow-in-the-dark plastic cup 2.00

Super Powers Cup Holders
Darkseid 4.00
Wonder Woman..4.00
Batman 4.00
Superman 4.00

1995

Gargoyles
Color transformation plastic cup 2.50

Disney's Pocahontas Glasses (over-the-counter)
Meeko & Flit 3.00
Governor Ratcliffe & Percy 3.00
Chief Powhatan & Kocoum 3.00
Pocahontas & John Smith 3.00

In 1999, Hardee's hooked up with NASCAR to deliver oversized cups featuring popular drivers.

Chick-Fil-A
1999

Thermal Cup (over-the-counter)
Insulated Cow cup 5.00

Dairy Queen
1976

Dairy Queen Collectors Series
Girl and boy with ice cream cones 7.00
Girl and boyon horse 7.00
Girl and boy on rail car 7.00
Girl and boy on swing 7.00
Set of 4 .... 40.00

Domino's Pizza
1975

Dick Tracy
Dick Tracy 225.00

1988

Christmas Noid
Noids, each 6.00

1989

Avoid The Noid
Noid at the beach 6.00
Noid playing golf 6.00
Noid playing tennis 6.00
Noid on water skis 6.00
Set of 5 .... 45.00

Godfather's Pizza
1975

Animal Crackers
Dodo 5.00
Eugene 5.00
Gnu 5.00
Lana 5.00

Louis 5.00
Lyle 5.00
Set of 6 .... 32.50

1985

The Goonies
Sloth and The Goonies 6.00
Sloth Comes To The Rescue 6.00
Goonies In The Organ Chamber 6.00
Data On The Water Slide 6.00
Set of 4 .... 25.00

Hardee's
1979

Ziggy
Be Nice To Little Things 7.00
Time For A Food Break 7.00
Smile 7.00
Try To Have A Nice Day 7.00
Set of 4 .... 30.00

1982

Smurfs
Brainy 4.00
Gargamel/Azreal 4.00
Grouchy 4.00
Hefty 4.00
Jokey 4.00
Lazy 4.00
Papa Smurf 4.00
Smurfette 4.00
Set of 8 .... 45.00

1983

Smurfs
Baker Smurf 4.00
Handy Smurf 4.00
Smurfette 4.00
Papa Smurf 4.00
Clumsy Smurf 4.00
Harmony Smurf 4.00
Set of 6 .... 35.00

1985

The Chipmunks
Alvin 5.00
Chipettes 5.00
Simon 5.00
Theodore 5.00
Set of 4 .... 32.50

A pair of Burger Chef glasses were handed out in the 1970s.

Mister Fantastic (circa 1975) and Ms. Marvel (1977) appeared at 7-Eleven.

1999

NASCAR Cups
Mark Martin/Jeff Burton.. 3.00
Other drivers 3.00

KFC
1978

Hot Air Balloon
Each.. 8.00

1984

Wizard of Oz
("Land of Ah's" series distributed only in Kansas.)
Dorothy and Toto.. 50.00
Scarecrow 50.00
Tin Woodsman 50.00
Cowardly Lion 50.00
Set of 4.. 220.00

1999

Star Wars: The Phantom Menace Cups
(Oversized, plastic cups with character toppers. This promotion was done in conjunction with sister companies Pizza Hut and Taco Bell.)
Boss Nass.. 5.00
Queen Amidala 5.00
R2-D2.. 5.00
Captain Tarpals... 5.00

McDonald's
1973

McDonald's Character Series
Big Mac... 14.00
Captain Crook 14.00
Grimace 14.00
Hamburglar 14.00
Mayor McCheese.. 14.00
Ronald McDonald 14.00
Set of 6, 5" glasses 95.00

1976

McDonald's Character Series
(These glasses are silk-screened versions of the above. There are some color variations.)
Big Mac (has different shades of blue) 8.00
Captain Crook (purple/lavender,black/red) 8.00
Grimace (dark blue, purple and lavender) 8.00
Hamburglar (both the top of cape and clothing are
    lighter)..8.00
Mayor McCheese (has different shades of blue) 8.00
Ronald McDonald (has red lettering) 8.00
Set of 6, 5-1/2" glasses 60.00

1977

McDonald's Series
(There is also a set of the same glasses, in a larger 6-1/4" size, put out the same year. Prices are the same.)
Big Mac on roller skates 5.00
Captain Crook on leaky boat 5.00
Grimace on pogo stick...5.00
Hamburglar on flat car 5.00
Mayor McCheese taking pictures 5.00
Ronald leapfrogging into lake 5.00
Set of 6 5-5/8" glasses 40.00

1980

Big Mac Multi Language
Each 6.00

Buck Rogers/Coca-Cola
Buck Rogers 30.00
Wilma Deering 30.00
Twiki...30.00
Draco 30.00
Set of 4 ....140.00

McDonald's Adventure Series
Big Mac nets the Hamburglar...8.00
Captain Crook sails the bounding main 8.00
Grimace climbs a mountain 8.00
Hamburglar hooks the hamburgers 8.00
Mayor McCheese rides a runaway train 8.00
Ronald McDonald saves the falling stars 8.00
Set of 6 ....60.00

Conan's main squeeze, Red Sonja, appeared on her own 7-Eleven cup in 1977.

This A&W cup came with a 1999 kid meal.

1981

The Great Muppet Caper

Happiness Hotel.. 2.00
Kermit... 2.00
Miss Piggy.. 2.00
The Great Gonzo 2.00
Set of 4... 18.00

1983

Peanuts: Camp Snoopy

Charlie Brown 4.00
Snoopy... 4.00
Lucy 4.00
Snoopy... 4.00
Linus 4.00
Set of 5.. 26.00
Charlie Brown glass promotional series: "Good Grief!
    McDonald's Camp Snoopy Glasses Are Coming" 45.00

1984

Disney Animated Classics

Peter Pan... 17.00
Cinderella... 17.00
Fantasia 17.00
Snow White and The Seven Dwarfs 17.00
Set of 4.. 85.00

Olympic Mugs

Red 5.00
White.. 5.00
Blue 5.00
Yellow.. 5.00
Set of 4.. 30.00

1986

McVote '86

McD.L.T.. 5.00
Quarter Pounder 5.00
Big Mac.. 5.00
Set of 3.. 25.00

1987

Garfield

Poetry In Motion... 5.00

Are We Having Fun Yet? 5.00
Home, James 5.00
Just Me and The Road 5.00
Set of 4.. 30.00

Garfield Mugs

I'm Easy To Get Along With When Things Go My Way 4.00
Use Your Friends Wisely 4.00
I'm Not One Who Rises To The Occasion 4.00
It's Not A Pretty Life But Someone Has To Live It 4.00
Set of 4.. 26.00

Hawaii

Catamaran and Outrigger............................... 8.00
Fisherman bringing in the nets 8.00
Surfing 8.00
Outrigger Racers 8.00
Set of 4.. 42.00

1989

Disney

Mickey at Tommorowland 8.00
Minnie at Fantasyland 8.00
Donald at Critter Country 8.00
Goofy at Adventureland.................................. 8.00
Set of 4.. 45.00

Mac Tonight

12 oz. Glass.. 5.00
16 oz. Glass.. 5.00
32 oz. Cooler 6.00

Mac Tonight Mugs

Set of 4 .... 30.00

1990

Camp McDonaldland

  (Part of a Happy Meal promotion.)
Ronald collapsible cup................................... 3.50

Pizza Hut
1976

Happy Days

Set of 6 .... 50.00

1978

C.B. Lingo Series

Bullwinkle in green truck................................ 45.00
Bullwinkle in police car 45.00
Bullwinkle in blue truck 45.00

McDonald's came out with a Batman glass in 1991.

Bullwinkle with fishing pole 45.00
Underdog holding C.B. mike 45.00
Dudley Do-Right in helicopter 45.00
Set of 6 .... 310.00

1982

E.T. Collector Series

Be Good 4.50
Home 4.50
I'll Be Right Here 4.50
Phone Home 4.50
Set of 4 .... 30.00

1983

Care Bears

Cheer Bear 2.00
Friends Bear, scarce 15.00
Funshine Bear 2.00
Good Luck Bear, scarce 15.00
Grumpy Bear 2.00
Tenderheart Bear 2.00
Set of 6 .... 50.00

1986

The Flintstone Kids

Barney 4.00
Freddy 4.00
Wilma 4.00
Betty 4.00
Set of 4 .... 26.00

Popples

Set of 4 .... 20.00

1999

Star Wars: The Phantom Menace Cups

(Oversized, plastic cups with character toppers. This promotion was done in conjunction with sister companies KFC and Taco Bell.)
Jar Jar Binks 5.00
Nute Gunray 5.00
Yoda 5.00
Mace Windu 5.00

Popeye's
1978

Popeye Sports Scenes

Popeye 15.00

Queen Amidala, Jar Jar Binks and Darth Maul were on top of things at KFC, Pizza Hut and Taco Bell in 1999.

Plastic racing cups were given out with kid menu items at Red Lobster in 1999.

Olive Oyl 15.00
Swee' Pea 15.00
Brutus 15.00
Set of 4 .... 70.00

1979

Popeye's Pals

Popeye 13.50
Olive Oyl 13.50
Swee' Pea 13.50
Brutus 13.50
Set of 4 .... 65.00

1982

Popeye's 10th Anniversary

Popeye 20.00
Olive Oyl 20.00
Swee' Pea 20.00
Brutus 20.00
Set of 4 .... 90.00
Olive Oyl-beaker shaped glass (company giveaway) 25.00

Red Lobster
1999

Plastic cup 2.00

7-Eleven
1970s

Major League Baseball Player Slurpee Cups

(Images and statistics on back.)
All cups, each 4.00

1975

Marvel Superhero Slurpee Cups

(16-oz. plastic cup.)
Angel 4.00
Black Knight 4.00
Black Widow 4.00
Daredevil 5.00
Doc Savage 4.00

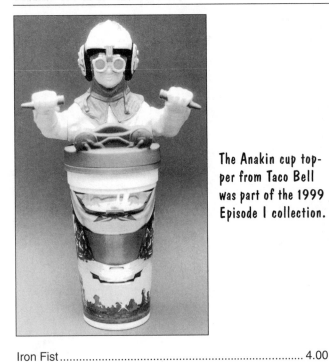

The Anakin cup topper from Taco Bell was part of the 1999 Episode I collection.

Iron Fist...4.00
Ka-Zar...4.00
Killraven..4.00
Mister Fantastic..4.00
Silver Surfer..4.00
Red Sonja 4.00
The Thing..4.00
Thundra...4.00
Yellowjacket (Hank Pym) 10.00
Warlock (Him) 10.00
The Watcher 10.00
Set of 16..185.00

1977

Marvel Superhero Slurpee Cups

(15-1/2 oz. plastic cup.)
The Avengers (Scarlet Witch, Vision, Iron Man, Beast, Yellow-
    jacket, Captain America, & Thor vs. the Overlord) 9.00
Captain America & the Falcon 9.00
Captain America & the Red Skull....................9.00
Captain Marvel...9.00
The Champions (Ghost Rider, Johnny Blaze, Angel, Hercules,
    Black Widow, & Iceman)..............................9.00
Conan #1 ....9.00
Conan #2 ....9.00
The Black Panther 9.00
Daredevil...9.00
Dracula...9.00
Dr. Strange & the Dread Dormammu...............9.00
The Fantastic Four..9.00
The Fantastic Four & Doctor Doom 9.00
Howard the Duck #1 ....9.00
Howard the Duck #2 ....9.00
The Hulk & the Abomination 9.00
The Hulk & Wendigo 9.00
The Inhumans 9.00
Iron Fist...9.00
Iron Man..9.00
Ms. Marvel 9.00
Nova...9.00

Red Sonja...9.00
Silver Surfer & Mephisto..................................9.00
Spider-Man 9.00
Spider-Man w/Kraven & Sandman 9.00
Thor on Rainbow Bridge...................................9.00
Thor & Frost Giants 9.00
Thor & Loki 9.00
Set of 29 ....320.00

1977

Marvel Superhero Glass Slurpee Cups

(15 oz. It is not known how many of the glass Slurpee cups
were produced, only Spider-Man & Thor can be verified, but it is
believed to have been a local run only in the Orlando, Florida,
area and that as many as four different glasses were made.)
Spider-Man 10.00
Thor & Frost Giants 10.00
Slurpee cup #3 ....10.00
Slurpee cup #4 ....10.00
Set of 4 ....55.00

1981-82

Marvel Superhero Glass Slurpee Cups

(This was just one cup featuring four heroes — Spider-
Man, Captain America, Hulk, & Spider-Woman — and issued
in conjunction with a contest.)
Each cup..5.00

Sneaky Pete's
1975

Al Capp Series

Daisy Mae...70.00
Joe Btsptflk...70.00
Li'L Abner 70.00
Mammy Yokum..70.00
Pappy Yokum...70.00
Sadie Hawkins...70.00

Taco Bell
1984

Star Trek III: The Search for Spock

Spock Lives 7.00

This serious-looking Watto cup topper was also part of the '99 Episode I collection at KFC.

Thor struck a mean pose on this 1977 cup from 7-Eleven.

Lord Kruge 7.00
Fal-Tor-Pan 7.00
Enterprise Destroyed 7.00
Set of 4... 40.00
Set of 4, in box... 185.00

Star Wars: The Phantom Menace Cups
   (Oversized, plastic cups with character toppers. This promotion was done in conjunction with sister companies KFC and Pizza Hut.)
Sebulba.. 5.00
Watto... 5.00
Darth Maul 5.00
Anakin Skywalker.. 5.00

Wendy's
1981

NY Times Limited Edition
Set of 4... 20.00

1982

1982 World's Fair
Each 10.00

1984

"Where's The Beef?"
Clara Peller "Where's The Beef?"....................8.00
Clara Peller...8.00
Newspaper advertisement for Wendy's...........8.00

1990

Jetsons the Movie
Beverage cups
Each 4.00

Whataburger
1989

Wizard of Oz
50th Anniversary etched crystal glass of Wizard of Oz
   characters 8.00

Burger King handed out several glasses featuring original Star Wars characters in 1977.

Web Addresses

In order to better hawk their wares, and to gain, preserve, protect, and promote an international identity in cyberspace, most of the major food chains have joined with the rest of the multinational community and have each staked out for themselves a niche on the Web. Since Web sites are the best place to acquire information about what toy is appearing where and when, we've decided to list as many of the fast-food Web addresses as are available.

For those new to the Web, all of the addresses listed below start with "http://www" (minus the quote marks), and are typed in all lower case unless otherwise indicated. It should also be noted that Triarc is the parent corporation of Arby's, T.J. Cinnamons, and Pasta Connection; CKE Restaurants, Inc. owns Carl's Jr., Hardee's, and Taco Bueno; IDQ owns Dairy Queen, Orange Julius and Karmel Korn; and Pepsi's Tricon owns KFC, Taco Bell, and Pizza Hut. Some of these "sister" sites are linked with each other.

Corporate Web Pages

A&W's .... no Web site
Arby's ....arbys.com
Baskin-Robbins............................ baskinrobbins.com
   (corporate site closed, local sites online)
Big Boy's .... bigboy.com
   (site under construction)
Burger Chef... no Web site
Burger King..................................... burgerking.com
Chick-Fill-A .... chick-fil-a.com
Carl Jr.'s ....carlsjr.com
Dairy Queen .... dairyqueen.com
   or idq.com/idq/dairyque.htm
Denny's ....dennys.com
Domino's .... dominos.com
Hardee's... hardee's.com
IDQ..idq.com
   (corp. site of DQ, Taco Bueno, & Karmel Korn)
IHOP..ihop.com
Jack in the Box ....jackinthebox.com
KFC.. kfc.com

Karmel Korn .... idq.com/idq/karmelko.htm
Long John Silver's .... longjohnsilver.com
McDonald's.. mcdonalds.com
Orange Julius .... idq.com/idq/orangeju.htm
Pizza Hut ....pizzahut.com
Popeye's.. popeyes.com
Roy Rogers..................... no Web site for food chain
Sonic Drive-In .... sonicdrivein.com
Subway ....subway.com
Sneaky Pete's.................site name has been reserved
Taco Bell ....tacobell.com
Taco Beuno.. no Web site
Triarc .... triarc.com
   (corporate site of Arby's, T.J. Cinnamons, & Pasta Connection)
Tricon .... http://tricon.softshoe.com
   (corporate site of KFC, Pizza Hut, & Taco Bell)
Wendy's ....wendys.com
Whataburger...................................whataburger.com
White Castle .... whitecastle.com

Fan/Collector & Other Web Sites

It should be noted here that the following Web pages are not sponsored by any of the fast-food franchises listed in this book. The following Web sites are private pages that offer news, information, and links to other privately held Web sites dealing with fast-food toys and collectibles. They also serve as places to go for people who are looking to buy and/or sell fast-food toys and collectibles. While these pages are being offered as a way for collectors to find and stay in touch with each other, the authors, editors, and publishers of this book do not endorse any of these sites over any others. However, we do feel that these sites offer good information and have been quite helpful to us in the compiling and verifying of information for this book.

http://members.aol.com/booneclan/FastFoodNews.html
   (Fast-food news)

http://www.thetoyzone.com
   (The Toy Zone information)

http://happytoy.com
   (News and information about Happy Meal toys)

http://www.geocities.com/EnchantedForest/6176/index.html
   (Reference for fast-food toys)

http://www.islandnet.com/~kpolsson/mugs.html
   (Mug Shots, an unofficial A&W listings page)

http://www.burgerchef.com
   (Unofficial Burger Chef page)

http://www1.tip.nl/~t150368/index.html
   (Rick & Daphne's Web Guide)

http://www.ebay.com
   (e-Bay auctions)

http://www.amazon.com
   (Amazon auctions)

http://www.mcdclub.com
   (McDonald's Collector's Club)

Fast-Food Fan Clubs & Magazines

Not all fan clubs are on the Web. Below are some of the fast-food fan clubs (both corporate-sponsored and independent) and their addresses. Again, the authors, editors, and publishers of this book do not endorse any of these clubs over any others. However, we do feel that these clubs do offer up good information, and have been quite helpful to us in the compiling and verifying of information for this book. Some toy magazines that discuss fast-food toys are also listed.

Fast-Food Toy Clubs

Burger King Kid's Club
Main Club House
P.O. Box 1527
Tucker, GA 30085-1527

Drinking Glasses Collectors
Collector Glass News
P.O. Box 308
Slippery Rock, PA 16057

Even films that stiff at the box office can generate very cool toys at the drive-up window. Witness the films Wild Wild West (BK – above, left), and Inspector Gadget (McDonald's – above, right). In spite of the fact that both of the 1999 films were critically pasted, the fast-food toy tie-ins were well-received by customers.

This ad ran in several comic books in 1995 alerting fans to Hardee's X-Men promotion.

This Rugrat item was issued by Burger King in 1998 in conjunction with the release of the Nickelodeon movie.

Nickelodeon's animated Cat Dog proved to be yet another popular BK Kid's Meal toy in 1999.

McDonald's Collectors Club
115 South Lee Street
Suite 200
Des Plaines, IL 60016

BK's Wild Wild West bag, from 1999.

Toy Magazines & Newsletters

Toy Shop Magazine
700 E. State St.
Iola WI 54990

Collecting Tips (McDonald's newsletter)
P.O. Box 633
Joplin, MO 64802

About the Authors

Robert J. Sodaro has been writing professionally longer than McDonald's has been selling Happy Meals. His published works include: *Trivia Mania: Commercials and Ads* (Zebra Books), and the comic book espionage series *Agent Unknown* (Renegade Press). He is also the features editor for Comics Values Annual. Over the years he has worked for Marvel Entertainment, DC Comics, Image Comics, Dark Horse Publishing, and others. He is a life-long resident of Connecticut, and has seriously considered petitioning the FDA to create a fifth food group that would include fast food. His long-term ambition is to one day grow up and become a Jedi Knight...OK, OK, so the growing up part is a bit far-fetched, but we had to put that in because his parents might read this.

Alex G. Malloy is a 30-plus-year dealer in ancient coins and antiquities. He has authored books on comic books, toys, and games, along with books on ancient coins, medieval crusader coins, and ancient antiquities. He founded Attic Books in 1969 and published several magazines about the comics hobby, including *Comics Values Monthly*, *Toy Values Monthly*, and *Triton*. He is also author of *Comics Values Annual*, a yearly price guide for comic books.